THE WISCONSIN

THE WISCONSIN

RIVER OF A THOUSAND ISLES

AUGUST DERLETH

The University of Wisconsin Press

Published 1985

The University of Wisconsin Press
114 North Murray Street
Madison, Wisconsin 53715

The University of Wisconsin Press, Ltd.
1 Gower Street
London WC1E 6HA, England

ISBN 0-299-10374-9

The illustrations prepared by John Steuart Curry for
the original edition of *The Wisconsin* are no longer
available. The present edition incorporates other
Curry illustrations: *The Valley of the Wisconsin*,
on pages 202–203, and the original jacket illustration,
on pages 298–299, both illustrations courtesy
Kennedy Galleries, Inc., New York.

Library of Congress Cataloging in Publication Data

Derleth, August William, 1909–1971.
  The Wisconsin, river of a thousand isles.

    Reprint. Originally published: New York: Farrar &
Rinehart, 1942. (The Rivers of America) With new introd.
    Bibliography: pp. 339–345.
    Includes index.
    1. Wisconsin River (Wis.) 2. Wisconsin River
Valley (Wis.)—History. I. Curry, John Steuart, 1897–
1946. II. Title.
F587.W8D4 1985   977.5 85–40367
ISBN 0–299–10374–9

To Dr. LOUISE PHELPS KELLOGG,

pre-eminent among historians of the old Northwest, with admiration and gratitude.

Contents

Introduction

CONSTANCE Lindsay Skinner conceived the idea for what became *The Rivers of America* series early in the 1930s during the worst period of the depression. A poet, dramatist, writer of popular history, and author of adventure stories for children, Skinner had been raised at a fur trading post in British Columbia, and most of her stories were told against a background of rivers and river valleys, where the "unending rhythm" of nature shaped the lives and character of the people who lived in such places. As the depression deepened, she concluded it was necessary to bolster the spirits of Americans by reminding them of their unique and natural heritage. "When American folk have troubles which do not end swiftly," she wrote in a prospectus announcing *The Rivers of America* series, "they begin presently to examine their own sources as a nation and their own story as a people." She prophesied that this series of books would "kindle imagination" and renew hope through a "retelling of the American story as a Folk Saga," based upon the great rivers of America and the people who lived along them. Her original intention had been to write a series of books herself describing the role of the world's great rivers in shaping history. "It was the rivers themselves that thrilled me," she wrote in 1935, "I was convinced that rivers—the perpetual motion in the quiet land—had had, and must ever have, a powerful influence on the temperament and imagination of mankind." But at the suggestion of Frederick Jackson Turner, the Wisconsin-born historian of the frontier whose ideas and work Skinner much admired, she decided instead on a series limited to the rivers of North America, each book to be written by an author intimately identified with the particular river, writers who "had it in their blood."

Skinner very specifically made the point in her prospectus that this was to be "a literary and not an historical series," and that the authors were not to be academic historians but rather novelists and poets: "On them, now in America, as in all lands and times, rests the real responsibility of interpretation." She argued that the "average American has been prevented from a profound self-knowledge . . . because the epic material of America has been formulated by the scholastics instead of by the artists." (She exempted Turner from this condemnation: "a great scholar without being scholastic.") She was particularly incensed by those historians such as Charles A. Beard who had advanced an "economic interpretation" of American history. "Everyone, apparently, has his 'revolution' today," she wrote in 1937, "and American writers and illustrators are entitled to theirs against the 'economic interpreters' with their foolish notion that the belly is the hub of the universe and America's own bright and morning star. If, as we hear shouted from the soap boxes, the old America with its customs and ideals is on the way out, we can march to intercept it and seize its baggage for our own purposes."

The New York publishing house of Farrar & Rinehart accepted Skinner's proposal and launched *The Rivers of America* series in 1935, with Skinner overseeing and promoting the series as general editor. Until her death in 1939, she had what her publishers termed "the final say" on which rivers were to be included in the series and who would write each volume. The first volume, Robert P. Tristam Coffin's *Kennebec: Cradle of Americans,* appeared in 1937. During the next twenty-five years nearly fifty volumes were published, twice the number Skinner had originally proposed. Each book included original drawings done by an established or aspiring artist. As a whole the series was a commercial success, and most of the individual volumes were well received by the reading public.

This might suggest that such traditional ideas and values as Skinner propounded had some currency among Americans in the years of the depression, the Second World War, and immediately thereafter. It would be foolish indeed, a half-century later, to dismiss her particular viewpoints as simply naive or hyperpatriotic. On the contrary, at the time and particularly during the war, such ideas constituted the consensus. Not all the authors in the series, August Derleth included, shared all of Skinner's viewpoints. But as a group they were writers who, like her, found great beauty in the natural surroundings of river valleys, were fascinated and knowledgeable about the people who lived their lives in such places, were strongly inclined to rank traditional values more highly than material success, and were proud of the history of their own locales and their country.

Farrar & Rinehart first approached August Derleth about doing a book for the series on the Wisconsin River in June 1937. But if the surviving evidence is to be believed, it was not until October 1940, in the year after Skinner's death, that the group of editors who had assumed Skinner's responsibilities decided it "would be nice" to have a book on the Wisconsin and asked Derleth for his ideas. He responded four days later with a proposal that was accepted, as was his recommendation that his friend at the University of Wisconsin, the artist-in-residence John Steuart Curry, be commissioned to do the accompanying illustrations.

Derleth was the ideal author to write the volume on

the Wisconsin for such a series. In 1852 his family settled in Sauk City, "a small largely German village pleasantly situated on the west bank" of the Wisconsin River near that point where the river ends its southern descent through the state and turns to the west to flow on to the Mississippi. He attended the local parochial and public schools, and graduated from the University of Wisconsin in 1930 with a bachelor's degree in English. Other than those four years in Madison and six months after graduation spent working as an editor for Fawcett Publications in Minneapolis, he was to live his entire life in Sauk City. "I am much attached to this corner of the earth," he wrote early in the 1960s, "not only because it possesses great natural beauty in abundance, but because it affords me a necessary continuity." He hiked the hills and low country around Sauk City almost every day and in all the seasons of the year, gathering morel mushrooms in May, swimming in the river in the summer, always carefully observing and noting anything that attracted his attention. "Of all aspects of life," he once stated, "nature alone offered the only constant." But he also walked every day from his large stone home on the outskirts into town to talk with relatives, old friends, and acquaintances. He missed little on these ramblings and recorded much in his daily journals, gathering material for future use. For more than sixty years, Sauk City and the countryside of the Sauk Prairie and the Wisconsin River were his Walden.

"My career had been decided upon before I left St. Aloysius parochial school," he recalled many years later. At age thirteen he began to write stories, one of which, "Bat's Belfry," was published in 1926 in *Weird Tales* magazine. He continued to write through the years in Madison and upon his return from Minneapolis, beginning with detective stories and supernatural tales, but then "gradually expanding into realistic studies of life in my home milieu." It was during this period in the early 1930s that he "evolved the plan to tell the story of Sauk City and its twin village, Prairie du Sac, in a sequence of approximately fifty books, combining novels, novelletes, short stories, poetry, journal extracts, [and] miscellaneous prose, under the collective title of the Sac Prairie Saga."

The extraordinary thing is not so much the presumptuousness of an unestablished author in his early twenties setting such a goal but the fact that he accomplished what he had set out to do . . . and a great deal more in addition. Before he died in 1971 at the relatively young age of sixty-two, he had written more than one hundred books and several thousand stories and articles published in some five hundred different magazines and newspapers. In addition to his novels, short stories, and poetry, he wrote history, biography, fantasy and science fiction, detective stories, and stories for juveniles. In 1941 and 1942, the years in which he researched and wrote the book on the Wisconsin, he commonly wrote a novel or another major piece of work at the rate of 5,000 words a day, at the same time composing a book of poetry while commuting the twenty-five miles back and forth to teach his class in Madison, as well as carrying on his journals, correspondence, and business affairs. When necessary he could write 15,000 words a day.

As if this were not enough, he established three publishing imprints for his own work and that of other authors: Arkham House, whose business he managed for many years from his home in Sauk City; Mycroft and Moran; and Stanton and Lee. For nearly twenty years he was the literary editor of *The Capital Times* of Madison. He privately reviewed the work of dozens of other authors at their request. He regularly taught courses at the University of Wisconsin and lectured throughout the state. Still, he found time to serve as clerk and president of the local board of education and as a parole officer for the county court, to help organize and serve in a local men's club and parent-teacher association, and to "meddle in village politics" when "a) some rank injustice is being practiced on people who can't defend or help themselves; [or] b) some ruling or individual has got in my way." In his free time he enjoyed a large record collection of classical, jazz, and Dixieland music, and accumulated what he claimed was the world's largest collection of comic strips (*comic* strips, "not adventure strips for morons"). "If I had to define myself," he wrote Sinclair Lewis in the mid-1940s, "I would say that I was possibly the most successful lazy man I knew."

Inevitably one asks why Derleth maintained this frenetic pace for more than forty years. "I write so much," he once explained, "because it is economically necessary for me to do so, and . . . the variety of my writing keeps me from tiring of the creative process." But perhaps the key is that Derleth did not seriously strive to be "the great writer" that Sinclair Lewis and others thought he had the potential to become. Although he fiercely and joyously defended his work when it was criticized, he was privately willing to concede otherwise. He frequently referred to his detective and fantasy stories as "tripe," quick exercises often produced at a rate of a story a day, written only to provide the income he needed for his other activities. In one of his rare moments of humbleness, he was heard to say: "Less than five percent of my work is worth a second glance." But in the case of Derleth's serious work, there was no necessary correlation between the speed at which he worked and the quality of what he produced. *Walden West* (1961), generally thought to be his best book, is one of the few exceptions, handwritten in blank books carried with him during his ramblings. But nearly all his other good books were written over very short periods of time.

One should not thus be either surprised or put off by the fact that Derleth wrote *The Wisconsin: River of a Thousand Isles* in only about two months. He began writing on April 4, 1942, and he mailed the first draft to Farrar & Rinehart on May 12. He completed the revisions and the final draft, while working on other manuscripts, exactly a month later. Despite his other commitments, he was the only one of the first eighteen authors in the series to prepare his own index. Such was the way Derleth worked.

Derleth's choice of John Steuart Curry to do the illustrations was a particularly happy one. At the time Curry was artist-in-residence at the College of Agriculture, where Derleth frequently taught in the school's short course. The two had become friends. Curry had been raised in rural Kansas, and like his contemporaries Thomas Hart Benton and Grant Wood who came from similar backgrounds, he took his images from the life of rural America, pictorially narrating themes of a local or regional nature. This school of American Regionalists flourished artistically if not financially during the decade of the depression, and it had its counterpart among American writers, of whom Derleth considered himself one. Curry's best known work was his portrayal of the abolitionist John Brown, a driven figure with arms thrown out against the violent background of a cyclone, created first as part of a mural Curry painted in the state capitol in Topeka and then done in closer focus as a lithograph. But "John Brown" was not typical of Curry's work; he preferred themes that portrayed the stolid strength of rural people combating and accommodating to the forces of their natural surroundings. In the summer of 1941, Curry and Derleth explored the Wisconsin River from the Sauk Prairie to its mouth near Prairie du Chien by canoe and motorboat, making sketches and taking photographs as they moved downriver. Curry's original drawings were done in a sepia tone, a matter of some concern to Farrar & Rinehart, who because of wartime ink curtailments had planned to print them in black. However, both John Farrar and Curry were fully satisfied with the printing. In mood and composition, Curry's illustrations beautifully complemented Derleth's text.

One other detail in the preparation of the manuscript deserves particular attention. Derleth dedicated *The Wisconsin* to Louise Phelps Kellogg, a distinguished historian of Wisconsin and the Old Northwest best remembered for her books on the French and British regimes in Wisconsin. In so doing, Derleth made it clear that he did not share Constance Lindsay Skinner's scorn for scholarly history and its academic practitioners. On the contrary, he admired the work of Turner, Kellogg, Merle Curti, and others who had dealt with various aspects of Wisconsin's history. Moreover, in advising other authors he insisted that "the writer of regional prose must know what has gone into the history of his region, what has influenced his people, what is responsible for their thought patterns; he must know, in short, what specific problems determine what they say and do, and fix the patterns of their lives." Although not professionally trained, Derleth was a very competent regional historian who based his historical writing upon research in the primary documents, and who regularly sought the help of professionals like Kellogg. By the time he agreed to write the book on the Wisconsin, he had already published one of two books on the life of Hercules Dousman, a leading citizen in the early history of Prairie du Chien, as well as two novels which traced the history of Sac Prairie to 1850 and incorporated many historical persons and events. Much of the content of *The Wisconsin* was derived from material gathered for these earlier books. In addition, he spent a good deal of time throughout the year 1941 doing more research. In short, there was a much greater invest-

ment of time and effort in this book than is suggested by
the two months or so it took to actually write it.

Professional historians can challenge some of Derleth's interpretations and conclusions (as they can and do
those of other professionals). Readers should not take this
book as the definitive or final word on Black Hawk,
Frank Lloyd Wright, or even Sauk City. In his historical
writing, Derleth was sometimes guilty of oversimplifying
complex situations and portraying contending forces in
sharp contrasts more clear than warranted. But in those
first months of American involvement in World War II
following the bombing of Pearl Harbor, that was a fault
that was common to most American writers. Indeed, one
of the benefits and pleasures of reading between the lines
of this book is the insight it offers into the values and
attitudes of a people who are reexamining their historical
heritage while in the midst of a war.

The books that constitute *The Rivers of America* series
were not intended to meet all the criteria of professional
historians. Derleth acknowledged that he had made "no
attempt to write a comprehensive history of the Wisconsin or its valley," although he did insist that he had "adhered as closely as possible to history, and to the best of
my knowledge there are no historical inaccuracies in this
book." For the most part, he was quite successful in this.
More to the point—and in this Derleth did share common ground with Skinner—he brought to the writing of
this book something very few professional historians
could provide: a lifetime of residency and involvement
and of study and reflection about the lower Wisconsin
River valley and the people who lived there. He dearly
loved Sauk City and its people. Even when critical, as in
his delightful account of a century of petty bickering between Sauk City and Prairie du Sac, he had deep affection
for the frailties of those involved. No other writer, of

whatever background or training, knew and understood his particular "corner of the earth" better than August Derleth.

January 1985   William F. Thompson
                                      State Historian

PART ONE

The Mark of History

Spotted sandpipers haunt the shallows, the herons drowse where once the curlews flew, crying wildly, where paroquets once made tropic color in the river bottoms, where the sky was darkened by the clouds of passenger pigeons in migration. Opossums, raccoons, the foxes and minks and otters still inhabit the Wisconsin's shores; the barred owls make their cacophony of cries suddenly in the twilight and the dark; but the bears are gone, the buffalo that once roamed its shores, the timber wolves—all are gone; and the lynx going, thinning before the white man's coming. In the lowland places along the blue waters, the golden prothonotary warbler nests in the spring, the pileated woodpecker challenges man with his proud, fierce cry, hawks wheel and soar upon the air currents, magnificent as ever. There are aspects of wilderness still, at its headwaters as well as near its mouth: in the wooded islands, the hill slopes, the forest country—and a kind of nostalgic wildness in its name: Wisconsin. Its waters, rising in a country of evergreens, birch, aspen, oak and ash, flow into the Father of Waters among honey locusts, chinquapin oak, black maple, and sycamores: once these were forests, reaching skyward, and they are only now beginning to come back—something starting over, something coming again, as if time were turning back to say that the prairie grass, the oak groves, the wilderness will return, not revenants of past time, but reality once more, to erase the marks remembered now, the ways the Indians went, and the trappers after, and the voyageurs, the engagés, the traders and the miners, the raftsmen and lumberjacks, the pioneers. . . .

EAGLE RIVER
HODAG
RHINELANDER
TOMAHAWK
PAUL BUNYAN
MERRILL
RIB HILL
RIB R.
WAUSAU
MOSINEE
KNOWLTON
STEVENS POINT
PLOVER R.
WISCONSIN RAPIDS
STAND ROCK
GREEN BAY
FORT HOWARD
FOX R.
LAKE WINNEBAGO
OLD SWIMMING HOLE
WISCONSIN DELLS
PORTAGE
FORT WINNEBAGO
BARABOO
VILLA LOUIS
RICHLAND CENTER
KICKAPOO R.
EAGLES CAVE
MUSCODA
TALIESIN
SAUK PRAIRIE
MAZOMANIE
BLACKHAWK
BOSCOBEL
WAUZEKA
ARENA
SPRING GREEN
PRAIRIE DU CHIEN
FORT CRAWFORD
MISSISSIPPI R.
CAVE OF THE MOUNDS

Wisconsin River

F. UTPATEL

1. Discovery

THAT part of New France which lay beyond the lakes was an unexplored wilderness in 1634—a land of forests beyond which lay a country, an ocean, a westward passage to Cathay, perhaps—no one knew. It was a year in a momentous time: in the mother country Cardinal Richelieu watched the affairs of church and state with hawk's eyes, and managed still with sardonic amusement to keep himself informed about the difficulties of Charles I and the English Civil War, presaging the rise of the upstart Cromwell. Things went none too well in the American colony of the British, with Governor Winthrop forced to deal with Anne Hutchinson and Roger Williams, and the powerful Iroquois on a war of extermination against their enemies, fancied or real.

In that year, too, a child of the sea, Cherbourg-born Jean Nicolet, late of Nipissing, recently promoted to the position of clerk and interpreter in the Company of New France, set out at the direction of the aging Governor Champlain from the Huron villages at the foot of Georgian Bay for those of the Ottawa on Manitoulin and other Georgian Bay islands, and from there went into the unknown—a lone white man with seven Indians, discovered Lake Michigan, and found a new western land. He thought it might be Cathay, since he had heard wondrous tales of this western land; so he put

3

on "a grand robe of China damask, all strewn with flowers and birds of many colors," which he had brought for the purpose of impressing the savages in "the land of les Puans," as this country was called, and also to be prepared in case these distant Winnebago Indians should be not savages, but Asiatics. He landed on the shores of what is now Green Bay, clad in his gorgeous robe, and carrying pistols in his hands, and the Winnebago called him *Manitouiriniou*—man of wonder—and his pistols, the thunder in his hands. He learned from the Indians that there were openings to westward "to the Big Water"; he could not ascertain whether this was an indication of the westward route to Cathay, or another tale of the "Father of Waters," or the "Great Water," which he felt reasonably sure led to some sea. He undertook to journey up the Fox River, but he did not go far—possibly as far as Lake Winnebago—and then turned back: only a day or so away from the Wisconsin. There is nothing to show that he did not actually see the greater of the two rivers, the link between the lakes and the Mississippi; but all presumptive evidence is on the side of the belief that he did not travel far enough to have seen the river, for, having seen it, he would certainly have pushed on to the "Big Water."

The Wisconsin was not long to remain undiscovered, and its discovery was imminent. The increasing wars of the Iroquois were the despair of their peace-loving "enemies," particularly the Hurons, among whom the Jesuits had established successful missions, and, rather than fight without end, the Hurons and allied tribes began to move westward, and the Algonquian tribes living in lower Michigan, including the Sauk, the Fox, the Mascouten and the Kickapoo, soon followed. When their charges uprooted themselves, the Jesuits did likewise.

Yet it was not Jesuits who first saw the Wisconsin River. It was a fellow Frenchman, one of the first fur traders—though he was not at that time committed to the trade: Pierre Esprit Radisson, who, with his brother-in-law, Médart Chouart Sieur de Groseilliers, followed Nicolet a quarter of a century later. These enterprising travelers were at the time making, as closely as can be determined from a study of Radisson's journal, what was Radisson's third voyage, and the first of his more westerly travels. The two men were possessed of a desire "to be knowne with the remotest people"—though they were also anxious to learn where the best furs might be obtained—and were not disposed to stop in their travels if stopping could be avoided. Nevertheless, the journals of Radisson, while bearing evidence of having been written considerably after the occurrence of the events therein chronicled, seem to indicate beyond doubt that he and Groseilliers were the first white men to see the Wisconsin.

The year was apparently 1659—two years before the death of the astute Cardinal Mazarin and the ascendancy of Colbert to the colonial administration of New France. Radisson writes of spending the winter of 1658-1659 among the Potawatomi near Green Bay, and of visiting the Mascouten, who were on the south shore of the Fox. In the course of his disjointed account, Radisson put down one of the most controversial paragraphs in the history of exploration in the Old Northwest Territory, when he wrote:

"We weare 4 moneths in our voyage without doeing anything but goe from river to river. We mett several sorts of people. We conversed with them, being long time in alliance with them. By the persuasion of som of them we went into ye great river that divides itselfe in 2, where the Hurons with some Ottanake & the wild men that had warrs wth them had retired. There is not great difference in their language, as we weare told. This nation have warrs against those of the forked river. It is so called because it has 2 branches, the one toward the west, the other toward the South, wch we believe runns towards Mexico, by the tokens they gave us."

There are today many historians who believe that Radisson thus records his discovery of what, to them, must have been the Mississippi, though there is no more evidence than this to indicate it. In any case, there is no doubt but that Radisson and Groseilliers did one day come to a flat, marshy country at the upper reaches of the Fox, a region that gave evidence of the presence of a greater river in the vicinity, and, making the portage of slightly over a mile and a half, they came to a broad river of many islands flowing into the south, and thus became the first white men to see the Wisconsin. There is nothing to show that either Radisson or Groseilliers at this time was aware of the potential value of the Fox-Wisconsin waterway for the fur trade. But Radisson liked the country of the rivers, for he wrote of it: "I can assure you I liked noe country as I have that wherein we wintered; ffor whatever a man could desire was to be had in great plenty; viz. staggs, fishes in abundance, & all sort of meat, corne enough."

Even before Radisson and Groseilliers had completed their voyage of discovery in the west, the first Jesuit had set foot in what was to become northern Wisconsin, sent to follow Ottawa and Huron neophytes who had established a village on Chequamegon Bay on Lake Superior: Father René Ménard, already then no longer a young man, and a veteran of the Huron mission. In 1660, the time of his coming to the shore of Lake Superior, Ménard was fifty-six years of age, and no longer strong, having lived among the Iroquois not long before, and being fully aware of the dangers and hardships he faced. Doubtless Father Ménard had opportunity to decline the appointment to the mission on Lake Superior, but he would not; yet his conviction that this would be his last undertaking was given to words in a letter to a friend, when he wrote: "In three or four months you may include me in the Memento for the dead, in view of the kind of life led by these peoples, of my age, and of my delicate constitution. In spite of that, I have felt such powerful promptings and have seen in this affair so little of the purely natural, that I could not doubt that if I failed to respond to this opportunity I should experience an endless remorse."

The Jesuit was a little short in his estimate of the span that remained to him, but he was not far wrong. After almost a year of great hardships, Ménard learned of the existence of a Huron village deep in the pineries of northern Wisconsin, a village in which the Indians were dying of starvation and want. Forthwith, the missionary set out in the company of some young Hurons and Pierre Levasseur dit l'Espérance, for the village on the Black River. What took place after that is somewhat obscured by time. Whether Ménard and l'Espérance went to Lac Court Oreilles or Lac Vieux Desert over the land trail is debated still. In any case, to one of these lakes they went, and there waited for Huron guides promised by the impatient young Hurons who went on ahead. If it was to Lac Vieux Desert that Ménard and l'Espérance went, they were unwittingly at the source of the great river which made its way for over four hundred miles through wilderness fastnesses to join the Mississippi as its largest northern tributary. Failure of their guides to come prompted the two men to trust themselves to an old canoe they found, and so they set out. Somewhere in the course of that voyage, along one of the tributaries either of the Chippewa or of the Wisconsin, Father Ménard stepped out into the forest to lighten the canoe for a perilous rapids journey—and vanished from the face of the earth, lost or murdered by Indians, no one ever discovered.

There is some basis for doubt about the route of Ménard; there is a monument to Ménard on the Grandfather Falls road at Merrill; but it is the considered opinion of Dr. Louise Phelps Kellogg, pre-eminent among authorities on the history of Wisconsin, that Ménard's route lay along one of the tributaries to the Chippewa—the Jump or Yellow, beside one of which Ménard disappeared.

There is no question, however, of Father Allouez's presence on the upper Wisconsin. Claude Jean Allouez was a younger man than Ménard; he had come to Canada in 1658, and was sent into Wisconsin in midsummer of 1665, leaving Three Rivers in one of an impressive flotilla of canoes, most of them carrying Indians, though six French traders were also in the company; and by autumn, he had reached Chequamegon Bay. The settlement there had expanded since the time of Ménard, so that there were almost a thousand Indians representing seven different tribes living on the shores of Lake Superior at that point. Four years Allouez remained at Chequamegon, making occasional trips to the Sault, before he entered into the valley of the Wisconsin.

The reason for his turning toward the settlement at Green Bay was the activity of the Sulpitians, missionaries who had their North American seat at Montreal and were preparing an expedition designed to begin mission work on the bay at the mouth of the Fox. For the purpose of forestalling the Sulpitians, Father Allouez, accompanied by Father Claude Dablon, superior of the northwest missions, left the Sault

November 3, 1669, under escort of two canoeloads of Potawatomi. After a winter spent on the Fox, Allouez went into the interior of Wisconsin, following the Fox and Wolf rivers into the valley of the Wisconsin. This was in 1670; how far down the Wisconsin Father Allouez went cannot be determined, but it is certain that the activities of Allouez and Dablon during their stay in the interior of Wisconsin were confined for the most part to the Indians in the valley of the Fox.

Apart from Father Allouez, it was 1673 before the Wisconsin was seen again by white men who left records, for it was in that year that Père Jacques Marquette and Louis Joliet appeared on the scene. Anxious to discover the Mississippi River, Jean Talon, the "great intendant" of Canada, prepared an expedition to be led by Joliet, who had discovered the deep-water route from Mackinac to Lake Ontario, and chaplained by Marquette, before the voyage of discovery could be begun, both Talon and Courcelles, the cogovernor of the colony, were recalled, and Louis de Buade, Count de Frontenac, was sent by Louis XIV to carry on Talon's policies. Count Frontenac immediately supported the Mississippi River expedition, while at the same time striking memorably at the warlike Iroquois, who menaced the French in the north and west. Père Marquette had been chosen, over the heads of older and presumably more experienced men, because of his youth, his skill in mapmaking, his knowledge of Indian languages. Moreover, while at the mission of the Sault, Marquette had learned in 1669 from a Shawnee Indian that the Shawnee village was but five days' journey from the "South Sea," near a "great river," which came from the country of the Illinois and discharged its waters into that sea. The Shawnee's reference was undoubtedly to the Gulf of Mexico; but Marquette believed that he

meant the Pacific Ocean, and, still hoping that the
"great river" might prove to be the long-sought route
through North America, he was eager to begin his
journey. They set out from the mission of St. Ignace on
May 17, 1673—"Monsieur Jollyet and myself, with five
men—in two bark canoes, fully resolved to do and suffer everything for so glorious an undertaking," and by
June 7th, they had reached the village of the Mascouten
on the upper Fox.

They were furnished guides by friendly Miami
Indians, and soon crossed the portage and came to the
southward flowing river. In his journal, he recounts
that their party had now "left the waters flowing to
Quebeq, four or five hundred leagues from here, to float
on those that would henceforth take us through strange
lands." It was manifest to Marquette and Joliet that it
was not true, as had been believed, that the rivers flowed
from the Great Lakes toward the western sea; it was not
yet manifest to them that the easiest route from the
basin of the lakes to the Father of Waters had been discovered. The Indian guides informed the explorers that
the southwestward flowing river was named the Meskousing, and Marquette put down a description of the
Wisconsin which is timeless in its application to the
stream: "It is very wide; it has a sandy bottom, which
forms various shoals that render its navigation very difficult. It is full of islands covered with vines. On the
banks one sees fertile land, diversified with woods,
prairies, and hills. There are oak, walnut and basswood
trees; and another kind, whose branches are armed with
long thorns. We saw there neither feathered game nor
fish, but many deer, and a large number of cattle." By
June 17th, the canoes left the Wisconsin and entered
the "so renowned River ... The Mississippi," which
Marquette wanted immediately to name Conception,

in honor of the Virgin Mary, and Joliet, Buade, for the family name of Count Frontenac, the governor-general.

A few years later Robert Cavelier, Sieur de La Salle, armed with a royal grant and bent on a voyage of exploration with his lieutenant, Henry de Tonty, determined to combat the Iroquois (now beginning to raid the country that was to become Wisconsin) by allying all the Algonquian Indians—Illinois, Miami, Mascouten, Kickapoo, Abenaki, Mahican, and Shawnee—left the first precise description of the Wisconsin in a letter found in Margry's *Découvertes et établissements des Français,* a letter attributed to him, though the facts of the description very likely came from Hennepin or one of his party.

"Following the windings of the Mississippi, we come to the river Ouisconsing, Misconsing, or Meschetz Odéba, which lies between the bay of the Puans and the Great River. It flows at first from north to south to about the 45th degree of north latitude, and then turns to the west and west-south-west, and, after flowing sixty leagues, it falls into the Mississippi. It is nearly as wide as that of the Islinois, navigable to that bend (and perhaps below it) where the canoes are portaged across an oak grove and a flooded meadow to reach the Kakaling (Fox) river, which falls into the bay of the Puans (Green Bay). Misconsing flows between two ranges of hills which widen out from one another at times, leaving between them quite large meadows and lands without trees, sandy and of but little fertility. At other places the level land between the hills and the river is lower, and swampy in some spots; and then it is covered with timber, and flooded by the overflowing of the river. The mountains gradually diminish as the river is ascended; and finally, about three leagues from the portage, the land becomes level and swampy, without trees on the side of the portage, but covered with pines on the other side. The place where the canoes are carried over is marked by a tree, on which two canoes have been clumsily drawn by the Savages."

Approximately two years earlier, Daniel Greysolon Duluth, coming down the Upper Mississippi, overtook at the mouth of the Wisconsin a party of Sioux with whom there were two white captives, one of whom was Father Louis Hennepin, a Recollect monk, and a chaplain of La Salle's party. Duluth imperiously demanded the surrender of the captives on pain of dire retribution, reproaching the chiefs for their breach of faith in taking white captives, and carried Hennepin and his companion off by way of the Wisconsin and Fox rivers, thus making the first recorded journey up the Wisconsin and down the Fox. Thirteen years after, in 1693, Pierre Le Sueur took the Fox-Wisconsin waterway en route to build a fort in the Mississippi; he traveled by order of Count Frontenac.

Within the decade after the west to east journey of Duluth and Hennepin, while the first traders were beginning to come to the Green Bay area at the mouth of the Fox, Louis Armand, Baron de La Hontan, took the Fox-Wisconsin route, and left another fine description of the waterway. Of the Wisconsin River, to which he referred as the Ouisconsinc, he wrote that "its sides are adorn'd with Meadows, lofty Trees, and Firs." He went into great detail about the river and the country through which it flowed, the first of the travelers to have spent so much wordage on the route he followed.

He was not the last, by any means. However, only two of the accounts between La Hontan's and our own time merit attention. They are those of Jonathan Carver and Captain Frederick Marryat. The visit of Jonathan Carver is of especial interest since, so far as is known, he was the first English-speaking person to describe the river. Prior to his visit, the fleur-de-lis had ceased to fly over his route; it had been supplanted by the British flag, since the surrender of New France to Britain, September 8, 1760. Carver had been a colonial officer in the French and Indian War, and was now serving as a mapmaker for Major Robert Rogers, commander at Mackinac, whom Carver had met in Boston. Rogers was intensely eager to discover the Northwest Passage, and needed the services of a good mapmaker; Carver was adventurous and eager to go. His trip was made in 1766; he set out from Boston in June of that year, and by way of Albany and Niagara Falls went to Mackinac, which he reached in September; at Mackinac he was supplied by Major Rogers and then set out for Green Bay. By September 20th, he was en route along the Fox-Wisconsin waterway. His narrative of the journey takes precisely four pages in his *Travels Through the Interior Parts of North America in the Years 1766, 1767, and 1768* (by J. Carver, Esq. Captain of a Company of Provincial Troops During the Late War with France. Illustrated with Copper Plates, Coloured), published in 1778. His narrative is as follows:

"I observed that the main body of the Fox River came from the south-west, that of the Ouisconsin from the northeast; and also that some of the small branches of these two rivers, in descending into them, doubled, within a few feet of each other, a little to the south of the Carrying Place. That two such Rivers should take their rise so near each other, and after running such different courses, empty themselves into the sea at a distance so amazing (for the former having passed through several great lakes, and run upwards of two thousand miles, falls into the Gulf of St. Lawrence, and the other, after joining the Mississippi, and having run an equal number of miles, disembogues itself into the Gulph of Mexico) is an instance scarcely to be met in the extensive continent of North America. . . .

"On the 8th of October we got our canoes into the Ouisconsin River, which at this place is more than a hundred yards wide; and the next day arrived at the Great Town of the Saukies. This is the largest and best built Indian town I ever saw. It contains about ninety houses, each large enough for several families. These are built of hewn plank neatly joined, and covered with bark so compactly as to keep out the most penetrating rains. Before the doors are placed comfortable sheds, in which the inhabitants sit, when the weather will permit, and smoak their pipes. The streets are regular and spacious; so that it appears more like a civilized town than the abode of savages. The land near the town is very good. In their plantations, which lie adjacent to their houses, and which are neatly laid out, they raise great quantities of Indian corn, beans, melons, etc. so that this place is esteemed the best market for traders to furnish themselves with provisions, of any within eight hundred miles of it.

"The Saukies can raise about three hundred warriors, who are generally employed every summer in making incursions into the territories of the Illinois and Pawnee nations, from whence they return with a great number of slaves. But those people frequently retaliate, and, in their turn, destroy many of the Saukies, which I judge to be the reason that they increase no faster.

"Whilst I staid here, I took a view of some mountains that lie about fifteen miles to the southward, and abound in lead ore. I ascended one of the highest of these, and had an extensive view of the country. For many miles nothing was to be seen but lesser mountains, which appeared at a distance like haycocks, they being free from trees. Only a few groves of hickory, and stunted oaks, covered some of the vallies. So plentiful is lead here, that I saw large quantities of it lying about the streets in the town belonging to the Saukies, and it seemed to be as good as the produce of other countries.

"On the 10th of October we proceeded down the river, and... on the 15th we entered that extensive river the Mississippi. The Ouisconsin, from the Carrying Place to the part where it falls into the Mississippi, flows with a smooth but a strong current; the water of it is exceedingly clear, and through it you may perceive a fine and sandy bottom, tolerably free from rocks. In it are a few islands, the soil of which appeared to be good, though somewhat woody. The land near the river also seemed to be, in general, excellent; but that at a distance is very full of mountains, where it is said there are many lead mines."

After Carver's succinct account, Captain Marryat's may seem prolix. Between the dates of Carver's trip and Marryat's, the Stars and Stripes had replaced the British flag over the territory soon to become the state of Wisconsin. Captain Frederick Marryat was the popular English author of *Peter Simple*, *Jacob Faithful*, *Frank Mildmay*, and others. In the fashion of so many British authors of the last century, Captain Marryat set out to write a two-volume account of his visit to the United States, *A Diary in America, with Remarks on Its Institutions*, published in 1839. His trip along the Fox-Wisconsin waterway was made in the summer of 1838, and he seems to have had a hard time of it. He did not intend to go through Wisconsin at all, he confesses, but it so happened that, having reached Green Bay, with the intention of going on down to Chicago and thence by Galena to St. Louis, he fell in with a "Major F—, with whom I had been previously acquainted, who informed

me that he was about to send a detachment of troops
from Green Bay to Fort Winnebago, across the Wisconsin territory. As this afforded me an opportunity of
seeing the country, which seldom occurs, I availed myself of an opportunity to join the party." They made
good time to Fort Winnebago, where a further opportunity awaited him, "of descending the Wisconsin to
Prairie du Chien, in a keelboat . . ." of which, naturally,
he availed himself, "instead of proceeding by land to
Galena, as had been my original intention."

He does not seem to have regretted his trip along
the Fox-Wisconsin waterway, for he concedes ultimately: "I consider the Wisconsin territory as the
finest portion of North America, not only from its
soil, but its climate. The air is pure, and the winters,
although severe, are dry and bracing; very different
from, and more healthy than those of the Eastern
States." There is, incidentally, no record extant of Captain Marryat's having spent a winter day in the Wisconsin Territory. Be that as it may, his account of the journey down the Wisconsin from Fort Winnebago at the
portage to Prairie du Chien is a stimulating and colorful
account. With his customary eye for detail, the captain
begins his account by devoting some lines to the keelboat on which he had been offered passage, and then he
is off downriver in an excellent picture of river travel at
that place in the river's history when the fur trade was
declining before the coming in of agriculture.

"The boat had been towed up the Wisconsin with
a cargo of flour for the garrison; and a portion of the
officers having been ordered down to Prairie du Chien,
they had obtained this large boat to transport themselves, families, furniture, and horses, all at once, down
to their destination. The boat was about one hundred
and twenty feet long, covered in to the height of six

feet above the gunnel, and very much in appearance like the Noah's Ark given to children, excepting that the roof was flat. It was an unwieldy craft, and, to manage it, it required at least twenty-five men with poles and long sweeps; but the army gentlemen had decided that, as we were to go down with the stream, six men with short oars would be sufficient—a very great mistake. In every other respect she was badly found, as we term it at sea, having but one old piece of rope to hang on with, and one axe. Our freight consisted of furniture stowed forward and aft, with a horse and cow. In a cabin in the centre we had a lady and five children, one maid and two officers. Our crew was composed of six soldiers, a servant, and a French *half bred* to pilot us down the river. All Winnebago came out to see us start; and as soon as the rope was cast off, away we went down with the strong current, at the rate of five miles an hour. The river passed through forests of oak, the large limbs of which hung from fifteen to twenty feet over the banks on each side; sometimes whole trees lay prostrate in the stream, held by their roots still partially remaining in the ground, while their trunks and branches offering resistance to the swift current, created a succession of small masses of froth, which floated away on the dark green water.

"We had not proceeded far, before we found that it was impossible to manage such a large and cumbrous vessel with our few hands; we were almost at the mercy of the current, which appeared to increase in rapidity every minute; however, by exertion and good management, we contrived to keep in the middle of the stream, until the wind sprung up and drove us on to the southern bank of the river, and then all was cracking and tearing away of the woodwork, breaking of limbs from the projecting trees, snapping, cracking, screaming, hallooing and confusion. As fast as we cleared ourselves of one tree, the current bore us down upon another; as soon as we were clear above water, we were foul and entangled below. It was a pretty general average; but what was worse than all, a snag had intercepted and unshipped our rudder, and we were floating away from it, as it still remained fixed upon the sunken tree. We had no boat with us not even a *dug-out*—(a canoe made out of the trunk of a tree)—so one of the men climbed on shore by the limbs of an oak, and went back to disengage it. He did so, but not being able to resist the force of the stream, down he and the rudder came together—his only chance of salvation being that of our catching him as he came past us. This we fortunately succeeded in effecting; and then hanging on by our old piece of rope to the banks of the river after an hour's delay, we contrived to re-ship our rudder, and proceeded on our voyage, which was a continuation of the same eventful history. Every half hour we found ourselves wedged in between the spreading limbs of the oaks, and were obliged to have recourse to the axe to clear ourselves; and on every occasion we lost a further portion of the frame work of our boat, either from the roof, the sides, or by the tearing away of the stancheons themselves.

"A little before sunset, we were again swept on to the bank with such force as to draw the pintles of our rudder. This finished us for the day; before it could be replaced, it was time to make fast for the night; so there we lay, holding by our rotten piece of rope, which cracked and strained to such a degree, as inclined us to speculate upon where we might find ourselves in the morning. However, we could not help ourselves, so we landed, made a large fire, and cooked our victuals; not, however venturing to wander away far, on account of the rattlesnakes, which here abounded. . . .

"This river has been very appropriately named by the Indians the 'Stream of the Thousand Isles,' as it is studded with them; indeed, every quarter of a mile you find one or two in its channel. The scenery is fine, as the river runs through high ridges, covered with oak to their summits; sometimes these ridges are backed by higher cliffs and mountains, which half way up are of a verdant green, and above that present horizontal strata of calcareous rock of rich gray tints, having, at a distance, very much the appearance of the dilapidated castles on the Rhine.

"The scenery, though not so grand as the high lands of the Hudson, is more diversified and beautiful. The river was very full, and the current occasionally so rapid as to leave the foam as it swept by any projecting point. We had, now that the river widened, sand banks to contend with, which required all the exertions of our insufficient crew.

"On the second morning, I was very much annoyed at our having left without providing ourselves with a boat, for at the gray of dawn, we discovered that some deer had taken the river close to us, and were in midstream. Had we had a boat, we might have procured a good supply of venison. We cast off again and resumed our voyage; and without any serious accident we arrived at the shot-tower, where we remained for the night. Finding a shot-tower in such a lone wilderness as this gives you some idea of the enterprise of the Americans; but the Galena, or lead district, commences here, on the south bank of the Wisconsin. The smelting is carried on about twelve miles inland, and the lead is brought here, made into shot, and then sent down the river to the Mississippi, by which, and its tributary streams, it is supplied to all America, west of the Alleghanies. The people were all at work when we arrived. The general distress had even affected the demand for shot, which was considerably reduced.

"On the third day we had the good fortune to have no wind, and consequently made rapid progress, without much further damage. We passed a small settlement called the English prairie—for the prairies were now occasionally mixed up with the mountain scenery. Here there was a smelting-house and a steam saw-mill. . . . The *diggings,* as they term the places where the lead is found (for they do not mine, but dig down from the surface), were about sixteen miles distant. . . .

"On the ensuing day we had nothing but misfortunes. We were continually twisted and twirled about, sometimes without bows, sometimes with our stern foremost, and as often with our broadside to the stream. We were whirled against one bank, and, as soon as we were clear of that we were thrown upon the other. Having no axe to cut away, we were obliged to use our hands. Again our rudder was unshipped, and with great difficulty replaced. By this time we had lost nearly the half of the upper works of the boat, one portion after another having been torn off by the limbs of the trees as the impetuous current drove us along. To add to our difficulties, a strong wind rose against the current, and the boat became quite unmanageable. About noon, when we had gained only seven miles, the wind abated, and two Menonnomie Indians, in a *dug-out,* came alongside of us; and as it was doubtful whether we should arrive at the mouth of the river on that night, or be left upon a sand bank, I got into the canoe with them, to go down to the landing-place, and from thence to cross over to Prairie du Chien, to inform the officers of the garrison of our condition, and obtain assistance. The canoe would exactly hold three, and no more; but we paddled swiftly down the stream, and we soon lost sight of the

Noah's Ark. Independently of the canoe being so small, she had lost a large portion of her stem, so that at the least ripple of the water she took it in, and threatened us with a swim; and she was so very narrow, that the least motion would have destroyed her equilibrium and upset her. One Indian sat in the bow, the other in the stern, whilst I was doubled up in the middle. We had given the Indians some bread and pork, and after paddling about half an hour, they stopped to eat. Now, the Indian at the bow had the pork, while the one on the stern had the bread; any attempt to move, so as to hand the eatables to each other, must have upset us; so this was their plan of communication:—The one in the bow cut off a slice of pork, and putting it into the lid of a saucepan which he had with him, and floating it alongside of the canoe, gave it a sufficient momentum to make it swim to the stern, when the other took possession of it. He in the stern then cut off a piece of bread, and sent it back in return by the same conveyance. I had a flask of whisky, but they would not trust that by the same perilous little conveyance; so I had to lean forward very steadily, and hand it to the foremost, and, when he returned it to me, to lean backwards to give it the other, with whom it remained till we landed, for I could not regain it. After about an hour's more paddling, we arrived safely at the landing-place. I had some trouble to get a horse, and was obliged to go out to the fields where the men were ploughing. In doing so, I passed two or three very large snakes. At last I mounted somehow, but without stirrups, and set off for Prairie du Chien. After riding about four miles, I had passed the mountains, and I suddenly came upon the beautiful prairie (on which were feeding several herd of cattle and horses), with the fort in the distance, and the wide waters of the upper Mississippi flowing beyond it."

Wisconsin was spared Mr. Charles Dickens and Mr. Oscar Wilde, and two of America's greatest writers who passed along the river valley—Henry David Thoreau and Ralph Waldo Emerson—the former on that futile journey to Minnesota in an attempt to gain back his health, the journey on which he had only the joy of seeing in the Wisconsin River country as in Minnesota, the pink clouds of wild crabapples in blossom ("I began to notice from the cars a tree with handsome rose-colored flowers. At first I thought it some variety of thorn; but it was not long before the truth flashed on me, that this was my long-sought crab-apple ... the prevailing flowering shrub or tree to be seen from the cars at that season of the year—about the middle of May.... I succeeded in finding it about eight miles west of the Falls; touched it and smelled it, and secured a lingering corymb of flowers..."), the latter on a winter lecture tour of Wisconsin cities—left no word of the river or its valley in their prose or poetry.

2. THE BLACKROBES

Under the fleur-de-lis the Jesuits prospered—accepting without complaint their lot of hardship and death. It was Cardinal Richelieu, always much interested in New France, who sent the Jesuits to reinforce the few Recollect missionaries in the colony, but he was gone when the French church began its struggle with the papacy, and the Jesuits, rather than comply with the Pope's requirement of 1673 that all reports of mission work be authorized by the Congregation of the Propaganda, stopped publication of the famed *Jesuit Relations*, most authoritative source of information on the missions. Reuben G. Thwaites, in his *Jesuit Relations and Allied Documents,* gathered together various other summaries unpublished before his book appeared, but no comprehensive history of missions in central Wisconsin is available.

But it is clear that the majority of early Wisconsin missions were established either in the Chequamegon country of Lake Superior, or in the De Pere region, along the lower Fox River. From De Pere, penetration to the interior was sporadic, and even the visits to the Illinois mission were not made by the Fox-Wisconsin waterway. In so far as the interior of Wisconsin is concerned, the Jesuits—apart from Allouez and Père Marquette—rather followed the traders than preceded them. Moreover, their penetration of Wisconsin coincided with an evil time for the Jesuits in the mother country, a decline in their fortunes that affected the number of young priests coming to New France, and a conflict with the civil authorities regarding their methods. The Jesuits, in short, refused to attempt anything more than the preaching of the word of God; the civil authorities wished them to "civilize" the Indians—that is, draw the Indians away from the evils of their living conditions and give them in return the dubious benefits of the white man's civilization. The Jesuits, who were for the most part extremely well-educated men, were possessed also of a high degree of doubt regarding the quality of the civilization they were ordered to bestow upon the red men, and inaugurated the spirit of passive resistance.

The aspects of French civilization most manifest in that wilderness were those which were calculated to arouse the utmost disapproval in the breasts of the Jesuits; and the Jesuits, let it be remembered, were far from being unworldly. The Jesuits spoke their minds, and they were as one in believing that the white men's vices and liquor went far to counteract all the good the blackrobes could do among the Indians. It was an old story, of course; the Jesuits and other missionaries had told it before. And it was not to be supposed that these priests, who were scrupulously honest about their work among the Indians as well as about all their hardships and sufferings, would neglect to tell the unpleasant truth about the liquor traffic, the exploitation of the Indians by the traders, and the gross immoralities of the coureurs de bois. The missionaries remained hostile.

His hostility to his fellow white men—the traders with whom, at the cost of but a few baubles and a little firewater, the Indian easily made friends—puzzled the aborigine; he could not understand the things the black-robes did, he could find no point of contact, no comradeship in the representatives of the white man's manitou, and, because he failed to understand the blackrobe, the Indian tended to distrust him and to question his motives in coming. He understood the motives of the trader very well, and though he did not always understand his firewater, he enjoyed it.

No tribe in all Wisconsin was Christianized, and after the Fox Wars, early in the eighteenth century, the Jesuits closed their De Pere mission and withdrew from Wisconsin.

Not so the traders; nothing daunted them.

3. PERROT

Perrot followed Radisson and Groseilliers into the heart of Wisconsin.

Nicolas Perrot took the Fox-Wisconsin route in the summer of 1668. Though there is no evidence to support it, he had been reported on the way to the Grand Portage, most famous of the fur routes, leading from the eastern point of what is now Minnesota up through the boundary lakes and rivers between the United States and Canada through the Rainy Lake, Winnipeg, and Red River country to the headwaters of the Mississippi— a way that led also to the country of the Assiniboine and Saskatchewan rivers; but before reaching the Grand Portage, he paused on Lake Superior where he stopped at Chequamegon. He was with Toussaint Baudry, and there is some evidence to show that this was not his first trip into the Northwest. The Lake Superior country was at this time a center of trading, and Perrot and Baudry very likely spent the time from 1667, when they went out with the returning Ottawa fleet, until the following summer in the Lake Superior area. While they were at Chequamegon, Perrot and Baudry were asked to visit the Potawatomi village at Green Bay, a delegation of Indians from that village making the request—"so that they might have the advantage of direct contact with the French," writes Louise Phelps Kellogg in *The French Regime in Wisconsin and the Northwest.* Agreeing to do so, Perrot and Baudry returned with the Potawatomi.

In this way Perrot came into Wisconsin. He had not been born a trader, he did not ever become a great trader in the way that many of Astor's agents became widely known, but he performed an important service for the trade of his time and the traders who came after him. Though he had spent some time in the service of both the Jesuits and the Sulpitians, it was to the trade that he ultimately turned, and it was in the trade that his knowledge of several Indian languages, learned among the Jesuits, served him well, for it was immediately apparent to Perrot, when he came into Wisconsin south of the Ottawa country, that there was no reason why the Ottawa should have a monopoly of the western trade, and it was obvious also that alliances among the tribes of central Wisconsin and the Upper Mississippi country would work to the advantage of both the trade and French sovereignty.

Forthwith Perrot set out to accomplish the ending of the Ottawa monopoly and the Indian alliances. This was in the summer of 1669. He traveled not only by the Fox-Wisconsin route, but also over the land trails into central Wisconsin, evidently reaching the Mississippi at several points, for he was not ignorant of the lead mines in the region of the Wisconsin's mouth, and, spurred doubtless by this discovery, as well as the success of his mission, Perrot erected posts along the Mississippi and took possession of the country of the Sioux in the name of the king of France.

He was accepted by the Indians as no white man since Nicolet had been; he was even given the same name they had bestowed upon Nicolet—"man of wonder"— and he was given treatment that might have been accorded a visiting prince. In his *Histoire de l'Amérique septentrionale* (Paris, 1753), Bacqueville de La Potherie, who knew Perrot and had access to Perrot's journals for his account, tells how Perrot and his companions were hailed as gods, carried on the shoulders of the braves, viewed at a well-defined distance by the women and children, and praised by the smoke from the sacred calumet, which was made to cloud them and their goods.

The Indians understood him. He was shrewd, resourceful, fearless. On one occasion he was called from the winter encampment of voyageurs at St. Antoine on the upper Wisconsin to take part in the war against the westward-moving Iroquois. When he returned to St. Antoine, he discovered that the Indians had rifled the fort, taking all the trade goods. Forthwith he commanded the chiefs to come before him and accused them of guilt, demanding the return of the goods. The chiefs, however, certain that Perrot could not force them to surrender their spoils, refused to return the goods. Manifestly, Perrot and his men could not raise arms against the Indians for the purpose of bringing about the return of the trade goods; but Perrot was not done. He took water in a container, having secretly poured into it some eau de vie, struck his flint and, making the water flame, he promised grimly to set afire all the streams, the lakes, sloughs and marshes unless the Indians immediately complied with his demand. The chiefs were no match for this magic of Perrot's; they vanished into the forests of the upper Wisconsin valley, and soon the Indian women came to the fort, bent under the weight of the stolen goods.

However, despite the success of such trickery, the Indians were not such naïve primitives as to fail to realize that it would be far more to their advantage to deal directly with the French at Montreal than to serve the trade through the mediation of a neighboring tribe, such as the Ottawa. As a result of his travels into the heart of the Wisconsin country and along the Mississippi, Perrot returned to Green Bay with a great many furs, and, in 1670, accompanied a delegation of Indians from various tribes to Montreal, leaving behind him a reputation for integrity which, had it been repeated in the traders who followed him, might have made for a more lasting understanding with the Indians.

He left no permanent mark upon the Wisconsin River valley; he erected no posts there, he established no source of trade, but he made alliances with the Sauk, the Outagami, the Mascouten, the Miami, and he helped clear the way for the formal annexation of the territory of the Great Lakes by agents of Louis XIV.

4. First Settlement

It was inevitable that white men in the Wisconsin River valley should settle first at the meeting place of the rivers, the plain along the edge of which the Wisconsin flowed to empty into the Mississippi; and the fur trade made that inevitable, for it was to this confluence of the rivers that the various Indian tribes of the Upper Mississippi country came in the latter part of every May, bringing their furs to trade, meeting here always in amity. Its name—derived from Chien, the name of an Indian chieftain, and not from the prevalence of prairie dogs there—was first put down in 1766, when Jonathan Carver made reference in his account of his travels to the settlement of Indians he saw there, and added a description of the place in his usual manner.

"About five miles from the junction of the rivers, I observed the ruins of a large town in a very pleasing situation. On enquiring of the neighbouring Indians why it was thus deserted, I was informed, that about thirty years ago, the Great Spirit had appeared on the top of a pyramid of rocks, which lay at a little distance from it, towards the west, and warned them to quit their habitations; for the land on which they were built belonged to him, and he had occasion for it. As a proof that he, who gave them these orders, was really the Great Spirit, he further told them, that the grass should immediately spring up on those very rocks from whence he now addressed them, which they knew to be bare and barren. The Indians obeyed, and soon after discovered that this maraculous alteration had taken place. They shewed me the spot, but the growth of the grass appeared to be no ways supernatural. I apprehend this to have been a stratagem of the French or Spaniards to answer some selfish view; but in what manner they effected their purposes I know not.

"This people, soon after their removal, built a town on the bank of the Mississippi, near the mouth of the Ouisconsin, at a place called by the French La Prairies les Chiens, which signifies the Dog Plains; it is a large town, and contains about three hundred families; the houses are well built after the Indian manner, and pleasantly situated on a very rich soil, from which they raise every necessary of life in great abundance. I saw here many horses of a good size and shape. This town is the great mart, where all the adjacent tribes, and even those who inhabit the most remote branches of the Mississippi, annually assemble about the latter end of May, bringing with them their furs to dispose of to the traders. But it is not always that they conclude their sale here; this is determined by a general council of the chiefs, who consult whether it would be more conducive to their interest, to sell their goods at this place, or to carry them on to Louisiana, or Michillimackinac. According to the decision of this council they either proceed further, or return to their different homes."

This meeting place was thus a natural site of residence for the early traders, though there is no claim of residence on record until 1779, when some of the traders gave Prairie du Chien as their home place.

Six years before, Peter Pond had paused at Prairie du Chien to carry on a trade which was so profitable that he was able to retire in 1778 and return to Connecticut to live. Peter Pond was venturesome and bold. In his teens he already yearned for adventure, for he chronicled in his memoirs: "Beaing then sixteen years of age, I Gave my Parans to understand that I had a Strong Desire to be a Solge. That I was determined to enlist

under the Oficers that was Going from Milford & joine
the army. But they forbid me, and no wonder as my
father had a Larg and young family I Just Began to be
of sum youse to him in his affairs." It was not long before he struck westward to take part in the fur trade.
He spent two years in the wilderness, and kept an impressive account of his sojourn and activities. His spelling remained astrocious. In autumn of 1774 he and his
partner reached Prairie du Chien, which, in the eight
years since Carver's visit, seems to have grown remarkably.

"I ... Descended the River to the Mouth which
Empteys into the Masseippey and Cros that River and
Incampt. ... Next Morning we Recrost ye River which
was about a Mile Brod and Mounted about three Miles
til we Come to the Planes of the Dogs, the grate plase
of rondavues for the traders and Indans Before thay
Disparse for thare Wintering Grounds. Hear we Meat a
Larg Number of french and Indans Makeing out thare
arangements for the InSewing winter and sending of
thare cannoes to Differant Parts—Like wise Giveing
Creadets to the Indans who were all To Rondoveuse
thare in Spring ... this Plane is a Very Handsum one
Which is on the East Side of the River on the Pint of
Land betwene the Mouth of Wiscontan whare it Emties
in to the Masseppey & the Last River. The Plane is Verey
Smooth hear. All the traders that Youseis that Part of
the Countrey & all the Indans of Several tribes Meat
fall & Spring whare the Grateist Games are Plaid Both
By french & Indans. The french Practis Billiards—ye
latter Ball. Hear the Botes from New Orleans Cum.
They are navagated By thirty Six men who row as
maney oarse. Thay Bring in a Boate Sixtey Hogseats of
Wine on one ... Besides Ham, Chese & c——all to trad
with the french & Indans. Thay Cum up the River

Eight Hundred Leages. These Amusements Last three
or four weakes in the Spring of the Year. . . . The french
ware Veray Numeres. Thare was Not Les than One
Hundred and thirtey Canoes which Came from Mack-
enaw Caring from Sixtey to Eightey Hundred wate
Apease all Made of Birch Bark and white Seder for the
Ribs. Those Botes from Orleans & Ilenoa and other
Part ware Numeres. But the natives I have no true Idea
of their Numbers. The Number of Packs of Peltrey of
Differant Sorts was Cald fifteen Hundred of a Hundred
wt Each which went to Mackena."

On this voyage, too, Pond discovered a lone white
man at the second logical place for a settlement along
the Wisconsin—the portage on the Fox-Wisconsin
waterway. This was one Pinnashon, an ex-soldier, engaged in transporting boats and cargoes across the portage, and he had been at this place on the occasion of
Carver's trip down the waterway on his mapmaking
expedition for Major Rogers. Of Pinnashon comparatively little is known, save only that he must have been
enterprising, and had a healthy sense of humor, for he
told Carver a whopping tall tale with a straight face.
Carver records it:

"Mons. Pinnisance, a French trader, told me a remarkable story concerning one of these reptiles (rattlesnakes), of which he said he was an eye-witness. An
Indian, belonging to the Menomonie nation, having
taken one of them, found means to tame it; and when
he had done this, treated it as a Deity; calling it his
Great Father, and carrying it with him in a box wherever he went. This the Indian had done for several summers, when Mons. Pinnisance accidentally met with
him at this Carrying Place, just as he was setting off
for a winter's hunt. The French gentleman was surprised, one day, to see the Indian place the box which

contained his god on the ground, and opening the door give him his liberty; telling him, whilst he did it, to be sure and return by the time he himself should come back, which was to be in the month of May following. As this was but October, Monsieur told the Indian, whose simplicity astonished him, that he fancied he might wait long enough when May arrived, for the arrival of his great father. The Indian was so confident of his creature's obedience, that he offered to lay the Frenchman a wager of two gallons of rum, that at the time appointed he would come and crawl into his box. This was agreed on, and the second week in May following fixed for the determination of the wager. At that period they both met there again; when the Indian set down his box, and called for his great father. The snake heard him not; and the time being now expired, he acknowledged that he had lost. However, without seeming to be discouraged, he offered to double the bet if his great father came not within two days more. This was further agreed on; when behold on the second day, about one o'clock, the snake arrived, and, of his own accord, crawled into the box, which was placed ready for him. The French gentleman vouched for the truth of this story, and from the accounts I have often received of the docility of those creatures, I see no reason to doubt his veracity."

Peter Pond was not so easily taken in. "It was on this Spot," he wrote in his incomparably bad English, "that Old Pinnashon a french man Impose apon Carver Respecting the Indans haveing a Rattel snake at his call which the Indans Could order into a Box for that purpos as a Peat. . . . He found Carver on this Spot Going without undirstanding either french or Indan & full of Enquirey threw his Man who Sarved him as an Interptar & thought it a Proper Opertunety to ad

Sumthing more to his adventers and Make his Bost of it after which I have Haird Meney times it hurt Carver much hearing such things & Putting Confadens in them while he is Govner. He Gave a Good a Count of the Small Part of the Western Countrey he saw But when he a Leudes to Hearsase he flies from facts in two Maney Instances."

As a matter of fact, Pinnashon probably made a good thing of transportation at the portage. Long before his time the Fox, often surly and unruly, suspicious of the French invaders, had decided to take over the portage and levy tribute upon all who crossed, and until after the Fox Wars, the Indians collected. For a while some of the other Indians levied tribute, but the traders were traveling up and down the Fox-Wisconsin waterway in ever-increasing numbers, and it soon became difficult to collect, though some of the Winnebago attempted to make levies as late as the 1830's. What became of Pinnashon does not appear to be known, but in 1792 Laurent Barth took over and built a cabin at the portage: ostensibly the first dwelling erected along the Wisconsin above the river's mouth.

The traditional date for the settlement of Prairie du Chien has been put down as 1781, because it was in that year that Pierre Antaya, Augustine Ange, and Basil Giard were granted formal possession of nine square miles of prairie by Governor Sinclair, the commandant at Michilimackinac, who gained title to the land from the Fox Indians in council. However, traders had lived in Prairie du Chien before this time, and the family names of these first "settlers" had occurred a generation before among the traders for the Wisconsin region to whom license had been issued. The time between Pond's visit and the official "settlement" of Prairie du Chien was a hectic one—British dominion, begun in 1760, was challenged by the revolution; while Charles de Langlade of Green Bay led Indians to the defense of Montreal and Quebec, George Rogers Clark succeeded in allying the Wisconsin Indians with the Americans, and the British came along the Fox-Wisconsin waterway in May, 1780, to erect a fort at Prairie du Chien, to be used as a base for an attack against the Spanish at St. Louis and the Americans at Cahokia. In 1783 the Treaty of Paris was concluded, and all territory east of the Mississippi was ceded to the United States; ten years later the interpreter, Robert Dickson, could write of Prairie du Chien that a "good number of families are settled" there, and they "have lately got cattle from Illinois and begin to raise wheat."

By 1800 the valley of the Wisconsin lay open to settlement.

5. Meskousing to Wisconsin

Of the name, Wisconsin, and its meaning, there is speculation still. The first recorded printing of the name in its early form was in Père Marquette's *Journal*, which was published in 1681 in Paris. The priest spelled the name Meskousing, Miskous, and, on the map published with the *Journal*, Messc8sing—the 8 used in place of the *ou*. Of its Indian origin, there can be no question whatever. Writing in her *Old Forts and Real Folks*, published as recently as 1939, Susan Burdick Davis says that the second part of the word—"sing, sin, or san . . . was probably an Indian ending indicating 'place' or 'location.'" The second appearance of the river was on the 1683 map drawn by Father Hennepin; there it is spelled Ouisconsin, clearly indicative of the French pronunciation of the Indian name. Its evolution to Wiskonsan is obvious, this being the English spelling suggested by the French pronunciation of Ouisconsin. On July 4, 1836, the final change was brought about; Wiskonsan became Wisconsin, despite the objection of some substantial citizens to the use of *c* for *k*; and on January 30, 1845, the territorial legislature in a formal resolution fixed upon the spelling of 1836 as the authorized spelling for the territory and thus also for the river. The alternative spellings of the past, which are sometimes come upon—Ouisconsings, Miskonsing, Ouisconsink, Ouisconsinc, *et al*, are obviously only mutations of the earlier forms, Meskousing or Ouisconsin. The origin of La Salle's Meschetz Odéba is lost in history, and the name occurs nowhere else.

The matter of the meaning of the name is another argument altogether. The Chippewa on the headwaters of the Wisconsin called the river Wees-konsan, which, they explained, meant "the place of the gathering of waters." But there is also the belief that the word means "red cliff" to the Chippewa; this belief is recorded by Miss Davis, though her source is not given. As she points out, however, "where are there 'cliffs' of any importance along the Wisconsin River, with the exception of the Dells, and how red would we call these?" H. E. Cole, writing in *Baraboo, Dells, and Devil's Lake Region*, maintains that Wisconsin "is an Indian word, meaning 'wild, rushing river,'" while Marquette affirmed that the word meant "the river of flowery banks." Finally, as recorded by Carver, there is the meaning of "the river of a thousand isles."

Of these meanings, only two fit the facts, and one of these is questionable. Undoubtedly in the early days of the Wisconsin, the meadows and low places along the river abounded in flowers—but surely no less so than hundreds of other rivers. There are still countless flowers along the river—the white and blue violets, the loosestrifes and lobelias, the blue flags and arrowleafs and yellow pond lilies, the ground nut and bonesets and all the yellow glory of the sunflower family, wild ginger and columbine and honeysuckle, puccoon, spotted crane's-bill, thimbleweed, wild roses and scores of others. But there is one aspect of the river which has not changed from its earilest time to this—the islands. Truly, the Wisconsin is a river of a thousand isles.

Great and small, islands dot the Wisconsin from its headwaters to its mouth, some of them shifting sandbar islands, staying long enough to grow a few trees and shrubs before disappearing again, but most of them substantial bodies of land, heavily wooded, sometimes so long that it is impossible to see from end to end, or even to ascertain that their nearer shore is not, indeed, the shore of the Wisconsin itself. Some of them retain the appearance they must have presented to the earliest explorers: hung with grapevines, bittersweet, carrion berry, greenbrier; abounding with trees, many of them tremendous in girth, here and there still a right-angled tree, hoary with age now, once bent by a passing Indian to make a trail-marking tree. For that reason, I am inclined to believe that the translation of Wisconsin as meaning the stream or river of a thousand isles is to be preferred above all others.

6. Downstream

The Wisconsin rises on the summit of the Archaean watershed, in the waters of Lac Vieux Desert, a shallow lake nowhere more than nineteen feet deep, almost equally divided by the border of Michigan and Wisconsin. The water area is approximately 6,400 acres, and in Wisconsin, 2,698 acres lie in Vilas County. "The country in the vicinity of this beautiful lake is called, in Chippewa language, Katakittekon," writes Captain Thomas Jefferson Cram in the *Wisconsin Historical Collections*, "and the lake bears the same name. On South Island there is an old Indian potato-planting ground; hence the appellation of Vieux Desert, which, in mongrel French, means 'old planting-ground.' There is more reason for calling it Lac Vieux Desert than for the appellation Lake of the Desert." Despite its shallowness Lac Vieux Desert is a large lake, one of the largest in northern Wisconsin, and, while the country immediately around it is flat, hills are not far away. It has a shore line of forty miles, with many well-hidden bays and islands, and on the shores, many Indian mounds.

The Wisconsin flows from Lac Vieux Desert at the southwestern end of the lake and proceeds in a northerly and westerly direction as a stream from six to twelve feet wide through level country which was once valuable timberland, has now been replanted, and will again yield timber in the future, pine, hemlock, tamarack, and cedar predominating, though there are birch and maple varieties, poplar and linden also. It soon establishes a southerly direction, and meanders for all but a hundred miles of its more than 400-mile length almost due south, bending in a wide, gracious curve to westward from Stevens Point to Strong's Prairie and back to Portage, its most easterly point, where it lies slightly over a mile from the Fox River, and is joined to it by a canal for the purpose of navigation. From Portage it pursues a more southwesterly direction until it discharges into the Mississippi a few miles below Prairie du Chien. In the northern part of the state, the river is widened slowly by the waters of almost fifteen hundred lakes and lakelets, which lie in the region covered by the most recent glacial drift. In the Merrill area, where the tributaries have the familiar tree pattern, the river flows through a region of older glacial drift. From Stevens Point to Wisconsin Dells the Wisconsin winds through a sandy plain which is comparatively recent in origin, geologically writing, and from the Dells to the Sauk Prairie, flows through drift region. H. E. Cole, writing in *Baraboo, Dells, and Devil's Lake Region*, points out that "the work of erosion is so incomplete, at the present time the swamp lands in the vicinity of Portage have not yet been drained." From the Sauk Prairie to the mouth of the Wisconsin, the river passes through a fourth type of country: the driftless limestone region, a country of comparatively few swamps and lakes. If there is another river system which presents four such distinct types of drainage, I do not know of it.

The drainage of the Wisconsin River includes 12,-280 square miles, which is just short of being twenty-five per cent of the total area of the state. Through its tributaries, it drains all of the major part of Vilas, Oneida, Lincoln, Marathon, Wood, Portage, Juneau, Adams, Sauk, Monroe, Vernon, Richland and Crawford counties and in addition part of Price, Taylor, Langlade, Clark, Jackson, Waushara, Columbia, Dane, Iowa, and Grant counties. Its major tributaries are the Rib River, the Eau Claire, the Big Eau Pleine, the Plover, the Yellow, the Lemonweir River, Roche a Cri Creek, the Baraboo and Kickapoo rivers. It begins flowing at an altitude of about 1,650 feet above sea level, and drops to 604 feet at the mouth, with the greatest fall—635 feet—in the one hundred fifty miles between Rhinelander and Nekoosa, first called Pointe Bas, a place which the Indians named Bungehjewin, "end of rapids."

In its natural state, the Wisconsin held to a good, level stage of water throughout the year, freezing over in cold winters, but since the stripping of the forests, particularly in the upper Wisconsin River valley, the water height has not remained consistent, sometimes going higher in flood (as on September 15, 1938, when it reached an all-time high of 20.5 feet above average summer flow) and lower in drought. The altitude of the Wisconsin above Lake Michigan varies from 951 feet at Lac Vieux Desert, to 34 feet at the mouth. There are no less than twenty-five power dams across the Wisconsin, the last of them being just above Prairie du Sac at the upper rim of the Sauk Prairie. Below Portage, the velocity of the water is remarkably uniform at something like two miles an hour, and the daily discharge of the river at Portage in times of very low water is approximately 259,000,000 cubic feet.

Before the dams, the Wisconsin was navigable to Pointe Bas, though boats usually stopped at Portage. However, navigation on the river was carried on for many years between Portage and Prairie du Chien, and the river in its time carried showboats as well as passenger boats, and even privately owned yachts, for the late Dr. Peter Fahrney of Chicago, famed for his Alpenkraüter (presumably good for all ills; I can remember as a child having to take this faintly bitter brown liquid under the pressure and assurance that it would be good for practically anything; since the chief component of its effectiveness was a healthy dose of psychology, it usually was!), used to bring his pleasure boat up the Wisconsin until, on one notable occasion, he stuck fast on a sand bar, whereupon the old gentleman made his way into Sauk City and telephoned the power dam above Prairie du Sac to let through enough water to float him. The rest of the story is legend—how the manager indignantly refused, how Dr. Fahrney, well aware of the federal statutes regarding navigation on navigable streams, telephoned Washington, how the water in due time came through and released his boat from the sand bar upon which it was so ignominiously stuck. Sand bars and the coming of the railroads together caused the river traffic to vanish on the Wisconsin as in all other areas of the United States.

The Wisconsin is spanned by sixty bridges (of these twenty-one are railroad bridges, thirty-eight highway, one a foot bridge) and the sixty-first is in process of construction; it is fed by ninety-six sizable tributaries, and there are fifty-four villages and towns either on its banks or within easy walking distance of it. The names of the Wisconsin's villages and tributaries bear their Indian origin in such as Tomahawk, Wausau, Mosinee, Brokaw, Somo Creek, Kewaykwodo Portage, Nekoosa, Dekorra, Okee, Muscoda, Wauzeka; they testify to the French occupation in names like Biron, Prairie du Sac, Prairie du Chien, Baraboo, Donil Creek, Lac Du Flambeau, Lac Vieux Desert, Big Eau Claire, Big Eau Pleine; to the influx of English and Cornish in Lewiston, McNaughton, Port Edwards, Port Andrews, English Prairie; to the Germans in Sauk City—the Germans preferring the ethnologically correct Sauk to the Frenchified Sac, so that the twin villages of the Sauk Prairie, where Carver found the great village of the Saukies in 1766 bear similar names, the upper being Prairie du Sac, the lower Sauk City, though, paradoxically, it was to the lower that those French who settled in the area came, rather than to the more Yankee upper village.

The development of the Wisconsin River valley from the time of the explorers through the fur trade and agriculture, lumbering and rafting to power, and the site of what is perhaps to be the largest ordnance plant in the world took comparatively little time. Close upon the heels of the explorers and missionaries—indeed, often with them—came the fur traders and the settlers after to open the valley of the Wisconsin, to the lovely land of which might come all those oppressed of Europe to find a "laborinth of pleasure," as Radisson wrote prophetically almost two centuries before they came— "the country so pleasant, so beautiful & Fruitful that it grieved me to see yt ye world could not discover such inticing countrys to live in. This I saw because the Europeans fight for a rock in the sea against one another."

PART TWO

White Men and Red

THE region from Bridgeport to the mouth of the Wisconsin was, typically, one of many islands, but in this area they were even more heavily wooded than in any other place, with more virgin timber, and all over the water there lingered that stimulating, refreshing pungence of the deep woods, a distillation of fragrant leaves and flowers, decaying vegetation, wet soil, and water itself; despite the heat, this lay coolingly upon the river, flowing from the woods, and presently, along the slopes of Wyalusing, where the islands are under protection as restricted areas, and wild life is not molested, the aspect of wilderness grew and the fragrant pungence was even more pronounced. Already the bluffs of Iowa rose up bluely before us, Pike's Peak and the ridges north and south, and the Wisconsin's current became steadily less strong, rebuffed a little by the Mississippi, as it were. In this late afternoon now, there was little sound but that of the water, though the spotted sandpipers were incessant in their fluted cries rising from shaded places, the birds restlessly moving from shore to shore; but apart from this and the water's sound along the shores, and the dipping of the paddles, nothing—only this aspect of wilderness and the wonderfully refreshing distillation of the woods in that place. All too soon, it seemed, we faced the last of the Wisconsin's beautiful islands, a wedge-shaped mound of sand heavily overgrown with willows, situated in the precise center of the river's mouth, so that two openings flowed water into the Mississippi, the channel following the more southerly of the two. In the mud and sand of the Wisconsin's mouth there were turtles in great numbers, in one place fully two hundred heads being above water at the same time, not the painted turtles which had rolled off logs and stumps into the river from Sac Prairie to the mouth, but the soft-shells—flat, muddy brown, yellow. To the north lay Prairie du Chien, to reach which we did not find it necessary to take the Mississippi, but only to move up through the countless sloughs between the Wisconsin's mouth and that higher land upon which the city stood, the place of meeting for white men and red for more than two hundred years. . . .

—*Sac Prairie Journal*
July 24, 1941

1. CONFIDENTIAL AGENT

HERCULES DOUSMAN was a man who knew his own mind.

Even at twenty-six in the twenty-sixth year of the nineteenth century, he was a commanding figure, and had repeatedly demonstrated his ability in the employment of the American Fur Company at Mackinac. The American Fur Company was Astor's company; Astor had incorporated it in 1808, and, while it was ostensibly a corporation, Astor was the company, dictating its policies from first to last. Of these policies Hercules had been well aware and had not always approved. Far from it. However, since his teens, he had been at work for the American Fur Company in one capacity or another, and he had long ago learned to keep his own counsel until an opportunity presented itself not only for the expression of his counsel but for the support of it. He was doubtless aware of Astor's methods; he must certainly have learned, as the Green Bay Indian agent had communicated to the United States Superintendent of Indian Affairs, that it was a British agent of Astor's who had made the British aware in 1812 that war would be declared, enabling the redcoats to take Mackinac before the commander of the fort there had even been apprised that war had begun. Of Astor's means to gain an absolute monopoly, Hercules knew; no one working long for the American Fur Company could be unaware of those methods, which included fraud, force, and government favoritism to such an extent that the only law prevailing in the Northwest and the regions bounding it, wherever the American Fur Company was supreme, was Astor's law. The government reports of that period indicate that Astor and his agents ignored all laws enacted by Congress in favor of the interests of the American Fur Company whenever they saw fit to do so. Indeed, so rapacious was the company, that it was freely said that for any unauthorized trader, individual or agent of a competitor, to intrude upon Astor's domain was to invite the reprisal of the American Fur Company, "not stopping short of outright murder," as Gustavus Myers puts it in his *History of the Great American Fortunes.*

Nor was the debauching of the Indians pleasing to many of those traders who had spent their lives in the trade. It was not Astor's company which had introduced liquor, and this must stand to his credit. In so far as his dealings with the Indians went, Astor's initial code had been fair enough. But Astor met competition on its own terms; for over a century the Hudson's Bay Company had been debauching the Indians; and, despite the strictest federal laws, Astor followed the same course, his company violating the law constantly, so that his agents could trick the Indians in the customary manner—that is, getting them drunk and swindling them of furs and land. Since Astor knew every detail of his business, it was manifest that however much he might protest that he knew nothing of his agents' doings, he was well aware of the policies they pursued. Moreover, this brigandage was carried to its logical end—when the Indian chieftains or individual Indians themselves complained of injustices, they were promptly dispatched to the happy hunting grounds, the government was petitioned to send soldiers and stop the "Indian uprisings," and with the utmost in sanctimonious hypocrisy, Astor could point to the courts and the army rising in his support!

By these methods, Astor made himself a millionaire.

By different methods, Hercules Dousman resolved to make himself another.

He came to Prairie du Chien in 1826 as an agent for the American Fur Company. The post was at this time in charge of Joseph Rolette, who was then also an executive officer of Prairie du Chien and Crawford County. Progress had been made at the meeting place of the rivers. The Americans had built a fort there, naming it Fort Shelby; a force from St. Louis had constructed this fort and held it until 1814, when a body of redcoats came along the Fox-Wisconsin waterway, surprised and took the fort, renaming it Fort McKay. The British held Fort McKay until they were ordered to abandon it following the Treaty of Ghent; news of the treaty, however, did not reach the garrison until May, 1815, and in that month it was abandoned. The redcoats were hardly out of sight up the river before the Indians burned Fort McKay. In the following year the second American fort was erected: Fort Crawford. But, at the time of the arrival of Dousman, this fort was beginning to be deemed inadequate, and a newer, rock fort was being contemplated. The establishment of a fort in this Indian territory naturally brought settlers, and, while the fur trade was still the dominant source of revenue, among the settlers were small farmers and lead miners, who were soon to have their turn in the development of the Wisconsin River valley. But their turn was not yet; agriculture was confined to little more than subsistence farms in the vicinity of the settlement, the lead miners had only begun to move up from the Galena country into the Wisconsin region.

Hercules, son of Michael Dousman, grandson of an old Baron van Dousman who had taken off from Holland many decades before and landed in New York, came into Prairie du Chien as a "confidential" agent for Astor. He was ostensibly only a clerk in the employ of the company, subject to Rolette's orders; but there may have been an unwritten motive for his coming, for complaints about Rolette had been reaching Governor Lewis Cass of the Territory of Michigan—that Rolette was actually still a British subject, that he quarreled constantly with Augustin Grignon, a well-known fellow trader of Green Bay, who claimed Rolette had fired the Sioux against him, that he wielded a great influence among Indians of all tribes, that he did not buy furs alone, but also game, feathers, meat, corn, ginseng, and whatever the Indians had to sell, that he was a close bargainer and always demanded five more skins, so that he had been called "Five More" by the Indians. Rolette had protested these slanders, but nothing had been done for or against him.

If Hercules had been sent with instructions to report on Rolette, his reports could not have been unfavorable; there is, in fact, every evidence among the Dousman papers that Hercules grew quite fond of Rolette; indeed, after Rolette's death, he married his beautiful young widow. His fondness for Rolette, however, had nothing to do with Rolette's wife. He learned that Rolette did indeed have a way with the Indians, that on the whole Rolette was opposed to debauching them, that he went off on long trips and lived among them, that he was extremely capable. So he settled himself to the trade, serving as Rolette's clerk.

By 1827, when the American Fur Company absorbed the Columbia Company, Astor's monopoly in the Northwest was practically unopposed by either individual traders or any rival company. Nevertheless, 1827 was late for the trade in the valley of the Wisconsin, and doubtless Astor was not unaware of it; however, Prairie du Chien was still the center of a great trading district, an area now taken up by four states— Wisconsin, Minnesota, Iowa and Illinois—and it was at this time the most important settlement in the Upper Mississippi Valley; not for three decades would Fort Snelling, now St. Paul, exceed it in importance; and, if Astor was beginning to see the handwriting on the wall, his view was that of a man already a millionaire, and it was not Dousman's view.

Hercules believed that there was still a good deal of wealth in the trading area of Prairie du Chien, and he meant to obtain as much of that wealth as possible for his own. Though he continued to function as Rolette's clerk, he found himself given more and more of Rolette's work, and, as he became familiar with the aspects of the trade at Prairie du Chien, he realized that, if the utmost were to be wrung from trappers and Indians alike, some kind of permanent peace would have to be established.

He could hardly have come to that decision at a worse time in the history of that portion of the Michigan Territory. The Winnebago had been complaining with mounting fury about the white invasion of their lead lands on the Fever River and elsewhere; the Sioux and the Fox were bickering about their boundary line; just across the Mississippi in Iowa, the Sauk were smoldering with anger about the seizure of their Rock River village and burial grounds by land-greedy white settlers, claiming that this land had never been ceded; and, to make matters worse, in the winter prior to Dousman's arrival, a trio of Winnebago, led by one Wamangoosgaraha, had wantonly murdered the Methode family, consisting of M. Methode and his wife, their five children and a pet dog, all of whom had gone to Painted Rock, a dozen miles above the settlement, to make maple sugar. The arrest of Wamangoosgaraha by Judge Boilvin, and the subsequent imprisonment of all three Winnebago so stirred the already irate Winnebago, that they took up arms and threatened to massacre the inhabitants of Fort Crawford and Prairie du Chien unless the instant release of the prisoners was forthcoming.

The result of this announcement was all that could have been desired by the Indians. The white population was thrown into panic; the commandant at Fort Crawford appealed to Colonel Josiah Snelling at Fort Snelling to reinforce the lower fort; this Snelling promptly did, and, as a result, nothing whatever happened. Until autumn of 1826. Then there occurred one of those inexplicable events that make the average citizen of the commonwealth tear his hair and usually addle him to such an extent that he votes for the party in power all over again—in the midst of the impending Winnebago uprising, the War Department blandly ordered the immediate evacuation of Fort Crawford, and the concentration of the Fifth Infantry from that fort at Fort Snelling. Suspected of complicity in this puzzling order was Colonel Snelling himself; he had quarreled with Rolette and other traders, and it was charged that he was now determined to leave them to their own devices. The Winnebago, of course, could not know this; the complexities of dealing with the white men were enough in themselves without the added burden of trying to understand what went on among them; they were simple people and made the obvious deduction when knowledge of the troop movement reached them—they decided that the soldiers were insufficient in number and were perhaps afraid of them, and the northward movement was tantamount to an admission that Prairie du Chien lay at their mercy.

This was the ridiculous situation that Hercules confronted. Moreover, as if these factors were not enough, Hercules encountered yet another difficulty; this was in the person of the subagent for Indian Affairs, Captain John Marsh, living with Judge Boilvin. Captain Marsh was a man of complex character; he was one of the most interesting inhabitants of Prairie du Chien at that time, and a man deserving of examination. He was both brave and cowardly, both honest and treacherous, courageous and devious. He had married a half-breed, Marguerite Decouteaux, whose Sioux background did much to determine the course of Marsh's actions, for, curiously, Marsh seemed to have caught from his wife the ancient Sioux enmity for the Fox and Sauk, and he could not prevent himself from siding with the Sioux even to the extent of condoning and aiding their murderous attacks on small parties of Fox. Ironically, he had just been made justice of the peace of Crawford County by Governor Lewis Cass—that same Governor Cass who had always manifested a fine partiality for the interests of Astor and his company—and he had made a splendid beginning by enraging both the civil authorities and the military.

Yet it was Marsh who undertook to do something about the dissatisfaction of the Winnebago.

Basically the trouble with the Winnebago could be laid directly to the occupation of their lead-mining country. Though Prairie du Chien was not itself in the lead region, it was just across the Wisconsin from it, and it was the most important of the settlements in that area of the Michigan Territory, the settlement to which residents of the lead-mining towns—Potosi, Mineral Point, Platteville, Dodgeville—looked for protection.

The history of the lead-mining region began with Nicolas Perrot, for it was he, sent by Governor de La Barre in 1683 on a mission to establish an alliance with the Iowa and Sioux near the mouth of the Wisconsin, who discovered the lead country by finding the mines of the Indians along what is now the Des Moines River. Radisson and Groseilliers had reported lead mines in the region of Dubuque, that is, among the Sioux in their time, and the journals of both Marquette and La Hontan make mention of the mineral wealth of the country south of the mouth of the Wisconsin, though there is no evidence that either explorer ever visited the mines. By 1687 a lead mine was marked on Hennepin's map in the vicinity of what was to become Galena, the capital of the lead-mining region, and in the same year Joutel's *Journal Historique* says that "travelers who have been at the upper part of the Mississippi affirm that they have found mines of very good lead there."

The area of the lead-mining region, save for scattered mines west of the Mississippi, was bounded on the north by the Wisconsin from its mouth to approximately the south line of the Sauk Prairie, on the east by a line drawn from that point southeastward to the Rock River, thence on the southwest and south by the Rock River to its mouth, and thence from the mouth of the Rock to the mouth of the Wisconsin along the Mississippi on the west. The heart of the region was thus along the Fever River.

In the Wisconsin portion of the Michigan Territory diggings were early established at settlements which were to become Mineral Point, Dodgeville, Platteville, but the center of activity in Wisconsin was for the most part well away from the valley of the river, though the bulk of the lead mined was shipped down the Wisconsin from the vicinity of Helena, the English Prairie, and other landings established specifically for the purpose of loading lead to be shipped down to St. Louis. The region included approximately ten thousand square miles, but lead was found away from its boundaries, indicating that the Indians had used lead even before the introduction of firearms demonstrated its use in warfare, for Jonathan Carver reported in 1766 that lead was to be found "in the streets" of "the Great Town of the Saukies" on the Sauk Prairie, but concluded that the lead had come from the deposits at the Blue Mound, south of the Wisconsin at that point.

By the time of Carver's visit, of course, the enterprising French were engaged in the lead trade. Captain Henry Gordon narrated that the French "have large boats of 20 tons, rowed with 20 oars, which will go in seventy odd days from New Orleans to the Illinois. . . . They . . . carry lead." The first application for a concession of lead-mine land along the Fever River was made by Martin Miloney Duralde in summer 1769. Soon thereafter lead stood second to fur as the most important and valuable export of the country.

The early lead grants were made by the government on land ceded by the Indians, and when mining was done on Indian lands, the early miners were careful to obtain the consent of the Indians. Julien Dubuque, that energetic and popular Mississippi Valley pioneer, obtained permission from the Sauk and Fox "to work lead mines tranquilly and without any prejudice to his labors"; this was as early as 1788. Dubuque's miners roamed Indian territory on both sides of the Mississippi unmolested, and freely showed the Indians how to mine and smelt the ore. Though the Indians had undoubtedly taken out lead for perhaps a century before Dubuque's time, there is nothing to show that they could smelt or cast the ore before they were instructed by white men. The Indian method of trading lead was in large unshapely masses, obtained by the crude means of reducing the mineral by throwing it into open fires. The Indians assisted Dubuque's miners, in mining as well as prospecting, miners roamed over the entire lead region from the Wisconsin to the Rock before the treaty of 1804, ceding Sauk and Fox owned mining districts to the United States. Dubuque's monopoly was shaken by the treaty of 1804 and the Louisiana Purchase, but it was not until 1819 that the French-Canadian hold on the lead trade with the Indians was broken.

In 1819 there was a general movement into the lead country. Almost a decade before, Nicolas Boilvin, then the government agent for the Winnebago, reported that the Indians had manufactured four hundred thousand pounds of lead, which they exchanged for goods from Canadian traders, and suggested that the government might wisely introduce a blacksmith and improved tools among the Indians to extinguish the Canadian trade. Indeed, the French-Canadian monopoly was so strong that early American miners invading the lead region in defiance of that monopoly were killed. Not until after 1819 was there any major amount of lead mining in the vicinity of the Wisconsin, but by 1822, hordes of squatters and prospectors from Missouri, Kentucky and Tennessee converged upon the region and flowed over all its territory, completely disregarding treaties and federal laws. In 1829 R. W. Chandler of Galena (the settlement had been named two years before) published a map of the "Lead Mines on the Upper Mississippi River" designed to bring to the region even more miners and settlers—an attractive map marking all the furnaces, deposits, diggings, roads, and even the location of a few copper (sulphuret) deposits found, he asserted, "over such an extent of this country, as to justify the expectation of that metal being produced in considerable quantities." Chandler had his map engraved in Cincinnati and distributed in the East. Not only was it a map, but it was also completely informative—about the country: "This tract of country upon the high lands is gently rolling, but as you approach the larger water courses it becomes more and more hilly, terminating in high, calcareous bluffs along their margins. About one third is first rate farming land. Not more than a tenth is covered with timber, which grows in detached groves; the balance prairie. Springs of the purest water are to be found in abundance. The interior is healthy; no local causes of fever exist except immediately on the Mississippi. The climate is pleasant and desirable except during the spring months. Snow seldom exceeds 12 inches in depth during winter. All the fruits, vegetables and grain which grow in the same latitude in our Eastern States, would succeed equally well here;" about the population: "In 1825—200 . . . 1828—10,000;" about the lead manufactured: "In 1825—439,472 lbs. . . . 1828—12,957,100 lbs."

The Indians and their claims were not considered to be of any consequence in the rush for wealth. If the treaty of 1804 had stood without challenge, there might have been no reason for listening to the protests of the Indians. But the treaty of 1804 was with the Fox and Sauk; there were also Winnebago and some Sioux in this country. Moreover, with that unerring instinct for doing the wrong thing, certain government officials had in 1816 concluded a treaty at St. Louis granted to the Ottawa, Chippewa, and Potawatomi "all lands lying north of a line drawn due west of the southern extremity of Lake Michigan to the Mississippi." The commissioners made an exception of a tract "five leagues square, to be designated by the President," presumably to be defined as including the lead mines as soon as the actual boundaries of the lead regions could be set.

Clashes between red men and white began to occur from the time of the 1804 treaty, increasing slightly after Dubuque's death in 1810, but not really becoming a major threat to settlement until after 1819. Before the end of the 1820's it was clear that something had to be done about the Indian trouble without delay—not only in regard to the lead mines. Captain Marsh recognized this as easily as anyone else in a position of responsibility, and he did it. He wrote to Cass to say that Fort Crawford had been abandoned, that the military had gone and taken the Winnebago prisoners along. "Several families have removed from this place to the mines, and if the Post is not re-established in the spring, it is probable the settlement will be nearly deserted. The miners at Fever River have been very successful and the prospects are better than ever. It is said by well informed persons that there are now 1500 Sauks at the mines and that the number will be at least doubled next season. Some of the most important discoveries of ore are on the lands of the Winnebagos, and some difficulty has occurred in consequence. The Indians are actively engaged in working their own mines and are jealous of the intruders. *I think some interference on the part of the government will be necessary.*"

Governor Cass thought so too. He announced that in July of 1827 he would hold a council of Indian representatives and civil authorities at Green Bay to settle the differences, and, if possible, purchase the lead country from the Winnebago.

No one thought to ask the irate Winnebago whether this was satisfactory.

2. RED BIRD

Something about the Sioux in Wisconsin conditioned them to make trouble. Perhaps word of Cass's
proposed meeting to arbitrate difficulties reached the
Sioux and caused them to believe that the impending
attack on the white population of Prairie du Chien
would not after all take place. The Sioux enjoyed a good
fight, particularly if they were at an obvious advantage
over their enemies; conversely, the prospect of losing
out on a fight was not pleasant. A party of Sioux went
to the village of Red Bird, on the Black River some
thirty miles above Prairie du Chien, and informed him
that the prisoners held for the Methode murders had
been cruelly put to death, their bodies "cut into pieces
no bigger than the spots in a bead garter!"

This was disgracefully untrue, but the Sioux were
possibly putting into practice a tactic learned from certain of their white brethren. Red Bird, best loved and
most pacific of the Winnebago chieftains, had been responsible almost alone for the delay in the uprising; he
did not wish to make war upon the whites; he was well
aware of the might the whites could summon from the
East, and he was not anxious to challenge them. The
code of the Winnebago demanded that two lives be
taken for every Winnebago slain, and, when word of
the Sioux story went around among the Winnebago, it
was impossible to prevail upon the Indians to still their
insistent demands for vengeance. Red Bird was especially subjected to pressure by Wekau and other lesser
chieftains, who demanded that Red Bird "take meat,"
and the pressure was apparently so great that Red Bird
assented, however reluctantly. He did not wish to be
called an "old woman," the greatest insult that could

possibly have been hurled at him by his braves if he refused to avenge his tribe.

But it was June before anything happened.

Hercules Dousman was at his desk on the 27th of that month, when he saw four Indians going toward the agency house. He was startled to observe that they were in war paint and regalia, but was somewhat less ill at ease when he saw that they were led by Red Bird, whose peaceful policies were well known to the traders. Their visit with Captain Marsh, however, was very brief. Then they went on to the tavern of Jean Brunet, and from this they emerged carrying a jug of whisky. Hercules watched them; they went on to the house of James Lockwood, a fellow trader, which Red Bird entered and left hurriedly; from there they wandered out of the village in the direction of McNair's Coulee, not pausing to stop at McNair's house.

Some time passed: an hour or a little more. Then the village was startled by the wild screaming of a woman. Marsh, Dousman, Brunet, Michael Brisbois— all popped out of their buildings; traders appeared in the streets, the half-breed engagés and voyageurs who were in Prairie du Chien at the time.

The woman was Mme. Registre Gagnier, who lived three miles down McNair's Coulee. She came running, stumbling into the village, clutching her three-year-old baby, and screamed that her husband had been murdered by Red Bird and Wekau. When she became coherent enough to think of it, she added that an old soldier, Solomon Lipcap, had also been killed. Of her baby she could not speak; she had taken the three-year-old and run; the baby had been left behind.

Fear and panic immediately struck the inhabitants of Prairie du Chien. There was no immediate realization that the episode represented a Winnebago vengeance murder and did not signalize a general attack. Captain Marsh, in the absence of Judge Lockwood, took charge; he raised a posse and galloped out to the Gagnier home, where they found Gagnier and Lipcap dead and scalped. Moreover, the baby had been scalped, too, but, though her neck had been cut to the bone, she was still alive, and was destined not only to recover, but to live to an advanced age.

The posse, failing to keep the track of Red Bird and his companions, returned to Prairie du Chien. By this time all the outlying farms had been abandoned; wagons rolled into the village carrying the farming population. Naturally, the fort was the first place of refuge; since it had been abandoned and partially dismantled, it could serve for the defense of the civilian population. Fortunately, a few damaged arms and an old brass swivel had been left. The walls and blockhouses needed repair, an earthwork had to be raised around the bottom logs of the fort—these things Marsh set the cowed inhabitants to doing at once. Then he lost no time in sending Indian runners out with messages for help, to all the garrisons up and down the Mississippi, from Fort Snelling to St. Louis; he sent word to Governor Cass, who was at the moment on his way to Green Bay to attend the council he had called for July 1st at the Butte des Morts on the Fox River; he dispatched to Lockwood, en route to New York, a simple, urgent message: "For God's sake return!"

Less than a hundred people were available to fight the Indians, women and men together. Fortunately, Marsh's message reached Lockwood, who came back at once. Moreover, Marsh energetically rounded up a hundred friendly Menominee, who could serve as express riders and messengers. At the same time, he had not forgotten the scheduled meeting at the Butte des Morts, and attempted to reach friendly Winnebago to send them upriver, himself to lead them to the council grounds. But four days out of Prairie du Chien the party met Governor Cass coming down the Wisconsin; the governor had been apprised of the situation, and, anticipating a general war in which Sauk, Fox, and Sioux might bury their differences long enough to join the Winnebago against the whites, had determined upon swift measures to counteract the uprising.

The shedding of blood was a concrete fact which could not be ignored, and the effect of it was to start troop movements converging upon Prairie du Chien. Naturally, the Winnebago were well aware of what was going on; their spies brought word of two keelboats of troops down the Mississippi from Fort Snelling, of others coming up from St. Louis, of volunteers from the lead-mining regions, of the arrival of Brigadier General Atkinson to take charge; they felt considerably less like carrying on a war, but followed the lead of Red Bird and began to gather in the vicinity of the Fox-Wisconsin portage, being careful to keep out of the way of the soldiers.

Having accomplished the gathering of troops at Prairie du Chien, Governor Cass returned to the Butte des Morts and on August 6th, opened his council before approximately a thousand Indians of all tribes, including the warring Winnebago. Cass made an impressive speech, crying out that unless the Gagnier murderers were surrendered to the military, he would order a wide path cut through their country, a path cut with guns.

The Indians were mindful of past history, and signed the treaty offered to them; this resulted in the withdrawal of some of Red Bird's support. It was the old game of dividing the enemy, and, as usual, it worked very well; the Winnebago were thrown into consternation and doubt; the deserters were ready and willing to give information to the army, looking forward to possible future favors; and the military were quick to take advantage of the moment.

Major William Whistler, with a force numbering over two hundred soldiers, militia, and Menominee, marched boldly through the Indian country toward the portage, while from the south General Atkinson began the 130-mile trek along the Wisconsin to that same point. So rapid and impressive were these troop movements that the Winnebago were astounded and panic-stricken. They had no alternative but to face the menace of the guns or surrender Wekau and Red Bird; they wished to do neither, but had to choose one.

Major Whistler, Captain Marsh, and their company reached the portage and made camp to await the arrival of General Atkinson and his men from Prairie du Chien. The day was the last of August. Accompanying Major Whistler's party was T. L. McKenney, the United States commissioner for Indian affairs, determined to avoid all unnecessary bloodshed. He had as his personal guide some Stockbridge Indians, who, on the following afternoon, gave the alarm to say that a hostile Winnebago was approaching McKenney's tent. Ever since their arrival at the portage, the encampment had received Indian scouts and spies, who reported that the Winnebago under Red Bird were near by, that the Winnebago did not want to fight, and yet did not want to surrender Red Bird and Wekau either. Major Whistler proposed to go out after them, to fall upon the Winnebago where they waited, but McKenney would not have it so, preferring to leave the first move up to the now hopelessly outnumbered Winnebago, a consideration unfortunately not always given the Indians.

The approaching Winnebago came directly to Mc-

Kenney's tent: clearly, the warring Winnebago had had spies of their own and were informed that McKenney was with the party at the portage; and, when the commissioner stepped from his tent, the Winnebago addressed him.

"Do not strike," he said, and, raising his arm slowly to point to a place in the sky where the sun would be in midafternoon, added, "When the sun is at that place tomorrow, Red Bird and Wekau will come in."

That was all; he wrapped his blanket around him and walked into the west.

In the course of the afternoon three more Indians came, one by one, to convey the same message: all deeply stirred, manifesting their sorrow at the need for surrendering Red Bird and Wekau.

On the following day, which was September 2nd, one of the Oneida scouts belonging to Major Whistler's command came in to report that the Winnebago were on the way. They were already within sight, in fact, and had been seen. The Winnebago made an impressive appearance, coming along a high bluff to the west in a long, colorful file: some thirty of them, led by an old chieftain carrying an American flag, followed by another carrying a white flag, in turn followed by a second chieftain bearing another American flag, and then a second Indian with again a white flag. Some of the company were mounted, some were not, but always the flag bearers, who were on foot, led the party along the ridge, descending the face of the bluff. While they approached, they sang: a sad keening, the death chant, causing a hush to fall upon the encampment, a hush broken only by the military band playing Pleyel's hymn. A detachment of soldiers rode out to escort the Indians through the ranks standing at attention to McKenney.

The leading chieftain, old Caramaunee, known to

all the men from the post at the mouth of the river, advanced to McKenney and addressed him: "Red Bird and Wekau are here. They have come in like braves. We know of no wrong they have done; they have but fulfilled the tribal law; to us they are heroes. We ask only this: treat them as braves; do not put them in irons."

Then he stepped aside and revealed Red Bird.

Red Bird had always been a handsome figure of a man, but on this day he was magnificent. He was dressed in white elkskin, fringed at the bottom; his sleeves were slit and likewise fringed, and his bronze arms showed through. His leggings were similarly of dressed elkskin, fringed at the seams, and decorated with blue-stained river shells. He wore a wide scarlet cloth about his neck and across his upper breast and back; upon this lay a collar of white and blue wampum, dangling polished lynx claws; and on his shoulders he wore still the preserved red birds (cardinals or scarlet tanagers) which symbolized his name. His head was uncovered, and his face unpainted, save for two crescents in green. He looked less like an Indian than many of the white men, standing six feet high, and with features that were so fine that they seemed almost feminine. He stood before McKenney while the commissioner told Caramaunee that he could promise nothing in Red Bird's favor, but presently the commissioner had finished, and waited to hear Red Bird.

The proud Winnebago chieftain spoke. "I am ready. I do not wish to be put in irons. Let me be free. I have given away my life"—as he said this, he caught up dust between his finger and thumb and blew it into the air—"like that. I would not take it back. It is gone." He then threw his hands behind him to signify that he was leaving all things of life and going forward into the unknown country that is death.

McKenney demanded to know why he had done this thing, and in reply Red Bird put the case for the Indians not only in the Michigan Territory, but wherever the white men had invaded their territory. After explaining that he had been deceived as to the murder of Wamangoosgaraha by the Sioux who "wished only to involve us in war so that they could fight against the Fox and the Saukenauk and the Chippewa," he went on to say: "I do not know that I have done wrong. I come now to sacrifice myself to the white man because it is my duty to save my people from the scourge of war. If I have done wrong, I will pay for it either with horses or with my life. I do not understand the white man's law, which has one set of words for the white man and another for the red. The white men promised us that the lead mines would be ours, but they did nothing to put the men who came to take possession away from them. If an Indian took possession of something belonging to a white man, the soldiers would come quickly enough. We have been patient. We have seen all this. We have seen the ancient burial grounds plowed over. We have seen our braves shot down like dogs for stealing corn. We have seen our women mocked and raped. We have seen the white men steal our lands, our quarries, our forests, our waterways, by lying to us and cheating us and making us drunk enough to put marks on papers without knowing what we were doing. When first the Long Knives came, the prophets told us they would never be honest with us. We did not believe them. We do now. When word came to us that Wamangoosgaraha was slain, I went forth and took meat. I did not know it was false; so I did no wrong. I fulfilled the law of the Winnebago. I am not ashamed. I would not be ashamed. I have come because the white men are too strong, and

I do not wish my people to suffer. Now I am ready. Take me."

With the arrest of Red Bird and Wekau, the Winnebago menace subsided. But the Indian trouble was not yet done, and there was little likelihood that it would be ended until the injustices to the Indians were rectified or the Indians were moved.

Moving the Indians was manifestly less expensive.

3. Fort Winnebago

The United States government was not sanguine about the settlement of the Winnebago uprising. There were already forts at both ends of the Fox-Wisconsin waterway—Fort Howard at Green Bay, Fort Crawford at Prairie du Chien—and it was entirely logical that a third fort should be constructed at the juncture of the two rivers, at the portage itself. It was almost a year later that the order came through to Fort Howard, August 19, 1828, reading: "The three companies of the first regiment of infantry, now at Fort Howard [are] to proceed forthwith under the command of Major Twiggs of that regiment to the portage between the Fox and Ouisconsin rivers, there to select a position and establish a military post." Logs for a temporary barracks were rafted down the Wisconsin for a distance of six miles or thereabouts, and moved by ox team across the portage to the high hill to the right of the river selected as the site of the fort.

The fort itself was constructed in the following spring, largely under the supervision of a young lieutenant only recently come from West Point: Jefferson Davis. Davis took a picked crew of soldiers and went up the Wisconsin for some fifty miles to a place along one

of the river's larger tributaries, the Yellow, and cut
lumber there, building a dam to flood out his rafts of
timber. The timber was cut by hand with whipsaws,
while bricks for the chimneys and fireplaces were being
baked by other soldiers not far from the fort along the
Wisconsin. Moreover, the soldiers constructed much of
the furniture themselves, planted a vegetable garden,
laid down parade grounds, dug a forty-foot well, built
an icehouse, a jail, and a wine cellar; and having done
these things resigned themselves to the discipline of life
in a military fort until a chance for action presented
itself.

This was in the offing, its nature almost farcical
were it not for the tragedy inherent in the situation
which ultimately commanded the services of the soldiers stationed at Fort Winnebago.

Meanwhile, events resumed their natural course at
Prairie du Chien. There Captain Marsh busied himself
by working with his wife on a dictionary of the Sioux
language, and, completing this, wrote a grammar entitled *Rudiments of the Grammar of the Sioux Language*. In the same time, Hercules Dousman was busy
with a multitude of small things, not alone the matters
of the trade. He had begun to ride around the country
on all sides of Prairie du Chien, and made an excellent
map of that region; he had learned Indian languages;
and, while King Rolette, as he was called, was increasingly often away among the tribes in upper Wisconsin,
he supervised the purchasing of supplies for the Rolette
household; he made a careful study of real estate in the
Prairie du Chien region as well as throughout those
places to which he traveled—Milwaukee, especially,
foreseeing a great future for that port. At this time he
began to invest in real estate.

It was not to be supposed that the Indians, following the surrender of their leader, would remain passive. They would not have minded if Red Bird had been granted an immediate trial, but that, unfortunately, was not done; Red Bird was cast into prison, where he had to languish until Judge Doty got around to appearing for the trial. There was, naturally, no regularity about the judiciary circuit in frontier Wisconsin. To the Winnebago, who regarded the white man's shackles with extreme distaste, imprisonment was an indignity far worse than the pronouncement and execution of the death sentence; and the longer Red Bird remained in prison, the more the Winnebago muttered. Moreover, word was passing among the Winnebago that the white men were ignominiously and slowly causing Red Bird to die in his cell while he awaited a trial.

In December, 1827, information came to Prairie du Chien that the Winnebago at Prairie La Crosse had exposed the bodies of the braves killed in the past summer on a scaffold, above which on a pole rode the scalp of Registre Gagnier, whose murder had precipitated the uprising; this was a symbol of Winnebago ill feeling, and was so understood by all the Indians and all those white men and half-breeds who had had any dealings with their red brethren. The new Indian agent, General Joseph Street, was of the opinion that the white men must answer this defiance of the Winnebago, and courageously Captain Marsh set out alone for Prairie La Crosse and, in the dead of night, took down and carried away the Gagnier scalp—an act which, for its boldness, astonished the Winnebago and for a time quieted their unrest.

But not for long, for it was only too apparent that Red Bird, his spirit broken, was dying. Judge Doty was not yet ready for Red Bird's trial, and while he delayed, the Indian medicine men foretold Red Bird's death.

Pierre Pauquette, the fearless, honest giant of a man who was the agent in charge of the trading post at the portage, sent word by other traders that the Winnebago were gathering again; he was himself the French child of a Winnebago mother, and he had learned from the Indians themselves that they meant to "take meat," in vengeance for the sufferings and indignity heaped upon Red Bird, who, they now believed, was being poisoned by the Americans. This was not their only complaint, however; despite all the fine words of Governor Cass and the treaty guarantees, the lead country of the Indians was still being mined. Indeed, young Henry Dodge —destined within a decade to become Wisconsin's first territorial governor—had led a company of militia into the regions just south of the Wisconsin River valley below Prairie du Chien for the express purpose of mining the lead. Only the past autumn, Major Rountree and J. B. Campbell, who had bought Metcalf's lead diggings, had taken out no less than $30,000 worth of lead; so rumor had it, and patently, according to Dodge and all the other white men in the region, it was crass stupidity to permit such wealth to fall to the Indians.

In mid-February of 1828 Red Bird died—without a trial. He was hastily buried somewhere within the fort, and so remained until a skeleton presumed to be his was unearthed just inside the fort gate in 1940 in excavations conducted by the Reverend Leland Cooper. Judge Doty was lost somewhere in the wilderness, though he turned up presently, much too late to be of any service to Red Bird. In the lead regions, Dodge thumped his chest and promised to protect the lead miners and the diggings. Exasperated beyond measure, and yet aware of the strength the whites had mustered in the previous summer, the Winnebago sent Corumna the Lame, an old chieftain, to lay their grievances before

General Street. Corumna could not avoid pointing out to Street that there was a curious difference among the white man's laws. Each time an Indian went on the land of a white man, he was driven off; but when a white man took an Indian's land, nothing was done to him. How was it, then, that the Indian was called the white man's brother? He was not treated as a brother should be treated. Street promised to write to the governor. That was not enough, Corumna insisted; the Winnebago had no reason to believe in the words or papers of white men.

So pushed, Street decided on action. He ordered Marsh to serve a notice of eviction on Dodge and his men. Marsh set out at once and served the notice, to which Dodge replied that he was not aware of definite lines of demarcation setting the ceded territory of the Chippewa and Ottawa from that of the Winnebago, and he intended to stay where he was. For all that Dodge knew, the government had never defined that "five leagues square" from which the Indians were to be excluded; if Marsh and Street had any grievance, they might take it up with the officials at Washington, and perhaps someone might get around to laying out that "five leagues square." General Street could put that in his pipe and smoke it. Young Dodge was sure of himself and made no bones about it; he had no illusions about his own importance, either. He was cool, daring, altogether as colorful and handsome as a cinema star playing Anthony Adverse over a century later. General Street was incensed; he ordered Major Fowle to take a company of soldiers and forcibly evict Dodge and his miners. With all apologies, Major Fowle presented his compliments, he could not do it; he had only a little over a hundred men fit for duty, and the fort could not be abandoned.

Into this impasse came Governor Cass with the only obvious solution in keeping with the fixed policy of the white man toward the Indian: another council, this time held in Green Bay in August of 1828. The Winnebago parleyed, accepted presents, signed papers and transferred their lead lands in the face of governmental pressure and the plain fact that into that area from Galena on the Mississippi to Dodgeville in Wisconsin had poured no less than ten thousand lead-hungry settlers.

Once more the Indian trouble had abated. It was not for long. Rid of their grievances about the lead regions, the Indians could still cause trouble among themselves. In December the old war between the Fox and the Sioux broke out again. In midwinter Captain Marsh, after his record of courage and service, showed that paradoxical other side of his nature which was ultimately to bring about his downfall. He carried a war challenge to the Sioux from a band of Chippewa he had encountered on the Black River. General Street's ire at this act was sufficient to cost Marsh his office as subagent; unperturbed, Marsh opened a store to sell merchandise; and within a short time indeed, he was selling guns, rifles, and ammunition to the Indians in direct defiance of the law. His partiality to the Sioux was manifest, and he was soon at loggerheads with Dousman, Street, and the military. Unfortunately, the military were far more concerned over the progress of the new fort than over the affairs of Captain John Marsh. Outbursts of violence among the Indians continued until the treaty of 1829, which dealt directly for the cession of close to eight million acres of farm and mineral land in Wisconsin and Illinois and was designed to settle all grievances of the assembled Sioux, Fox, Sauk, Winnebago, Chippewa, Ottawa, Menominee, and Potawatomi, and there were present at this council, held at Prairie du

Chien, Indian agents and subagents, interpreters, the military, and many strangers, including, according to Caleb Atwater, one of the commissioners, persons from "Liverpool, London, and Paris."

But though Keokuk, hereditary chieftain of the Sauk, now residing in Iowa, was present, there was one Sauk leader who was not. That was the Black Sparrow Hawk; his absence was an expression of his anger against the whites, and was destined to give the restless military at Fort Winnebago an opportunity to go into action.

4. BLACK HAWK

The Black Sparrow Hawk was born to a lesser chieftain named Pyesa and his squaw, presumably on the great prairie of the Sauk at the bend in the Wisconsin below the greater bend at the portage. In his *Autobiography*, Black Hawk says that he was born on the Rock River in 1767; but in the same paragraph tells that his grandfather had been born in Montreal; presumably, then, his family followed the Sauk route through Wisconsin and lived on the Sauk Prairie in 1766, when Carver visited the village, and until shortly after, when the tribe moved to the mouth of the Rock. It is conceivable, in the light of these facts, that Black Hawk was brought to the Rock River village as a very small child, and, when the idea of the *Autobiography* was put to him not long before his death in 1838, he gave the Rock River village as the site of his birth without any investigation.

He was in 1832 no longer a young man, but one of commanding mien, fearless, and not a braggart. He was about five and a half feet tall, and not heavy, rather spare. Reuben Gold Thwaites in his *The Black Hawk*

War, describes him: "His somewhat pinched features exaggerated the prominence of the cheekbones of his race; he had a full mouth, inclined to be somewhat open when at rest; a pronounced Roman nose; fine 'piercing' eyes, often beaming with a kindly and always with a thoughtful expression; no eyebrows; a high, full forehead; a head well thrown back, with a pose of quiet dignity, and his hair plucked out, with the exception of the scalp-lock, in which, on ceremonial occasions, was fastened a bunch of eagle feathers." He was fearless, honest, idealistic, but not too intelligent; in another century he would have been called a Red or a radical; in whatever he did, he was sincere, though it was the custom of the whites to doubt the sincerity of any Indian leader.

The Black Sparrow Hawk had a strong and valid grievance; this was that the white settlers at the mouth of the Rock River in Illinois had torn up not only the Sauk's cornfields, but had taken possession of their village there—the village which had been founded after the removal of the tribe from the Sauk Prairie in Wisconsin—and even their burial grounds in defiance of any treaty. Neither Keokuk nor Black Hawk had ever signed a treaty permitting this region to be taken. The position and answer of the whites was that in 1804 the Sauk chieftains had signed away this land. Unfortunately, Black Hawk's retort was only too true: in the customary procedure, the whites had persuaded secondary leaders to sign this treaty—Pashepaho, Quashquame, Outchequa, and Hashequarhiqua—in the place of those leaders whom the Indians would follow.

Black Hawk had been smoldering for some time. It was the unfortunate tendency of the white men to look upon him as an upstart, in any case; he was not an hereditary chieftain, he had no right to supersede Keo-

kuk; and Keokuk was a peace-loving Indian who could
be counted on to deal with the whites in the manner the
whites arrogated unto themselves. Nevertheless, it was
Black Hawk who led the Sauk, very possibly because his
cause was sound. The treaty of 1804 was nothing short
of ridiculous in its skulduggery—for an insignificant
yearly payment of a thousand dollars, the government
persuaded the Sauk and Fox to cede to the whites no less
than fifty million acres of land in the heart of the continent. It was article seven of this compact which Black
Hawk seized upon, for this article did not oblige the Indians to vacate the territory, but permitted them to
"enjoy the privilege of living or hunting" there "as long
as the lands which are now ceded to the United States"
remain public lands. The land included the Sauk village
near the mouth of the Rock River, then a village of some
five hundred families, and thus one of the largest Indian settlements on the continent. In tribal fashion, the
Sauk cultivated three thousand acres of rich alluvial
soil, and on it raised great crops of corn and pumpkins,
an accomplishment of which they were very proud.

It was from this village that the Sauk were driven.
In 1830 the squatters, illegally on the ground, had
almost completely ruined the Sauk town, had plowed
over their graves, and were as insolent as might be expected of the kind of riffraff who would desecrate a
plainly marked burial ground. Black Hawk, furious,
went to Malden to vent his indignation to his "British
Father," who naturally agreed with him; moreover,
Black Hawk received the encouragement of White
Cloud, self-styled "the Prophet," who had no love for
the whites. Thus fortified, Black Hawk returned to the
site of the Sauk village and served notice upon the
squatters there; in his *Autobiography,* he says that he
did not threaten them with bloodshed, but only with

physical eviction, and complains (the old, old story):
"The white people brought whiskey into our village,
made our people drunk, and cheated them out of their
homes, guns and traps. This fraudulent system was carried to such an extent that I apprehended serious difficulties might take place unless a stop was put to it. Consequently I visited all the whites and begged them not
to sell whiskey to my people. One of them continued the
practice openly. I took a party of my young men, went
to his home, and took his barrel and broke in the head
and turned out the whiskey. I did this for fear some of
the whites might be killed by my people when drunk."

In anger, then, he gave the squatters until the middle of the following day to remove themselves from the
country; most of them cleared out—only to go to Governor John Reynolds of Illinois and set up such a hullabaloo about Black Hawk's "war of extermination" that
the doughty governor, addled by visions of bloodshed,
issued a proclamation calling for volunteers to "repel
the invasion of the British band"—a harking back to the
time of Black Hawk's support of Tecumseh and the
British against the Americans in 1812.

The fat was in the fire.

Volunteers raced to the colors—hundreds of them
—to co-operate with ten companies of regulars under
General Gaines, and, after a demonstration before the
Sauk village, the Sauk were forced to capitulate and
retreat across the Mississippi, where, it being now too
late to raise crops, they suffered from want for the rest
of that year. The Sauk were soon in an ugly mood, and
were naturally receptive to word from the British at
Malden sent through Neapope, another Sauk chieftain,
that aid would come to them in the spring of 1832, and
to the constant mutterings of White Cloud against the
whites. Black Hawk was easily led; he believed in the

sincerity of every man, save that of the whites, about whom he had learned as bitterly as many an Indian leader before him; but he was gravely wrong to put his trust in the cupidity of White Cloud, who told Black Hawk that "he had received wampum and tobacco from the different nations on the lakes—Ottawa, Chippewa, Potawatomi; and as for the Winnebago, he had them all at his command."

Deluded, misled into believing that all the tribes which had belonged to Tecumseh's federation would join the Sauk, told by White Cloud that the Prophet was guided not alone by the British Father, but also by the lost bones of Tecumseh, the venerated Indian leader who had fallen at the Thames in 1813, despite specific warnings in 1831 from the military at Fort Crawford, delivered to Black Hawk and the Sauk by Lieutenant Jefferson Davis, Black Hawk led the Sauk across the Mississippi into the Rock River territory in the spring of 1832. The country into which he led them was one still sparsely settled, but honeycombed with Indian trails, of which two led up along the Fox-Wisconsin waterway, one to Fort Winnebago, the other to Fort Howard, apart from the route to Prairie du Chien. While a large proportion of the settlers in this area were respectable, hard-working people in the prime of life, there was also a lawless element composed of loafers and thieves, to whom a war was welcome, since it would give some of them occupation and pay. The trek back across the Mississippi was begun on April 6th; the warriors in the tribe, chiefly Sauk, numbered about half a thousand; with them went squaws, old men, children, belongings —clearly not a war party. Black Hawk's intentions were pacific at this time; he wanted to raise a crop near the Prophet's town, and prepare for war in the fall. Nevertheless, he had sent messages to the Potawatomi, some of whom, under the leadership of Big Foot and the despicable renegade, Mike Girty, serving as a British agent, were for taking the warpath. The Potawatomi chief, Shaubena, notified the whites of the approach of Black Hawk, whereupon General Henry Atkinson, known to the Indians as "White Beaver," apprised Governor Reynolds that his force of regulars could not meet the emergency and that he needed the help of a detachment of the militia. Once more Governor Reynolds issued a fiery proclamation, and sixteen hundred men assembled at Beardstown to form into four regiments, in one of which served Captain Abraham Lincoln. By May 9th the pursuit of Black Hawk and his band began.

The rest of the saga of Black Hawk is a monument to human stupidity and error.

The volunteer militia numbered almost two thousand men when the whites caught up with Black Hawk and the Sauk on May 14th, not far from the mouth of Sycamore Creek in Illinois. The meeting was between a small band of less than fifty Sauk, under Black Hawk, and two regiments of militia under Major Isaiah Stillman, proceeding in advance of the bulk of the militia. Apprised of the encampment of the militia near by, Black Hawk determined upon a difficult course; by this time, after conferences with the Potawatomi, who had sent only about a hundred braves, and the wily Winnebago, he had begun to realize that White Cloud had deceived him, and knew that he could never stand up against the force the whites had assembled against him; so he determined to ask for a truce, and forthwith dispatched three of his braves bearing a flag of truce into the white camp. These were followed by a small party of spies. The whites, some of whom were drunk, promptly dispatched as many Indians as there were in sight, quite regardless of the rules of war, so scrupulously observed by Black Hawk. Thus enraged, the Hawk ordered a suicidal attack by his braves, resolved that all should die to avenge this gross misconduct of the whites. The brave whites, who had not hesitated to display their courage in slaying the Indian truce-flag bearers, were astounded and frightened at sight of more Indians, and, not stopping to reconnoiter, set off helter-skelter for the main body of the whites; moreover, they left everything behind them, and reaching the main camp, did not stop, but went right on through, so that the entire militia was alarmed, and, beset by fear, took out also, many of them riding steadily for fifty miles and more to their own firesides, and all bearing tales of "two thousand bloodthirsty warriors" sweeping all Illinois with destruction. Had he been in camp that day, presumably Honest Abe would have ridden as hard in retreat as those others in what was to become known as Stillman's Run; but Lincoln's regiment was at the time at Dixon's Ferry, and reached the scene next day, where he assisted to bury the dead left by the troops so ignominiously put to flight by a scattered band of Indians.

The result of this farcical encounter was to throw the entire Midwest into a state of the utmost terror and confusion. "I never was so surprised, in all the fighting I have seen—knowing, too, that the Americans, generally, shoot well—as I was to see this army of several hundreds, retreating without showing fight, and passing immediately through this encampment," wrote Black Hawk later. "I did think they intended to halt here, or the situation would have forbidden attack by my party, if their number had not exceeded half mine, as we would have been compelled to take the open prairie, whilst they could have picked trees to shield themselves from our fire." Moreover, Black Hawk, almost destitute, captured all the supplies left behind, and was given the impetus to go forward on his march, despite the fact that he had since his first disillusionment learned that the British Father at Malden had, contrary to White Cloud's report, warned the Sauk to stay at peace. Terror sped throughout the territory along the Upper Mississippi and its tributaries, and from all sides the settlers hurried away from their fields to take refuge in the nearest forts.

Volunteers had to be called all over again, and throughout the Illinois and Michigan Territory country irregular hostilities—the murder of isolated whites by marauding Indians, largely Sioux and Winnebago, the depredations of the Potawatomi led by Girty—broke out. In all, some two hundred whites and easily as many Indians were slain apart from battles. Black Hawk and his Sauk moved up the Rock River to Lake Koshkonong and presently reached the Four Lakes country near the site of Madison, in their approach to the Wisconsin River valley, Black Hawk now debating whether it would not be best to recross the Mississippi and cease fighting. Meanwhile, up from the lead-mining country just south of the valley of the Wisconsin came a body of rangers under the command of the dashing Colonel Henry Dodge, striving to assure the neutrality of a village of Winnebago near the Four Lakes. Gathering more volunteers, to the number of some two hundred, Dodge moved toward the Blue Mounds country, at the eastern edge of the Wisconsin River valley southeast of the Sauk Prairie. There Dodge learned that Black Hawk had made his main encampment in the vicinity of Lake Koshkonong; indeed, at this time, the last week in June of that year, Black Hawk and his band had just returned from an unsuccessful sortie at Kellogg's Grove just over the Wisconsin-Illinois border, pursued by General Atkinson and a large company of regulars. By the time the Koshkonong camp was reached, however, the Sauk had fled.

Thus the Black Hawk War came to the Wisconsin River valley. Fully cognizant that his defeat was inevitable, Black Hawk sought to deliver as many of his people as possible across the Mississippi, and for that reason he fled directly westward, intending to cross the Wisconsin near the Sauk Prairie and pass southeastward along the Wisconsin to cross the Mississippi above Prairie du Chien. Meanwhile, with the arrival of the Sauk in Wisconsin, the forts along the river became beehives of activity, their commanders almost daily receiving scouts—whites and Indians—with advice and information. On July 10th, Colonel Dodge was dispatched to Fort Winnebago, with the brigades of Generals M. K. Alexander and James D. Henry, to obtain badly needed provisions for the regulars and militia pursuing the Sauk. There Pierre Pauquette offered to guide the soldiers to Black Hawk's stronghold, but Black Hawk had fled by the time Henry and Dodge reached the place to which Pauquette guided them, but several days later the trail of the Sauk band toward the Wisconsin River valley was accidentally discovered, and forthwith Henry and Dodge set out in pursuit, encountering straggling Winnebago, who were deserting the Sauk, and by the night of the 20th, a short skirmish was fought with retreating Sauk just beyond the last of the Four Lakes to the west, at the site of Pheasant Branch.

Late in the afternoon of July 21st, the whites caught up with the band under Black Hawk. About fifty warriors under Black Hawk and Neapope had fallen back to cover the flight of the main body of the Sauk to the bluffs and across the Wisconsin. The place they had chosen to engage the enemy was a shallow valley, bounded on the north by low, rolling moraine, and on the south by craggy bluffs known as the Wisconsin Heights, marking the beginning of the driftless area. The Wisconsin lay approximately a mile to the westward, over a low swampy area and the heavily wooded river's edge itself, and it was necessary that the Sauk cross the river and move westward with dispatch, Black Hawk believing that the regulars would not follow the Sauk, once the band had crossed the Mississippi and returned to Iowa.

"I would not have fought there but to gain time for our women and children to cross to an island," wrote Black Hawk in his *Autobiography*. "A warrior will duly appreciate the embarrassments I labored under . . ." Indeed, Black Hawk was more than embarrassed; he was grievously outnumbered, but he had no alternative, he had to make a stand and fight if his people were to effect the passage of the Wisconsin. He still had with him such of the old men and women who had not fallen back (and been shot by the advancing whites); his band was short of provisions to the point of starving; and all were exhausted by their rapid travels.

The place at which he had chosen to stand and fight was admirably suited to such a delaying action as Black Hawk hoped to accomplish. The valley itself was covered with grass to a height of six feet, and the slopes of the bluff to the south were heavily wooded; more than this, the north slope of that height formed a rude descending semicircle, its configuration of slowly rising mounds and ridges to the top of the hill and the ridge; finally, a similar semicircular formation began at the top of the hill and swept around into the south to even higher hills, this giving the Sauk the advantage of a high point of land which the whites could neither encircle nor very well storm. In addition to these natural advantages, rain was falling, with its attendant difficulty in keeping muskets dry, and night was not far distant. It was approximately five o'clock when the first shots were exchanged.

It was Black Hawk's plan that the main body of the Sauk should continue through the valley and the marsh beyond to the belt of trees that marked the Wisconsin's edge, but it was soon apparent that the direct route through the valley could not be so easily defended, and the remainder of the band mounted the rise, safe from bullets among the trees. Despite the advantage of the grass, the Sauk braves were forced steadily back until finally the whites were in command of the valley, and the Sauk on the slope. Black Hawk, mounted on a white pony, climbed boldly to the top of a little knoll slightly to eastward of the slope where the Sauk now took their stand behind trees, ready to snipe at the whites.

From where he sat, Black Hawk could look into the rain-misted north and see the paw of land which had for many decades been the home of the Sauk; he could see the curve of the Wisconsin as it swung around that land, skirting the moraine ridge less than two miles north of the Heights; he could see how it divided not far below for the long island there, the island Black Hawk had hoped his band might reach. However, he felt now, however much he believed his delaying action would be successful, Black Hawk knew that his cause was lost, and he himself in jeopardy. Even while they fought here, the remnants of his band slipped noiselessly away among the trees, down the ravines and declivities beyond the ridge, and went silently across the marshes to the river's edge and a fording place there.

The whites charged the slope, and met the fire of

the Sauk. They retreated, reformed their lines, charged again; again they were beaten back. There were casualties on both sides—how many, no one seems able to say with authority. Black Hawk writes that he lost six men, but a loss of fifty was reported to Fort Winnebago; this latter is obviously untrue, and, since the tactical position of the Sauk in the battle was the better, Black Hawk's statement must be regarded as more nearly correct. "The loss of the enemy could not be ascertained by our party," he writes; "but I am of the opinion that it was much greater, in proportion, than mine."

By this time darkness was falling. The Sauk still held the ridge; the whites, having had reports of their scouts and realizing that the Indians could take a further stand on the Wisconsin's shore, decided to make camp for the night, confident of driving the Sauk from their positions in short order at dawn. If they had known it, the majority of the Sauk had already left the Heights. Black Hawk retreated up the slope and ordered fires built, to deceive the soldiers into thinking the Sauk were camping there. In the night, Neapope, acting doubtless on instructions from Black Hawk, took his stand on one of the points of the Heights and, in a loud voice, addressed the militia in the Winnebago tongue, suing for peace, saying they wished only to retreat across the Mississippi and would harm no one; evidently the harangue was meant for the ears of Pauquette and the Winnebago known to be with the militia; but Pauquette and his Winnebago had parted from the company in the course of that day, and the Sauk scouts had not brought in this information. Thus, for the second time, an attempt by Black Hawk to halt the war came to nothing.

It was not the last attempt.

In the night the last of the Sauk slipped away to

the river, forded the Wisconsin below the long island, and moved on down the Wisconsin. A minor mystery was left in their wake; not far below the Heights, on the west bank of the Wisconsin, the Sauk doubtless came to a similar ridge of hills at the mouth of one of the oldest streams in Wisconsin—untouched by the glaciers —known then as the De Tour River, now Honey Creek. What happened there is not known; there is no account of it; but within the past decade R. S. Babington of Prairie du Sac, the upper of those twin villages destined soon to be founded on the Sauk Prairie, discovered on the boles of the old trees there evidence of battle— scars, bullets from a past time—leading to some speculation as to whether the Sauk might not have had another encounter at the Ferry Bluff, first of those bluffs past the mouth of Honey Creek, or whether, indeed, the battle of Wisconsin Heights might not have been an error of placement. All the available accounts, however, from the whites and the red men, fix the site of the battle of Wisconsin Heights at the hills on what is now Fasbender's farm, southeast of Sauk City. Whatever took place at the Ferry Bluff is shrouded in history.

As for the strategy of the battle of Wisconsin Heights, the honors went to Black Hawk. The delaying action—for it was little more than this essentially— which enabled the squaws to tear bark from the trees and make shallops in which to float their papooses and their burdens across the Wisconsin while they swam beside them, while the old men and warriors swam after them, holding their weapons over their heads, was alleged to have been described fifty years later by Jefferson Davis, made rich in experience since Wisconsin Heights by the Mexican and Civil wars, as "the most brilliant exhibition of military tactics that I ever witnessed—a feat of most consummate management and bravery, in the face of an enemy of greatly superior numbers. I never read of anything that could be compared with it. Had it been performed by white men, it would have been immortalized as one of the most splendid achievements in military history."

The saga of Black Hawk does not end with the battle of Wisconsin Heights. Arriving at the west shore of the Wisconsin, the Sauk band divided. Knowing that the movements of the braves were seriously hampered by the presence of the old men, the women, and the children, Black Hawk ordered the construction of a large raft, and obtained canoes from friendly Winnebago to carry those who wished to go down the Wisconsin. The Sauk hoped that so obviously harmless a band would be allowed to cross the Mississippi in peace. Unfortunately, the humanity of the whites was again sadly overrated. One of the militia's scouts, aware of the division of the band, sent word to General Joseph Street at Prairie du Chien, who in turn ordered Lieutenant Ritner with a small detachment of regulars from Fort Crawford to "intercept" this band. Lieutenant Ritner's concept of interception was to fire upon the helpless Sauk, killing fifteen men, drowning as many others, capturing thirty-two women and children, and four men. Some of the rest escaped to the woods, but less than a dozen ultimately got away with their lives, either starving in the woods or massacred by Menominee from the Green Bay country, acting under Colonel Stambaugh.

The whites at Wisconsin Heights, discovering in the morning that the Sauk had gone, decided not to follow them, but rather to make for Blue Mounds for provisions, and on July 23rd, they set out for the fort at that place, there encountering General Atkinson, who assumed command. On the 27th and 28th the militia crossed the Wisconsin in pursuit of the Sauk; they crossed at Helena, a deserted log village near which Dan Whitney of Green Bay had begun the construction of a shot tower the year before. The militia tore down the cabins of Helena and made rafts on which to float across the river. Regulars and militia were now together again, though not always on the best of terms. The Sauk trail was discovered leading away from the Wisconsin toward the Mississippi, turning slightly northwest and passing through country which was completely unknown to white men, thus making progress extremely difficult among the swamps, small rivers, heavily wooded hills and valleys which lay between the Wisconsin and the Mississippi there. The Sauk trail was clearly, if gruesomely, marked by the corpses of Sauk who had died of wounds and starvation, evidence of bark having been eaten, and of the devouring of tired ponies.

"Myself and band having no means to descend the Wisconsin, I started over a rugged country to go to the Mississippi, intending to cross it and return to my nation. Many of our people were compelled to go on foot for want of horses, which, in consequence of their having had nothing to eat for a long time caused our march to be very slow. At length we arrived at the Mississippi, having lost some of our old men and children, who perished on the way with hunger." That is Black Hawk's sparse account of what must have been a painful and heart-rending journey; what he thought can be well imagined; he had misled his people, bringing them to death; that he had been misled was his own fault alone; he put the blame on no one, since he permitted the Prophet, White Cloud, to ride with him still, though he knew full well that had it not been for White Cloud's grandiose promises of British and Indian ally aid, he would never have led the Sauk back across the Mississippi.

The next to last act of this tragic "war" took place just beyond the Wisconsin River valley, below the mouth of the Bad Axe River. Ready to cross the Mississippi with the pitifully small remnant of his band, Black Hawk spied the steamer *Warrior* approaching, and since he "knew the captain (Throckmorton) and was determined to give myself up to him, I then sent for my white flag. While the messenger was gone I took a small piece of white cotton and put it on a pole and called to the captain of the boat and told him to send his little canoe ashore and let me come aboard." This was the third specific attempt of Black Hawk to end the war. He spoke in the Winnebago tongue; on board the *Warrior* were some two dozen soldiers, who, with Captain John Marsh, had been up the river to enlist the aid of the Sioux—Marsh's old friends—in the campaign against Black Hawk. Captain Marsh understood the Winnebago tongue but there is nothing to show that he made any effort to prevent the slaughter that followed, and even his biographer, George D. Lyman, does not quibble about his weakness at this point. There was also present a Winnebago, who translated what Black Hawk had said; but whether the captain did not wish to believe the Winnebago or misunderstood, the result was another abrogation of the rules of war. The Sauk were fired upon, fifteen killed at once, and many more wounded.

The *Warrior* proceeded to Prairie du Chien, and from there, on the morning of August 2nd, an army of annihilation set out against the Sauk, who had for so long sought peace, and had tried on three successive occasions to obtain peace by the rules of war understood alike by red men and white, but clearly not ob-

served by the whites. To write of it as an army of annihilation is no exaggeration. Marsh had played his part
in talking the Sioux into taking up arms against the
Sauk; moreover, he had made a good thing of selling
arms to the red men, and the Indians were savage warriors against their old enemies. The Sauk were in the
act of crossing the river, and they were literally
slaughtered; this was not without a battle, however,
which cost the whites approximately a score of men—
to the miserable, weakened and starved Sauk's hundred
and fifty—and as for those who had reached the opposite shore of the Mississippi, they were set upon and
butchered by the Sioux, who did not discriminate (any
more than the whites) between women and men, children and braves. The result of this carnage was that out
of a thousand Sauk and allies who had left for the Rock
River country in the spring, only a little more than
a tenth lived to tell the tale of their wanderings.

The Black Hawk War was over—but Black Hawk
was not yet captured. Indeed, leaving careful instructions for the disposition of the braves in the event of
battle on the 2nd, Black Hawk, the Prophet, a handful
of warriors, and some squaws and children, had set out
on August 1st for a retreat at the dells of the Wisconsin,
but next day, conscience-stricken at having left his
band, he returned, in time to witness the carnage and
recognize that he could do nothing; so, embittered and
angry, he turned back into the forest, and, guided by
the Winnebago chieftain, Winnieshiek, of La Crosse,
left the scene of the three-hour massacre of his people
and fled to the Wisconsin once more.

From his retreat just above the present site of Wisconsin Dells, Black Hawk, together with White Cloud,
was led voluntarily by Chaetar and One-Eyed Decorah,
two Winnebago braves, and delivered on August 27th

to General Joseph Street and Colonel Zachary Taylor, in command of Fort Crawford at Prairie du Chien. Fully expecting the death penalty, Black Hawk in surrender was dignified, proud, aloof. Confronting his captors he made a speech that was second only to Red Bird's.

"I loved my cornfields and the home of my people. I fought for them. Know that and remember it and do not speak untruths of the war after I am gone. The war is done. My warriors fell around me, and I saw my evil day at hand. The sun rose clear on us in the morning, and at night it sank in a dark cloud, and looked like a ball of fire. This was the last sun that shone on Black Hawk. He is now a prisoner of the white man. But he can stand the torture. He is not afraid of death; he is no coward. Black Hawk is a Sauk; he has done nothing of which an Indian need be ashamed. He has fought the battles of his country against the white men, who came year after year, to cheat us and take away our lands. You know the cause of our making war—it is known to all white men—they ought to be ashamed of it. The white men despise the Indians and drive them from their homes. But the Indians are not deceitful. The white men speak bad of the Indian and look at him spitefully. But the Indian does not tell lies; the Indian does not steal. Black Hawk is satisfied. He will go to the world of spirits contented. He has done his duty—his Father will meet him and reward him. The white men do not scalp the head, but they do worse—they poison the heart; it is not pure with them. His countrymen will not be scalped, but they will in a few years become like the white men so that you cannot hurt them; and there must be, as in the white settlements, as many officers as men, to take care of them and keep them in order. Farewell to my nation. Farewell to Black Hawk."

But he was not sentenced to death, even though he was to die six years later. He was imprisoned, given in charge of Lieutenant Jefferson Davis to transfer him from Fort Armstrong on Rock Island to Jefferson Barracks in St. Louis, and of this acquaintance Davis's biographer says: "He entirely won the heart of the savage chieftain, and before they reached Jefferson Barracks there had sprung up between the stern red warrior and the young pale face a warm friendship which only terminated with the life of Black Hawk." While the Black Hawk was at Fortress Monroe, a striking portrait of the old warrior was painted by Robert Sully; the portrait is now in the Wisconsin Historical Museum.

In April of the following year Black Hawk was taken to Washington, where he met the Great White Father; and after this he was taken on a tour of the East, so that he might be impressed with the might of the whites and take the story of that might back to his people. He died in peace along the Des Moines River in what is now Davis County, Iowa, but he lived long in the memory of the men who had fought him in the brief war which took his name, men who were to rise in the annals of the nation's history—not only Lincoln and Jefferson Davis, but still another president, Zachary Taylor, the Confederate General Albert Sidney Johnston; Governor, and later, Senator Henry Dodge; the sons of Alexander Hamilton and Daniel Boone (Billy Hamilton and Nathan Boone); Generals W. S. Harney, John J. Hardin, and E. D. Baker.

With the end of the Black Hawk War, trouble between the white men and the red in the Wisconsin River valley was ended, though Indians remained in the valley of the Wisconsin for many years thereafter, chiefly Winnebago, of whom the largest body was forcibly removed from the Wisconsin's shore in the Baraboo valley

north of the Sauk Prairie in 1840. In 1844 the wily
Winnebago Chief Dandy was taken at the head of the
Baraboo, and with ox chains to his legs under his horse's
belly, was removed from the valley. Dandy, however,
was determined to stay and demanded to see Governor
Dodge at Mineral Point. He was taken before the governor and asked to be allowed to talk in council. There
Dandy took a Bible from his bosom and held it up for
Governor Dodge to see. "This good book," he said. "You
do like say in good book?" The governor, mystified,
agreed that he could not have a better book in his hands.
"Then, if a man do all it say in this book, what more
should he do?" The governor said no more would be
required of such a man. "Then look at good book; if
you find in it Dandy should go to Turkey River, Dandy
will go today; but if not, he will never go to stay."
Nor did he; shortly after, he escaped his captors, and
he lived his life out along the Wisconsin, dying at Peten
Well, a rocky peak, two hundred fifty-five feet above
the surface of the Wisconsin, near Necedah, in 1870, a
symbol of the unconquerable spirit of the Indians who
loved their land, the red men like Yellow Thunder, Red
Bird, and Black Hawk.

5. WAU-BUN

Even before the Black Hawk War life along
the Wisconsin had become comparatively settled. True,
that life extended for only a fourth of the river's length
—from the portage to the mouth of the Wisconsin—
and its focal points were at the ends of that distance,
centering around Fort Winnebago and Prairie du Chien.
Here and there, however, enterprising pioneers began
to move farther and farther away from the settlements,

and near the site of the high hill Dan Whitney of Green Bay had selected for the construction of his shot tower, a cluster of cabins had sprung up briefly: the village of Helena, abandoned in the face of the Black Hawk War, and destroyed by the military in that war. Helena had been platted in 1828, a village at the edge of the lead-mining region, and when, after the Black Hawk War, the shot tower was completed, Helena sprang up again to exist until the Civil War. Laurent Rolette, brother of King Joe, had a trading post at what was then known as English Prairie, later to become the site of Muscoda.

Life at the settlements centered around the military posts; this was especially true at Fort Winnebago, whose *Record Book* reveals aspects of life in that time. Of a council of administration held on September 14, 1832, the *Record Book* discloses: "Camp Women of this Post will wash for the officers & soldiers and at the following Rates. 50 Cents per dozen or two dollars per Month for single gentlemen, four dollars per Month for Married officers, 50 Cents per Month additional for every Child or Servant. They may wash for 50 Cents per Month for the soldiers. . . . The Ice House will be opened every Morning at Fatigue drum after Revelly by Sergeant Van Camp when families will supply themselves for the day. . . . Not more than Three men per Company will go on pass at the same time, and on their return they will report in person to their Company Officer, should they not return punctually at the expiration of their permission or should be in a state of intoxication, they will be refused passes for the next 30 days, or confined for trial or *not* at the discretion of their Company Officers." They kept accounts of the weather, many of them, noting that in one summer the weather never got higher than ninety degrees, nor lower than thirty-one "with some frost"; that the river froze over as early as November 25th; that "snow, hail, and sleet" still fell in April; and one of the soldiers nostalgically recorded the arrival of the spring birds: "March 19—five pigeons seen this day. April 10— Meadow lark appears. April 12—English snipe appears. April 14—Barn Swallows appear. April 17—Robins appear. April 19—Wood cock appears." Whether the English snipe was Wilson's snipe, commonly called jacksnipe, or the killdeer is not made clear by the amateur ornithologist.

But it is not the recorded life of Fort Winnebago that is of paramount interest in the life of early Portage. From 1830 to mid-1833, the Indian agent at Fort Winnebago was John H. Kinzie, and it is to his wife, Juliette Kinzie, that we owe the best narrative of life in those years at the portage of the Fox-Wisconsin waterway. *Wau-Bun—The "Early Day" in the North-West*, was first published in 1856, dedicated "To the Hon. Lewis Cass, in the 'Early Day' the Tried Friend of the Pioneer and the Red Man," which is a masterpiece of overstatement. However erroneous Mrs. Kinzie's concept of Governor Cass's integrity, her dedication was well meant, and there is no cloud upon her observation. She was a woman with a fine sense of humor, keen observation, and a capacity of enjoying whatever life she lived. She included in her book many anecdotes about the early Wisconsin settlers, some of whom were destined later to play important roles in the growth of the state; among them was the famed story which more than anything else brought home the degree of casualness with which King Joe Rolette treated his beautiful young wife, Jane Fisher, who was to marry the enterprising Hercules Dousman soon after her first husband's death.

"Then there was a capital story of M. Rolette

himself. At one point on the route (I think in crossing Winnebago Lake), the travellers met one of the Company's boats on its way to Green Bay for supplies. M. R. was one of the agents of the Company, and the people in the boat were his employés. Of course, after an absence of some weeks from home, the meeting on these lonely waters and the exchanging of news was an occasion of great excitement.

"The boats were stopped—earnest greetings interchanged—question followed question.

" '*Eh! bien*—have they finished the new house?'

" '*Oui, Monsieur.*'

" '*Et la cheminée, fume-t-elle?*' (Does the chimney smoke?)

" '*Non, Monsieur.*'

" 'And the harvest—how is that?'

" 'Very fine, indeed.'

" 'Is the mill at work?'

" 'Yes, plenty of water.'

" 'How is Whip?' (his favorite horse)

" 'Oh! Whip is first-rate.'

"Everything, in short, about the store, the farm, the business of various descriptions being satisfactorily gone over, there was no occasion for farther delay. It was time to proceed.

" '*Eh! bien—adieu! bon voyage!*'

" '*Arrachez—mes gens!*' (Go ahead, men!)

"Then suddenly—'*Arrëtez—arrëtez!*' (Stop, stop!)

" '*Comment se portent Madame Rolette et les enfans?*' (How are Mrs. Rolette and the children?)"

The Agency House to which they were assigned was a poor affair, indeed, but the government had promised them a new house. The new house, however, did not materialize, despite repeated attempts to obtain permission for its construction. However, Mrs. Kinzie writes: "Permission was in time received to build a house for the blacksmith—that is, the person kept in pay by the Government at this station to mend the guns, traps &c. of the Indians. It happened most fortunately for us that Monsieur Morrin was a bachelor, and quite satisfied to continue boarding with his friend, Louis Frum, dit Manaigree, so that when the new house was fairly commenced, we planned it and hurried it forward entirely on our own account.

"It was not very magnificent, it is true, consisting of but a parlor and two bedrooms on the ground-floor, and two low chambers under the roof, with a kitchen in the rear; but compared with the rambling old stable-like building we now inhabited, it seemed quite a palace. . . .

"The workmen who had been brought from the Mississippi to erect the main building, were fully competent to carry on their work without an overseer, but the Kitchen was to be the task of the Frenchmen, and the question was, how could it be executed in the absence of *the bourgeois?*

" 'You will have to content yourselves in the old quarters until my return,' said my husband, 'and then we will soon have things in order.' It was to be a long and tedious journey, for the operations of government were not carried on by railroad and telegraph in those days.

"After his departure I said to the men, 'Come, you have all your logs cut and hauled—the squaws have brought the bark for the roof—what is to prevent our finishing the house and getting all moved and settled to surprise Monsieur John on his return?' . . .

"Building a log-house is a somewhat curious process. First, as will be conceived, the logs are laid one upon another and jointed at the corners, until the walls have reached the required height. The chimney is formed by four poles of the proper length, interlaced with a wicker-work of small branches. A hole or pit is dug, near at hand, and with a mixture of clay and water, a sort of mortar is formed. Large wisps of hay are filled with this thick substance, and fashioned with the hands into what are technically called 'clay cats,' and then are filled in among the framework of the chimney until not a chink is left. The whole is then covered with a smooth coating of the wet clay, which is denominated, 'plastering.'

"Between the logs which compose the walls of the building, small bits of wood are driven, quite near together; this is called 'chinking,' and after it is done, clay cats are introduced, and smoothed over with the plaster. When all is dry, both walls and chimney are whitewashed, and present a comfortable and tidy appearance.

"The roof is formed by laying upon the transverse logs, thick sheets of bark, and around the chimney, for greater security against the rain, we took care to have placed a few layers of the palisades that had been left when Mr. Peach, an odd little itinerant genius, had fenced in our garden, the pride and wonder of the surrounding settlement and wigwams."

This was in 1832. It is this structure which is today kept in an admirable state of preservation after restoration and redecoration by the Colonial Dames of Wisconsin. For many years, this house was the only social center for West Point graduates stationed at Fort Winnebago; moreover, Mrs. Kinzie, who hailed from the East, did not long mean to be without the best things of life, for she brought to the Agency House the first piano to enter Wisconsin, having it shipped up the Fox to the portage. In view of the way in which their furniture had come to them earlier—soaked and broken—one can imagine with what pleasure, Mrs. Kinzie could write at its receipt: "To our great joy, we found it entirely uninjured. Thanks to the skill of Nunns and Clark, not a note was out of tune. The women, to whom it was an entire novelty, were loud in their exclamations of wonder and delight. '*Eh-h-h! regardez donc! Quelles inventions! Quelles merveilles!*'" Thereafter, Mrs. Kinzie gave almost weekly musicales.

The domestic life of the Kinzies doubtless paralleled that of many another pioneer couple in their circumstances; Mrs. Kinzie had a little Negress to serve her, and the life at the Agency House was novel and constantly entertaining for all that it offered comparatively little variety. "We were now settled down to a quiet, domestic life. The military system under which everything was conducted—the bugle-call, followed by the music of a very good band, at 'réveille;' the light, animated strains for 'sick-call,' and soon after for 'breakfast;' the longer ceremony of guard-mounting; the 'Old English Roast-beef,' to announce the dinner hour; the sweet, plaintive strains of 'Lochaber no more,' followed most incongruously by 'the Little Cock-Sparrow,' at 'retreat;' and finally, the long, rolling tattoo, late in the evening, made pleasant divisions of our time, which, by the aid of books, music, and drawing, in addition to household occupations, seemed to fly more swiftly than ever before. It was on Sunday that I most missed my eastern home. I had planned beforehand what we should do on the first recurrence of this sacred day, under our own roof. I felt that it would be very pleasant, and perhaps profitable, for all the inmates of the garrison to assemble on this day; one of our number might be found who would read a portion of the church-service, and a sermon from one of our different selections.

"I approached the subject cautiously, with an inquiry to this effect:

"'Are there none among the officers who are religiously disposed?'

"'Oh, yes,' replied the one whom I addressed, 'there is S——; when he is half-tipsy, he takes his Bible and "Newton's Works," and goes to bed and cries over them; he thinks in this way he is excessively pious.'

"With an occasional dinner or tea-party to the young officers, sometimes given at the Major's quarters, sometimes at our own, our course of life passed pleasantly on. At times I would amuse myself by making 'something very nice' in the form of a fruit cake or pie, to send to the quarters of the young officers as a present, it being supposed that possibly, without a lady to preside over their mess, it might be sometimes deficient in these delicacies. Mrs. Twiggs was so fortunate as to have well-trained servants to do for her that which, thanks to my little dark handmaid, always fell to my share."

Apart from the Black Hawk War, the greatest excitement to prevail at the post was the coming together of the Indians for their annuities, payment of which was made at the fort. Mrs. Kinzie left some carefully observed descriptions of the chieftians on the first of those visits which never failed to fascinate her in the variety of the braves and squaws who presented themselves.

"There was Naw-kaw, or Kar-ray-mau-nee, 'the Walking Rain,' now the principal chief of the nation, a stalwart Indian, with a broad, pleasant countenance, the great peculiarity of which was an immense under lip, hanging nearly to his chin. There was the old Day-kau-ray, the most noble, dignified, and venerable of his own, or indeed of any other, tribe. His fine Roman countenance, rendered still more striking by his bald head, with one solitary tuft of long silver hair neatly tied and falling back on his shoulders; his perfectly neat, appropriate dress, almost without ornament and his courteous demeanor, never laid aside, under any circumstances, all combined to give him the highest place in the consideration of all who knew him. It will hereafter be seen that his traits of character were not less grand and striking, than were his personal appearance and deportment.

"There was Black-Wolf, whose lowering, surly face was well described by his name. The fierce expression of his countenance was greatly heightened by the masses of heavy black hair hanging around it, quite contrar͵ to the usual fashion among the Winnebagoes. They, for the most part, remove a portion of their hair, the remainder of which is drawn to the back of the head, clubbed and ornamented with beads, ribbons, cock's feathers, or, if they are so entitled, an eagle's feather for every scalp taken from an enemy.

"There was *Talk-English,* a remarkably handsome, powerful young Indian, who received his name in the following manner. He was one of a party of sixteen Winnebagoes, who had, by invitation accompanied their Agent and Major Forsyth (or the Chippewa as he was called), on a visit to the President at Washington, the year previous.

"On the journey, the question naturally addressed to them by people not familiar with Western Indians was,

" 'Do you talk English?'

"The young fellow being very observant, came to his 'father.' 'What do they mean by this? Everybody says to me, *talk English!*'

"The Agent interpreted the words to him. 'Ah, very well.'

"The next place they arrived at was Lockport, in the State of New York. Jumping off the canal-boat upon the lock, he ran up to the first man he met, and thrusting forward his face cried out, 'Talk Eengeesh?'

" 'Yes,' said the man; 'do you talk English?'

" 'Ya-as.'

"From that time forward, he always bore the name of *Talk-English*, and was registered on the pay-rolls by a title of which he was not a little proud."

Throughout her charming narrative, she put down descriptions of the wild country that was the Michigan Territory of that time, soon—within less than half a decade, to become Wisconsin Territory. "The woods were now brilliant with the many tints of autumn, and the scene around was further enlivened by groups of Indians, in all directions, and their lodges, which were scattered here and there, in the vicinity of the Agency buildings. On the low grounds might be seen the white tents of the traders, already prepared to furnish winter supplies to the Indians, in exchange for the annuity money they were about to receive.... Our road, after leaving the lake, lay over a 'rolling prairie,' now bare and desolate enough. The hollows were filled with snow, which, being partly thawed, furnished an uncertain footing for the horses, and I could not but join in the ringing laughter of our Frenchmen, as occasionally Brunët and Souris, the two ponies, would flounder, almost imbedded, through the yielding mass. Even the vain-glorious Plante, who piqued himself on his equestrian skill, was once or twice nearly unhorsed, from having chosen his road badly. Sometimes the elevations were covered with a thicket or copse, in which our dogs would generally rouse up one or more deer. Their first bound, or 'lope,' was the signal for a chase. The horses seemed to enter into the spirit of it, as 'halloo' answered 'halloo;' but we were never so fortunate as to get a shot at one, for although the dogs once or twice caught, they were not strong enough to hold them. It was about the middle of the afternoon when we reached the 'Blue Mound.' . . . Our afternoon's ride was over a prairie stretching away to the north-east. No living creature was to be seen upon its broad expanse, but flying and circling over our heads were innumerable flocks of curlews, 'Screaming their wild notes to the listening waste.' Their peculiar shrill cry of 'crack, crack, crack—rackety, rackety, rackety,' repeated from the throats of dozens as they sometimes stooped quite close to our ears, became at length almost unbearable. It seemed as if they had lost their sense in the excitement of so unusual and splendid a cortége in their hitherto desolate domain. The accelerated pace of our horses as we approached a beautiful, wooded knoll, warned us that this was to be our place of repose for the night. These animals seem to know by instinct a favorable encamping-ground, and this was one of the most lovely imaginable. The trees which near the lake had, owing to the coldness and tardiness of the season, presented the pale-yellow appearance of unfledged goslings, were here bursting into full leaf. The ground around was carpeted with flowers —we could not bear to have them crushed by the felling of a tree and the pitching of our tent among them. The birds sent forth their sweetest notes in the warm, lingering sunshine, and the opening buds of the young hickory and sassafras filled the air with perfume."

So much for *Wau-Bun*. The book was out of print for many decades before the Caxton Club of Chicago reprinted it in 1901, with annotations by Dr. Reuben Gold Thwaites, and the ladies of the Colonial Dames sponsored the printing of its 1930 edition, edited by Dr. Louise Phelps Kellogg. No better picture of life in the Wisconsin River valley for the years 1830 to mid-1833 is in existence.

6. Four Men of Prairie du Chien

The period of the 1830's left its mark on Prairie du Chien, and the valley of the Wisconsin. Under Colonel Zachary Taylor, Fort Crawford was rebuilt on a new site; the old site passed into the possession of Hercules Dousman, together with other real estate the trader was quietly purchasing throughout the territory. When it was discovered at the close of the Black Hawk War that Captain John Marsh had been selling guns and ammunition to enemy Indians as well as to the allies of the whites, Marsh was forced to flee to the west, to avoid arrest, and Dousman lost an enemy. One of the earliest of the traders in the Prairie du Chien country died—Michel Brisbois—and was buried high on the bluffs east of Prairie du Chien, where his large sarcophagus shows whitely still on the tree-girt slope, giving rise to two legends—that Brisbois had had himself buried there so that (a) he might avoid the high waters of the Mississippi which occasionally flooded the French cemetery in the spring; (b) might be on this high place to look down upon the resting place of his rival, Rolette. Rapidly now, after the war, other Indian lands in Wisconsin were ceded by the Fox, the Chippewa, the Ottawa, the Potawatomi, and the Winnebago, and the news of the cessation of hostilities brought an influx of settlers.

By 1834 land offices were opened at Mineral Point and Green Bay, and the first public land sale was held at

Mineral Point. In that year, too, the first public road was laid out, and in the following year the Military Road was built to connect Green Bay and Prairie du Chien. The settlers came eagerly now. In 1800 there were but 200 whites in all the territory that was to become Wisconsin; forty years later the population of Wisconsin was 30,945. Within that time the mark of history had already been made distinctively at the meeting place of the rivers. Not only by the Indians or by the early traders, not only by the missionaries and explorers, not only by Black Hawk and Colonel Zachary Taylor, but by others.

There was, for instance, Dr. William Beaumont—

Dr. Beaumont was a Connecticut man. At Mackinac one day in June, 1822, he was called to attend a half-breed trader, one Alexis St. Martin, part of whose stomach had been torn away by a gunshot wound. Dr. Beaumont gave St. Martin thirty-six hours, at the longest, to live; he was sorry for the impending death of the nineteen-year-old trader, but there was nothing he could do. However, St. Martin was made of stern stuff; he was still alive the next day; and the doctor hopefully trimmed the ragged edges of the wound. For ten months Dr. Beaumont treated St. Martin, and after that time the doctor took the trader into his own home, where, after two years, St. Martin's wound had healed, save for an aperture into the stomach, covered by a mobile, valvelike fold of flesh.

"In this situation I retained St. Martin in my family for the special purpose of making physiological experiments," Dr. Beaumont stated in a formal report prepared some years later for Congress. In summer, 1825, Dr. Beaumont began to experiment with St. Martin, introducing various kinds of food into his stomach through the stomach wall, the valvelike flap of flesh easily lifted, and the doctor spent all his leisure watching the movements of the stomach and noting the secretions therein. His first report must have thrilled him to put down, for all its dry precision: "EXPERIMENT I August 1, 1825. At 12 o'clock, M., I introduced through the perforation, into the stomach, the following articles of diet, suspended by a silk string, and fastened at proper distances, so as to pass in without pain—viz: a piece of high seasoned *à la mode* beef; a piece of raw, salted, fat pork; a piece of raw, salted, lean beef; a piece of stale bread; and a bunch of raw, sliced cabbage; each piece weighing about two drachms; the lad continuing his usual employment about the house.

"At 1 o'clock P.M., withdrew and examined them —found the cabbage and bread about half digested; the pieces of meat unchanged. Returned them into the stomach.

"At 2 o'clock, P.M., withdrew them again—found the cabbage, bread, pork, and boiled beef, all cleanly digested, and gone from the string."

Then for four years St. Martin was lost to Dr. Beaumont, but joined him again in 1829. By that time Dr. Beaumont was at Prairie du Chien, stationed at Fort Crawford, and there, for two years more, he carried on the most exhaustive experiments. His conclusions are historic; the photographic records of X-ray experiments after 1897 proved that the conclusions of Dr. Beaumont made seventy years before were accurate. For, as a result of his experiments on St. Martin, to whom he paid a salary higher than St. Martin could have earned in the trade, this indefatigable medical man was able to announce in detail just how the stomach digested food, that emotional disturbances adversely affected digestion, that overeating delayed digestion, that carefully chewed food digested more easily, that vegetables took longer to digest than animal food; and he made a dietetic table which has stood over a century without notable change.

For two years he experimented without pause on St. Martin, and it was here, at Prairie du Chien, that Dr. Beaumont "did his fundamental work, and all his future work was based upon what he accomplished at Prairie du Chien," wrote Dr. William Snow Miller, professor emeritus of anatomy of the University of Wisconsin a century later.

There was Father Samuel Mazzuchelli—

Father Mazzuchelli was a Milanese, born in 1806; by 1830 he was in Mackinac, the most remote point of the diocese of Cincinnati. Twenty-four and newly ordained. A poet, too, by all accounts, with soft brown eyes, and a head of curly hair, obsessed by a passionate zeal for his service in Christ. And an architect—it is this fact that is important, and perhaps the equally important one that the history of Catholicism in Wisconsin for the next thirty years is the story of Father Mazzuchelli's life. For to Father Mazzuchelli was shortly assigned the whole of Wisconsin, which achieved territorial status in 1836.

Father Mazzuchelli took over from the Fox-Wisconsin route. He stopped first in Green Bay, and built a church there, that of St. John the Baptist. Then he moved on up the Fox, crossed the portage, and came to Prairie du Chien; by 1840 he had built the church of St. Gabriel there. He built churches away from the valley of the Wisconsin as well—in Galena, Dubuque, Davenport, Potosi, and planned churches for various smaller settlements. By 1839, too, he was vicar-general to the newly appointed Bishop Mathias Loras of Dubuque. Though his work after 1840 centered in Iowa, he found time to build churches in Shullsburg and Sinsinawa, Wisconsin, to travel throughout the territory, to serve as chaplain for the first meeting of the territorial legislature in Wisconsin. He was a tireless missionary, and the Wisconsin was his highway, save for those times he traveled the more difficult way: on horseback. He used the Wisconsin as his route even in the heart of winter on his first mission to Prairie du Chien in 1835.

Writing of himself in the third person, with excessive modesty, he says in his *Memoirs, Historical and Edifying, of a Missionary Apostolic*, published in Milan in 1844: "On the first of February he left Fort Winnebago in company with one of the traders, and traveled by sleigh down the frozen Wisconsin River for one hundred and fifty miles; thence crossing a tongue of land he found himself at his destination." His trip was not without incident, which he faithfully records. "On the journey the travelers saw in the distance a fine buck attacked by nine greedy wolves, who cunningly contrived to force the fleet-footed creature flying for its life, to cross the river; here on account of the ice, it could not keep up its swift flight, slipped, and fell into the ravenous jaws of its famished pursuers. They were tearing it to pieces and devouring it alive, when the whip was laid to our horse and the two travelers came up to the poor victim. The wolves with mouths full of the yet warm flesh, taking fright at the sudden rush of the horse, fled off the ice to the bank nearby, leaving behind them more than two-thirds of their prey. In this unforeseen manner did Providence supply needy travelers, who this time shared the game caught by the cunning and skill of the very wolves. The night was spent in the woods on an island in the Wisconsin, and as a company of traders reached the same place of encampment at evening, most of the night was devoted to roasting and feasting on the venison."

He pursued his work with unabated zeal, and, lest his finely constructed churches be not enough to signify his devotion to Christ, he founded a congregation of nuns to serve Catholic education—the Congregation of the Most Holy Rosary at Sinsinawa. He labored steadily until his death in 1864.

There was the Reverend Alfred Brunson—

He was a Connecticut Yankee from Pennsylvania, one of the first Methodists in Wisconsin. He came into the state and to Prairie du Chien during a sleet storm in late autumn of 1835, "the first Methodist preacher who ever trod this soil, but even here I found friends," his diary tells us. He undertook to serve a parish that reached from Rock Island, Illinois, to St. Paul, Minnesota: a strip of land seventy-five miles in width and five hundred miles in length, and it was his purpose, nay, his mission, to carry the gospel to every cabin and community in that territory, in whatever manner occasion demanded.

What he saw, he liked; he returned to Meadville, Pennsylvania, the following year, having made a journey of over three thousand miles very largely in his saddle, and by July 16, 1836, he was back in Prairie du Chien with his family and their belongings; this time he came by keelboat, spurred by his rugged physique and his mountainous faith. He made his influence felt immediately after his arrival when he discovered that some of the post officers held Negroes, one of whom was a mulatto who could speak the Indian tongue. Mr. Brunson was not an abolitionist, but he could not abide slavery; nor could he sway the officers at Fort Crawford. He could, however, free the mulatto, and he did so by buying him for $1,200—the money supplied by his Pennsylvania friends—and setting him up in his own household as an interpreter. Through the mulatto the Reverend Alfred Brunson found his way to the Kickapoo and other Indian tribes, and exhorted them.

The Reverend Alfred Brunson exhorted until his retirement in 1873—traveling with astonishing vigor through his great parish, in summer and in winter, holding camp meetings, baptizings, weddings, buryings. Moreover, he rested upon his missionary labors by being elected to the territorial legislature, which met in Madison where "The vice and wickedness of the whole territory seemed to be concentrated." The Reverend Alfred Brunson rolled up his sleeves and fell to, the first in a long tradition of reformers which was to reach its fullest flower in the late great Senator Robert Marion La Follette a half century later. He became the symbol of all Protestant preachers in Wisconsin.

And, of course, there was Hercules Louis Dousman—

In 1834 events in the East changed the pattern of his life. Up to this time Hercules Dousman had been seemingly content to serve King Rolette as a clerk in the American Fur Company, though he did most of the work, and was already as well loved by the Indians as Rolette. Back in New York, shrewd old John Jacob Astor compared his income from the trade in the Upper Mississippi valley and the Territory of Michigan with the income from the same source a decade and two decades before. He was not pleased, and there rose up before his mind's eye a vision of the country to the west— the land of the Miniconjou, the Ute and the Hunkpapa —and of the land beyond them: another empire of furs. The profit from the trade in the Great Lakes region was no longer sufficient to repay him for his trouble in sponsoring and protecting that trade.

The sale of the Northern Department of the American Fur Company was made to Ramsay Crooks in 1834; but Crooks did not buy the debts of traders to Astor. Astor had a better plan than that; he simply took mortgages and presently foreclosed them. In this way he became the owner of much real estate in Green Bay and Prairie du Chien—just in case this territory should some day boom—and managed to clean out a good many of the traders. Among those who suffered in Prairie du Chien was King Rolette. In the new American Fur Company which superseded Astor's company, the leading men, apart from Crooks, who kept to Mackinac and the East, were Hercules Dousman, in charge at Prairie du Chien, and Henry Sibley, in charge at Mendota, Minnesota.

Thus, at last, the positions of Dousman and Rolette were reversed—now it was Dousman who was openly in control. But this made little actual difference; if anything, it added more to Dousman's burdens, for Rolette, insolvent, needed assistance, and Hercules gave it. Moreover, Rolette was no longer a well man; he had taken to liquor, and spent more and more of his time away from Prairie du Chien. Hercules had no illusion about the fur trade; he knew it was on the decline; but he realized also that such profits as Astor scorned were still a good profit to him, and he meant to reap it as long as the trade could be maintained. But, because he foresaw that, with settlers coming in in ever-increasing numbers, the fur trade must inevitably move westward, he invested in more land, and as the trade fell away he exposed himself as prepared to sponsor agriculture, to ship grain, to finance railroading.

He grew rich. He had always wanted to. In 1842 King Rolette died; in 1843 Hercules began to build his famed mansion on the mound that had been the site of the old Fort Crawford; in 1844 he married Jane Fisher Rolette and brought her to live in the house which was destined to become the Villa Louis and one of the most widely known show places in Wisconsin. The fur trade held for twenty years more, until 1864.

When, four years later on a summer day, old Louis LeBrun came to where Hercules Dousman rested in the shade of the maple he had planted at the southeast corner of his mansion and asked how to pronounce an Indian name, and Hercules told him and fell dead, he died a millionaire—the first millionaire in the old Northwest Territory. He had always wanted to be rich; he had managed to become rich without following Astor's pattern; and he died the symbol of all the time between the explorers and the farmers, the dreamers, the rivermen who came after.

PART THREE

Always the Land

THE RIVER at this point enters upon that part of the Western Upland which was never covered by the glaciers, flowing into a region of rugged country around an outthrust table of land known variously as the Sauk Prairie or the Prairie of the Sacs, after the Sauk or Saukenauk who had a village along the Wisconsin there a century ago. The steadily broadening stream flows from among the hills of the Baraboo Range—hills of quartzite rock in the heart of which, not far from the river itself, the glacier, by a deposit of moraines, created Devil's Lake, which is in itself a place of singular beauty, and also an area of great geological interest—from among these hills, I say, the Wisconsin flows leisurely along a moraine which forms its eastern shore, around the Sauk Prairie, which is best described as a paw or a lip or a ledge of land, which has in many of its aspects the appearance of having at one time served in part at least as the bed of the river. It is variously called an oak opening and a prairie. Certainly it is an oak opening; there are groves here and there upon it—of oak, cotton-wood, birch, wild crabapple, poplar, (including the tulip tree sparsely), and a few sycamore at the river's edge; but it is not a true prairie, for it is apparent when one reaches the southern extremity of the Sauk Prairie that it is not flat land, nor even what is known as an "undulating prairie," but a series of terraces rising from the river into the northwest. Some idea of the rise may be obtained in considering that the river, which seems scarcely marked by the difference in the height of the land, enters upon its course around the prairie at a height of 172 feet above Lake Michigan, and leaves it at a height of 160 feet.

The river flows in from the north and almost immediately turns eastward, flowing among islands for a distance of several miles, in the course of which it again determines a southerly direction, and presently bends swiftly into the southwest, and thence again moves southward, away from the prairie. The Sauk Prairie is a wonderfully beautiful country, encircled as it is by hills on all sides, hills at one place as far as eight miles away from the Wisconsin in a westerly direction. From the southernmost extremity of the prairie to the Baraboo Range the distance is perhaps twelve miles. This prairie embraces, besides oak openings, marshes, alluvial sand, tamarack swamps, and some true prairie slope, and, in addition, it is watered by two streams, the Otter Creek, which has an interesting disposition of its waters, in that it vanishes into the sand shortly before it reaches the Wisconsin; and the De Tour River, recently being called the Honey Creek, an extensive drainage system which is said to be the oldest stream in the west because it alone was not affected or changed in any way by the glacier which changed the course of every other stream in the Midwest. A few houses stand upon the eastern edge of the paw of land; and it would seem, from all appearances, that the Sauk Prairie will some day be host to a great settlement, for it is so situated in a place of such great natural beauty, it is inevitable that settlers will ultimately cover its expanse.

—Ten Years in North America

1. Hungarian Count

Not all the pioneer settlers of the Wisconsin River country were practical men.

Count Agostin Haraszthy had his practical side, but the side of his personality which he nourished was that of the passionate dreamer. When, on a summer day near the middle of July, 1840, the count mounted the moraine ridge east of the Sauk Prairie, looked down upon his future home, and shouted, "Eureka! Eureka! Italia!" he already had a distinguished career behind him—a career as a liberal in a Hungary which was under the iron rule of Prince Metternich. Born in 1810 in the Comitat of Bacs-Bodrog on the east bank of the Danube, Count Haraszthy was at this time thirty years old. At twenty-two he had made his first trip to America. Already at that age he had taken up the cause of the downtrodden, incurred the anger of the aristocrats, and had found it prudent to take a vacation in America. If he returned to Hungary chastened, he gave no evidence of it; by the end of the decade of the 1830's, he was in trouble again, and it was freely rumored that Prince Metternich admired his leonine head, and would particularly like to see it parted from the rest of him.

This was naturally not a wish that Count Haraszthy could willingly gratify. He took off for the second time when it was apparent that it was either his head or his reformation Metternich wanted; since

Haraszthy would concede him neither, he found it expedient to look once again to America. But he had no illusions; he knew that Europe was ailing of more woes than he or a hundred like him could cure; he knew he would henceforth look upon America as his home. He had learned of the Sauk Prairie from the account of Captain Marryat; so it was directly to that place that he came in that summer of 1840.

Sauk Prairie was ready for him. It was at that time an incipient settlement little more than two years of age. Early in the spring of 1838, Berry Haney, a stage driver on the Military Road, "received private information from George W. Jones, who was then delegate in congress from Wisconsin Territory, that the treaty with the Winnebago Indians, for their lands north of the Wisconsin River, was ratified." So wrote Charles O. Baxter in recounting his memories of early Sauk City to William H. Canfield many years later. "On learning of the ratification of the treaty, Haney sent Jonathan Taylor to the Wisconsin River, opposite Sauk Prairie, there to await the coming of Solomon Shore, also in his employ, who went with Haney to Fort Winnebago to purchase a skiff to take down the river to Sauk Prairie, in order to get across. They met at that point according to previous arrangement, crossed and proceeded to mark out their claims. The first one marked out by them was for Berry Haney, on what is now Sauk City. Taylor claimed the next above Haney, and Shore the next. Haney, I believe, had the first land broke in Sauk County. In June, 1838, he employed James Ensminger and Thomas Sanser to break ten acres, for which he paid them one hundred dollars. The first place in the shape of a dwelling on Sauk Prairie was built by Ensminger and Sanser. They dug a pit in the ground about four feet deep, twelve by sixteen or eighteen feet square, logged it up and covered the hole with hay and earth, making a sort of root-house. This they did for the purpose of preventing the Indians from burning them out." Thus began Sauk City, and in January of 1839 came the first family in Sauk County, that of James S. Alban, to settle on the upper prairie and become the first settlers of Sauk City's twin village, Prairie du Sac.

If Sauk City is today typical of the agricultural communities that sprang up along the Wisconsin from the mouth to the portage, it was not always so, though it was land that brought its founders and those who came after. Count Haraszthy was the most colorful of the men who came in the village's first decade. When he rode up over the ridge along the east shore of the Wisconsin, and looked down to the valley below, he saw not only that it was a country that reminded him of northern Italy, but also that it was the ideal setting for a town. Forthwith he bought up as much land as he could and employed a courtly Virginian, Charlie Baxter, to survey all the land along the river and plat a village to be called Haraszthy, though its name was soon changed to Westfield, and then to Sauk City—in memory of the Sauk who had first occupied the prairie. Characteristically, once the plat was made, the count was in no haste to record it, and it was not until April 26, 1845 "at half past 12 P.M.," that the plat was recorded, bearing this information: "Proprietors' Names: Charles Haraszthy, Robert Bryant, by Charles Haraszthy, agent; Stephen Bates, by Agostin Haraszthy, agent." Charles was Agostin's father; Agostin had returned to Europe in the spring of 1842 and in summer of that year brought back with him his wife, Eleanora de Dodinsky, their sons Gaza, Attila, and Arpad, and his parents. Robert Bryant was an Englishman of means whom Haraszthy encountered in Milwaukee and induced by his eloquence to become his partner in the proposed town.

The name Haraszthy was soon known far and wide. Frankly, there was no enterprise worthy of attention into which Agostin did not put a finger—and very often capital to a ruinous extent. Throughout that first year, apart from enlisting the interest and capital of Robert Bryant and the surveying services of Charlie Baxter, the count indulged to the full his desire to hunt and fish. Haraszthy was a commanding figure, as the legends that were to follow his passing from the prairie testify. The only contemporary description of him in his first year on the site of the village he founded was put down by an itinerant preacher, the Reverend T. M. Fullerton, who, under date of June 23, 1841, wrote in his journal: "There is here an Hungarian Count—so he calls himself—who claims to have quantities of money and is spending it liberally on improvement. There is also an Englishman here (Bryant) who claims to have been a Lord in the old country. He is in partnership with the count. They both look like savages, wearing a long beard above as well as below the mouth. And they are the great men of the place, and others adopt their customs, and make themselves as ridiculous as possible."

For all Mr. Fullerton's belief that the count looked like a savage, Haraszthy was precisely the kind of man who would engender legend. He was six feet tall and very dark, with eyes that were as black as his hair. He invariably wore a stovepipe hat and, when on foot, carried a cane. However, he liked best to ride his horse, and as a hunter he was entirely picturesque, wearing a green silk hunting shirt and a wide silk sash of a crimson color, a garb which did not prevent him from walking or riding through brush and bramble, completely disdainful of damage to his manifestly expensive dress.

Decades later, Satterlee Clark said of him: "He was a nobleman in every sense, and he and his wife were among the most refined people I ever knew; and both were exceedingly good looking. I saw them both frequently, both at home and at Madison."

If the count had been comparatively idle until his family reached the prairie, he was so active after that that even today it is impossible to say when he ended one venture and began another. The story is that his ventures were made possible largely through his father's money. Charles Haraszthy, however, was a character in his own right, quickly and lastingly winning the esteem of the settlers, who called him either the Old General or the Old Count; he was interested in natural science and contributed his share to the Haraszthy ventures by opening soon after his arrival an apothecary shop, which he conducted until late in 1848, when the Haraszthys left for the West. He worshiped what he himself lacked and what was so manifest in his son: the intrepid daring.

Agostin began by opening a ferry across the Wisconsin; the date was October 14, 1842, and the earliest record of it appears in a deed of conveyance from Bryant. There had been two ferries established previously—one by Berry Haney and H. F. Crossman, in August, 1839, a second by James S. Alban, in October of that year. But Haney had sold out his interests to Haraszthy and left the prairie; Alban's ferry was presumably still running on the upper prairie. The count operated the ferry for many years, but this was perhaps the least of his enterprises. In that same month, Haraszthy and Bryant opened a brickyard, Bryant filing a mortgage covering all the brick in the yard, "seventeen cows, two yokes of oxen, a span of horses, sofa, and peanna." Shortly he constructed the first Haraszthy residence; but this was hardly completed before he was about the construction of a second. Sometime in 1842 or 1843, Haraszthy began a retail merchandising store, erecting his own building in which to accommodate it. As if this were not enough, he began a second store in Baraboo, just over the northern rim of the Sauk Prairie, putting up to house the business the first frame structure to be erected in the valley of the Baraboo River near its confluence with the Wisconsin.

Meanwhile, settlers began to flow to the townsite, and Haraszthy did a lively business selling property. A census taken in June, 1842, listed 393 "free inhabitants" for Sauk County, and Sheriff Bird's census included names which were destined to loom large in the history of Wisconsin—Prescott Brigham, Nathan Kellogg, Cyrus Leland, Thomas Kelsey, Abraham Wood; the Haraszthy name did not occur because the count was at that time in Europe arranging to bring his family over. Despite the time the affairs of his commercial enterprises must have taken, Haraszthy managed to indulge in agricultural experiments. The prairie called to him—alluvial soil, most of it within his ownership, and such as was not was owned by no one; so that he could use it as if it were his own. He began to raise grains; he experimented in growing swine; he raised sheep. He rode up to Fort Winnebago and made a contract to supply the fort with corn; on this memorable occasion, he put in the corn and left it to grow. Unfortunately, that season was a good one for hunting, and Haraszthy had to hunt. When he thought of the corn again, it was long past time for delivery, and also very late in the fall. Nothing daunted, the count summoned his neighbors and friends to a husking, arranged for flatboat transportation, and husked wagonfuls of corn en route to the river, where the corn was loaded into the flatboat and taken up to Fort Winnebago.

Nor did he forget his village. Among the transfers of property in the first volume of Sauk County records, is evidence that ground was set aside for a schoolhouse, and two lots were deeded to the Right Reverend John Martin Henni, Bishop of Milwaukee, for the establishment of the first Catholic church in the county. Moreover, Haraszthy agitated for a permanent parish priest, and not an itinerant. By 1845 the priest had come— Father Adelbert Inama of the Tyrol; on December 12th in that year he wrote to his superior enough to justify Haraszthy's extravagant praise of the country.

". . . by comparison, the climate here in the West is more moderate than in the East, and the seasons run their course more regularly. Since my coming on the twenty-fifth of last month, I made use of the fine weather to ramble through the surrounding country in all directions. I certainly maintain at present that few localities can outdo the environs of Sauk Prairie in fertility, variety, romantic beauty, and healthfulness of climate. Wood, water, freestone, clay, lime and sand— in fact, everything requisite for building—is found here in great plenty. Rich silver-bearing copper mines have been discovered this year a few miles west of here, and the opening of the mines has already begun; for several years copper and lead mines have been operating twenty-five miles south, stretching out southward through Illinois, Iowa, and Missouri. However, the richest silver and copper mines are near the Menominee River, north of this territory, and were detected first in the vicinity of Lake Superior. About here mineral land is at the same time the most productive soil; thus rich metallic veins run below the most fertile of top-soils.

"At this time I will add a bit about the locality where, if God wills, I contemplate building in the beginning of the year, with the assistance of the parish, my provisional hermitage and chapel. At this point the Wisconsin River, not one-half mile wide, incloses numerous thickly wooded islands, flows majestically and peacefully between scarped banks very like sculpture, which are covered to the water's edge with grass and overgrown with bushes. The hills upon which the chapel will be built, rise precipitously one hundred and ten feet from the river lowland. The side toward the river, a regular triangle, is covered with grass, and the other side with oak trees. Back from the river six or seven miles the land becomes level and has pools where from two mill streams rise. Nearly regular hills from a hundred to two hundred feet in height rise from this plain, wholly grass-covered or stocked with oaks and birch, ... from which one enjoys a perspective which can vie with the Rigi. So is the land on the east. The extensive Sauk Prairie stretches to the west, with a semicircular ridge in the distant background, where the mineral region commences. This, the land of my future residence and sphere of activity, for which I ask your blessing, and commend myself to the ever pious remembrances and prayers of my fellow religious and countrymen."

Beside a brook in a low valley among the moraine hills east of Sauk Prairie the Reverend Adelbert Inama erected a chapel, from which he sallied forth to serve several congregations, and subsequently he brought about the building of a church at the hamlet of Roxbury which came into being three miles east of the Sauk Prairie on the road to Madison—the site of Floyd's Folly, an eastern speculator, Charles Floyd, having bought up much of the land for the purpose of speculation and the establishment of Superior City. Like many others, Superior City never grew beyond the paper stage, but ultimately Roxbury sprang up on the abandoned site, and there in 1939 a tablet was unveiled to the memory of the tireless priest who followed the steps of Mazzuchelli.

Finally, Haraszthy invested in a steamboat, the packet *Rock River,* which undertook regular express and passenger service from Sauk City to Prairie du Chien, and north to Fort Winnebago, and even traveled on the Upper Mississippi, between Galena and Fort Snelling. But this venture was short-lived; the *Rock River* was frozen in one winter day at Prairie du Chien, and the ship was abandoned with the casual, almost heroic insouciance with which the firm of Haraszthy and Bryant abandoned any enterprise which seemed no longer profitable. In addition to all this, Haraszthy found time to write in Hungarian a two-volume account of his experiences in America; the book was published in Budapest in 1844.

Beyond question, Count Agostin Haraszthy left his mark on the prairie. But destiny did not mean for him to succeed in the town he had founded. One by one his ventures failed, and it developed that he had put comparatively little of his own capital into many of those ventures; the stores failed, the ferry's operation was undertaken by John C. Hawley of near-by Mazomanie for Robert Richards; the brickyard no longer paid for itself; and even his agricultural experiments failed, by no fault of his own, as the incident of his sheep-raising failure illustrates. He had as many as two thousand head of sheep when he engaged to tend them Edmund Juessen, a young Swiss who was destined to become one of early Chicago's leading lawyers; entirely by accident, young Juessen fired the prairie grass, which resulted in the death of almost a fourth of Haraszthy's sheep—an accident that so frightened young Juessen that he ran away and hid among the Baraboo bluffs until the following day, when he was convinced that Haraszthy would not have the loss out of his hide.

Yet it was not the failure of any one of these enterprises which ultimately drove Haraszthy from the prairie; it was the sterility of his dream. For Haraszthy had a dream of great vineyards in America, and he thought that the Sauk Prairie would ultimately be host to them. Unfortunately, something was lacking; the grapes did not do well enough to justify his dream; so late in 1848 the Haraszthys—without Agostin's mother, who had died of nostalgia soon after reaching the new home along the Wisconsin—pulled up stakes and set out for California, where the count managed to fulfill his dream to such an extent that a little more than a decade later he was selected by President Lincoln to proceed to Europe for the express purpose of obtaining hundreds of grape cuttings, and ultimately found himself put down by the historian, Bancroft, as the father of viticulture in the United States.

He left behind him a flourishing village, whose leading spirits were the men who had come with him or shortly thereafter—most of them the forty-eighters, refugees from the German countries in a turmoil of riot and revolt against oppression, a village which could harbor a group of men who could work together for the best interests of their community despite the variety of their interests. Charles Hallasz, styled the count's "cousin" (though he may as easily have been his stable-boy despite the count's magnanimous reference to him as "cousin," in conversation and direct address), was more quietly and successfully enterprising than Haraszthy, in his lumber business, which is still in existence today in the hands of his descendants, the Lachmund family. Charles O. Baxter preceded the count to the prairie as one of the first settlers; promising to follow

Berry Haney from the prairie, he did not do so, and, when asked by urgent letter why he had not come, replied, "I have found here a very delightful and well educated young lady, who can play the piano and speak French"—his reference being to his future bride, Ottilie Naffz, sister of Charles, who was one of the earliest Germans to reach the prairie. Edmond Rendtorff was the leader of the German migration to Sauk Prairie; he left letters and descriptions of his chosen home, one of which is particularly noteworthy in that it gives us a picture of the doughty Count Haraszthy hunting.

"Haraszthy, Hallasz, my brother and I, sometimes made hunting excursions. At one time, leaving the settlement, we started for Honey Creek Valley, in which at that time not one living soul could be found, but a plenty of rattlesnakes. We killed many of them; also lots of pigeons and prairie chickens, which made us fine soups. We found wild honey, too, but how to get it, we did not understand at that time. At another time, we started out, taking a horse to carry our tent and other things. Near that bluff where Merrihew's mill now stands, the Count shot a deer, but unluckily so that it escaped him. By and by we all four started after the buck, but in vain was all the trouble. In the chase we lost much time and greatly exhausted ourselves, and did not notice the tremendous thunderstorm coming over us. The Count was wounded in the head and we had nearly lost him. We arrived at last at camp, drenched to the skin, where, in the dark and rain, we found everything wet; the tent torn into pieces, and its contents swimming in water—no fire—cold and shivering. You can believe we made pretty sour faces that night; but never mind. The night passed; at daybreak we regaled ourselves as best we could. Fine sunshine warming us up again, we endeavored to cross Honey Creek. But to do this we had no idea what a difficult job it would be. We tramped up and down the creek, through mud, heavy underbrush, and were by thorns half torn to pieces. At last we were so lucky as to find a place where the trunks of fallen trees lay partly across the stream. Now we ventured out balancing. But such balancing I had never before done in my life. I used to balance in dancing saloons, in Hamburg, New York and even in a log cabin on the Wabash River, but here, surely it could not go very well, from sheer nervousness on account of being in such a critical position. I declare I was not afraid of the water, as in my former days I was called a pretty good swimmer; but that swampy mud by the shore!— if any shore was there, nobody could tell where, or whether a bottom could be found; then to swim in mud is a considerable piece of art, and I knew, not so easily done, as I had experienced before in a piece of Honey Creek swamp. However, over we must and did go.

"But oh! our travelling assistant had to come over yet, besides all our guns, tent, and baggage. Finally all crossed safely, which consumed half a day's labor. Now we travelled on, up hill and down hill, for hours until we struck an Indian trail, which set us in good spirits. Not understanding how to travel by compass, however, we took ours, which showed us (greenhorns) about the direction we wished to take, but on we travelled, following the trail. After many hours, up and down, round and about, we came out in an entirely contrary direction from that we wished to travel; we stood upon a height and saw our own Wisconsin River, where we finally camped. Being now not very far from Helena, we visited now, for the first time, the oldest settler in Sauk County, Mr. John Wilson. We travelled and camped out several times along Pine River, where we met a great many Indian braves, but no settlers. Near the head of this river we discovered a cave, in which we slept that night. The next morning brought us a most disagreeable affair. We soon noticed that over night our most worthy travelling companion, our horse, had got loose, and was now—who knows where? Here we sat in the wilderness, with kettle, coffee pot, blankets, tents and so forth, but the horse was gone. With empty stomachs, my brother and I started immediately in search of the four-leg. We searched and searched, and traced back where we had travelled the day before, not noticing how fast the time passed by. At last, fatigued and very near giving up all hope of finding the horse— there, there, we came in sight of him, far far away, so far we could hardly distinguish him. Really, we had to combine all our energy to advance with something like good humour. The four-leg was eating grass very comfortably while he kept walking slowly on, bound homeward. Noticing this, we had to march much faster to cut him off by and by, but to do this it cost us a heap of drops of sweat, until we got so far—now commenced a chase, and trying and trying over again to catch that four-leg. We learned now, if we had not learned it before, what independence means—that horse, really he showed himself an independent one. He tricked us out continually. On that day we learned some experience in western horse-catching. My legs seemed to me to have turned over to the age of fifty or more years; my brains —in what condition they were is hard to tell. At last we caught him, and almost dropped down, so exhausted we were...."

In the same account, Rendtorff leaves evidence of the individuality of the settlers, in his tale of the "Sauk Rebellion": "Provisions at one time being rather scarce, a civil rebellion broke out in the village among the workmen of the Count and Bryant. The motto of the rebels had previously been, 'Pork and potatoes for breakfast, potatoes and pork for dinner,' and so forth, and seldom anything extra. A procession was formed, headed by a stout man, carrying on a long pole a picked ham bone for a banner, the rest following in single file like geese, each one carrying a piece of the cooking concern, such as tea-kettle, tin pails, tin pans and so forth; beating on them, and shouting, joking and making a tremendous noise—which from the clearness of the evening, was echoed back from the bluffs upon the opposite side; and the reverberation came again and again from the numerous islands up and down the river, as though all pandemonium was there. When the procession was disbanded, the settlement was still and quiet. The supper horn was blown by the cook at an unusually early hour. In a short time a great hurrah was heard, the sequel to which was that the dishes were heaped with pies, cookies and cakes, and so ended the Sauk Rebellion."

Mrs. Rendtorff, too, kept a diary of her trip to Sauk City. The Rendtorffs, like many others of the early Germans, came by way of the Erie Canal, over the lakes to Milwaukee, and then overland to the Sauk Prairie; the water route up the Fox and down the Wisconsin did not appeal to the Germans bearing as many of their belongings as possible. On July 9, 1840, Mrs. Rendtorff writes: "Thank God, it's the last day, and tomorrow we shall be in Milwaukee. The sky, however, is beautifully blue, and the shores of Lake Michigan covered with woods—though I am sorry to say that we pass the most beautiful regions by night. . . . This evening several ladies and gentlemen danced an American dance to the music of a violin, and this afforded us a great deal of laughter." By the 11th, they were en route on the overland trail. "We made about sixty miles; the first twenty of them through a never ending woods,

over stones, stumps and swamps, and where these became too swampy, logs were placed one beside the other,
to form a sort of bridge which was, alas! very bumpy to
travel upon. Then the region became more pleasant,
beautiful prairies and small woodlands alternating agree-
ably.... The colorful prairie chickens were abundant,
and birds of every description attracted attention with
their beautiful plumage, but few of them sang, possibly
because of the heat, which was indeed unbearable from
one to three this afternoon." On the 13th, the prairie
was reached. "After we had traveled about twenty-four
miles from Madison, and were driving over a hilly road,
we saw the beautiful chain of hills which can be seen,
Ed told us, from Sauk Prairie. How inexpressibly great
was our joy when we arrived at the Wisconsin River,
where the ferryboat moved to meet us." By the 14th,
"the house was set in order, and we were twelve persons at table, with pork, lettuce and bread."

There were others. Joseph I. Heller, for instance.
Like Haraszthy, he had been interested in the liberal
movement, and had been so injudicious at a meeting in
the town hall of Königshofen on the Tauber as to turn a
picture of the Grand Duke of Baden to the wall with a
remark as to the superfluity of the duke even in likeness
at a meeting of members of the republican movement.
He had hardly reached his home when the Polizei were
on his trail. They knocked at his front door, where he
begged to be allowed to dress. He fled to the back; but
the Polizei were there also; to them he said that his
honor demanded that he should surrender himself at his
front door, as a gentleman. Fortunately, the Polizei had
forgotten the side window; so Heller made his escape to
Rotterdam, where his wife and family joined him, and
from there they proceeded to America and Sauk City,
where he had himself built (by Adam Clas, the young

German refugee architect who, too, lived in Sauk City)
a house of limestone, with walls two feet thick, a house
that was to serve as a refuge for the entire population
of the village on the occasion of a false Indian scare,
and was to shelter a variety of tutors for his children—
strange, homeless men who came to Sauk City, drawn
by reports of its intellectual life, in those first two decades of its existence, some of them to live out their
lives here, some for but a little while. They tutored and
taught to good effect in Sauk City, and one of Joseph
Heller's girls came briefly into the limelight thirty years
later when she wrote a militant and widely circulated
pamphlet entitled *A Woman's View of the Woman
Question.*

And F. G. J. Lueders—

Lueders came to Sauk Prairie in July, 1841, following the Fox-Wisconsin waterway, sometimes on foot, in
part by boat: a botanist sent out by the Academy of
Natural Science of Hamburg, fresh from a visit with
Dr. Asa Gray, and on his way to visit Dr. Engelmann
of St. Louis, a fellow horticulturist. After a trek westward, in the course of which he collected plants and put
down the peculiarities of the country, he lost his baggage and all his notes in the rapids below the Grand
Cascades of the Columbia River, he, his boat, and his
Indian guide overturning one November day in 1843
before the eyes of a far more notable traveler, Captain
John C. Frémont, who left an account of the accident
in his narrative of his expedition to Oregon and California: "A gentleman named Lueders, a botanist from
the city of Hamburg, arrived at the bay I have called
by his name while we were bringing up the boats. I was
delighted to meet at such a place, a man of kindred pursuits; but we had only the pleasure of a brief conversation, as his canoe, under the guidance of two Indians,

was about to run the rapids and I could not enjoy the satisfaction of regaling him with a breakfast, which, after his recent journey, would have been an extraordinary luxury. All his instruments and baggage were in the canoe and he hurried around to meet it at Grave Yard Bay, but was scarcely out of sight when, by the carelessness of the Indians, the canoe was drawn into the middle of the rapids and shot down the river, bottom up, with the loss of everything it contained. In the natural concern I felt for his misfortune, I gave to the little cove the name of 'Lueders' Bay.' " Lueders was discouraged; he returned to Hamburg, and then came back to Sauk City to settle on a little farm of ten acres just west of the village line, now the site of my own home, built after the pattern for his own chaletlike house, hidden like a refuge among the trees he planted; there he indulged his botanical leanings to his heart's content, he grew nursery stock of imported cuttings— much of which still stands—and carried on observations of the heavens to such good end that in 1884 he put down for the director of the Washburn Observatory at the University of Wisconsin, a *List of 608 Auroras Observed at Sauk City, Wisconsin, From 1859 to 1884,* and, three years later, submitted *A Memorial to the Representatives of Physical Astronomy and the Friends of the Progress of this Science.* Not long after, his son Herman was writing for the *American Journal of Science* such learned papers as *Floral Structure of Some Gramineae, Concerning the Structure of Caoutchouc, The Vegetation of the Town Prairie du Sac,* etc.

There is no question but that Sauk City in those first two decades was a mecca for many refugees who were drawn to it because of stories about its colorful Count Agostin Haraszthy; about its exclusive Turner Academy—which offered courses in riding, fencing,

Latin, Greek, French, etiquette, and reading; about its strange Humanist Society, whose members had Carl Schurz to speak to them, and attracted other speakers from the University of Wisconsin and points beyond, one of them an Austrian whose name was to become world famous when it appeared on a pencil of his manufacture: Faber. These self-styled humanists stemmed directly from the movement that had its beginning with the founding of the University of Prague; the society at Sauk City had its branches in Honey Creek and Merrimac; and similar societies existed in Milwaukee and near-by Painesville. They became known in Sauk City and far around as the Frei-Denker or the Freie Gemeinde —Freethinkers or Free Congregation. Writing in the *Pioneer Press* on the occasion of the Sauk Prairie Centennial in 1938, Karl Ganzlin justly wrote: "The self-styled Humanists... were largely responsible for the cultural development of Sauk City. It was speakers and lecturers like Lies from California, Kuhneman from Breslau, Reitzel from Washington, Friedrich Schoenemann-Pott of Philadelphia, the African traveler, Gerhardt Rholfs, Voss, Bruns, Hohlfeld, Otto and others from the University of Wisconsin, who contributed by lecture to the broadening of mental horizons in Sauk City." He might well have pointed to the evidential fact that no other village of the size of the Sauk Prairie community in the nation could boast of as many of its sons among the Guggenheim Fellows, and in the merit lists of Who's Who in America.

By 1853 Sauk City had a newspaper—*Pionier am Wisconsin,* and the agricultural pursuits of the community were carried on with such success that the six dry goods stores noted by a contemporary historian were selling $65,000 worth of goods a year. The newspaper survived to become the *Pioneer Press,* rivaled now by

Prairie du Sac's *Sauk County News,* and in 1939 there came into being in Sauk City, Arkham House, a publishing business unique in that it publishes only collections of uncanny stories. But after the Civil War, especially with the approach of the twentieth century, Sauk City's eminence declined.

2. TWIN VILLAGES

By 1840 the main currents of settlement in Wisconsin were apparent. Following the French down the Fox-Wisconsin waterway came the lead miners pushing up from Illinois; then came the influx of settlers following the end of the Black Hawk War; these settlers entered Wisconsin by way of Chicago and Milwaukee, establishing and holding for a decade the northern boundary of settlement as the old Fox-Wisconsin waterway. Not for a decade more was there to be a movement of settlers into the remainder of Wisconsin, and then it was to be from the Mississippi, up its tributaries, and up the Wisconsin.

The settlers of the 1830's and 1840's, apart from the German forty-eighters who made for Milwaukee, Janesville or the Sauk Prairie, included a large number of Easterners, commonly termed the "Yankee element" by settlers already on the land. Most of them came overland to Chicago, then by boat to Milwaukee, though some followed the land route all the way from New York, New England, Pennsylvania, Ohio, and Michigan. Joseph Schafer in *The Yankee and the Teuton in Wisconsin,* wrote in 1922: "New York's title to primacy in peopling Wisconsin is exhibited, most impressively in the statistics of the 1850 census. At that time native Americans constituted 63 per cent of the total, and

New Yorkers had 36 per cent of the native majority."
Next to the Germans in the 1840's, the Cornish in the
previous decade, occupying the lead-mining country,
were most largely represented; and the Norwegians and
Swedish were next to come in numbers, electing to settle
largely in the Koshkonong area and the northern part
of Wisconsin.

The Yankees, too, were attracted to the Sauk
Prairie. Captain Marryat was more widely read than
one would suppose in this day, in America as well as
in England. True, there was then at its height the wor-
ship of British and Continental authors, despite the
literary activities of the Concord-Boston group, and
this may have accounted for the influence of *A Diary
in America*. Manifestly, too, the Yankees had easier
access to Frederick Marryat than to Peter Pond or Père
Marquette. In any case, there soon began to invade the
upper Sauk Prairie increasingly large numbers of the
Easterners bearing such fine Yankee names as Mather,
Perkins, Fairchild, Conger, Bailey, Crocker, Lathrop,
Clark, Tripp, Seymour, Bates, Kellogg, Waterbury,
Kelsey, Abbott, Hill, etc. Simultaneously came a large
group of Swiss, including the Ochsners, the Ragatzs,
the Kindschis, the Kuonis, and others. The Yankees
tended in large part to live together in a town; the
Swiss to occupy rural areas. Their movement, since the
Germans already held to the lower prairie, was nat-
urally north and west.

To understand the farcical nature of the proceed-
ings that followed, it is necessary to realize that the settlement on the lower Sauk Prairie and that on the upper
were radically different from each other, almost anti-
podally so; the settlers on the lower prairie were upper-
and middle-class Germans in large part, many of them
aristocrats who had dropped their titles (of German,

Austrian, Hungarian, and French origin), and the majority belonged either to the Humanist Society or to the Roman Catholic faith; those on the upper prairie were almost entirely Protestant, and, in contrast to the broad and liberal concepts of the inhabitants of the lower prairie, tended to be dogmatic and conservative. In short, in no time at all the inhabitants of the upper prairie were downright suspicious of those below, and there is no doubt that the settlers in Haraszthy's town looked upon the Yankees of the upper town with scorn and not a little ire. By 1840 they were at loggerheads over the question of which site had first been settled, despite the clear title of Berry Haney months previous to James Alban's. The result was that, instead of the logical development of one town on the Sauk Prairie, there were two, Prairie du Sac rising as a twin village north of Sauk City, and adjacent to the earlier village's north line.

This ridiculous beginning was shortly followed by an even more ludicrous second chapter. The first bone of contention had hardly been abandoned when a second appeared. Ever since Crawford and Dane counties had surrendered their portions of land west of the Wisconsin River to form Sauk County, it was clear that the new county would have to have a county seat. What better place than Sauk City! cried Count Haraszthy. What about Prairie du Sac? retorted the villagers to the north. There was still Baraboo to consider; this settlement just beyond the bluffs marking the north rim of the Sauk Prairie was smaller than either Sauk City or Prairie du Sac and not yet even a village, but it was a contender, nevertheless. It was perfectly obvious to anyone who would see, that the twin villages were bound to grow together ultimately, if only a small part of the settlers each expected came to the site, and it was only

common sense that the two communities should unite
their forces to secure the seat of government for the as
yet undeveloped space between them. There were some
level heads in the area, but they were quickly shouted
down—the fate of most levelheaded thinkers, unfortunately—and all of them knew that it would be small
consolation to be able to say, as they could and did later,
"I told you so!" If it were not for the evidence of human
stupidity so manifested, the events that now took place
were nothing short of hilarious.

Sauk City magnanimously offered Haraszthy's
store, valued at three thousand dollars, for a courthouse,
in making its bid for the county seat. Prairie du Sac
countered by offering several vacant lots. Unfortunately, the Yankees were too shrewd; they concealed in
their deed of gift a proviso whereby under certain conditions the lots conveyed would revert to the donors.
When this was discovered, after the seat had been
awarded to Prairie du Sac, the citizens of Sauk City,
instead of pausing to reflect that the benefits of the
county seat must inevitably be shared by them, raised
such cries of anguish as to shake the rafters of heaven.
Moreover, they united with the citizens of Baraboo in
demanding that the county seat be relocated, and managed to stir up so much dust that relocation of the
county seat was taken under advisement. This time the
howl went up from Prairie du Sac, whose citizens con-
tended angrily that Baraboo was a wilderness, and virtually uninhabited. It was virtually uninhabited, all
right—when Haraszthy and another Sauk Citizen
joined with a group of Baraboo settlers to examine the
proposed site of the county seat, they were unable to
find enough game in this usually well-stocked country
to remain comfortably fed, existing for two days on a
single partridge before a deer was shot to end the period

of famine. The upshot of this trip of exploration was a report that Baraboo was ideally suited to be the county seat. So the county seat went to Baraboo and Sauk City and Prairie du Sac were left to hold the opposite ends of the same bag.

One might have thought that this experience would teach both villages a lesson. But nothing is so difficult to teach by experience as Homo sapiens; an animal, fortunately, needs only to experience something a few times and a habit pattern is formed; Homo sapiens, on the other hand, has the ability to rationalize even his most irrational actions—and can convince himself. In a remarkably short time, Sauk City was convinced that everything was the fault of Prairie du Sac; Prairie du Sac was as strongly convinced that it was Sauk City which did everything in a spirit of contentious animosity. The county seat controversy had hardly smoldered out before the twin villages were at it again with considerably more vigor than any other business of their respective communities ever managed to stimulate. This time it was a quarrel over the post office.

Prairie du Sac had a post office that was meant to serve both communities. There was no need for two post offices; one was adequate. Nevertheless, it was a great thorn in the side of Sauk City that its citizens needed to go all the way up to Prairie du Sac to get their mail. There was nothing the lower Sauk people could do but grumble and complain—until Simon Dean was appointed postmaster. Alas for the people of Prairie du Sac! Simon came from lower Sauk, and he had done his share of complaining. Simon solved the difficulty neatly by bringing the post office to his domicile instead of taking up his position in the post office; one day he appeared in Prairie du Sac with something like two dozen of the most stalwart fellow citizens he could muster and removed the post office building in toto. It was a body blow, and Prairie du Sac had no intention of tolerating it. Now it was their turn to wail and gnash teeth, and their caterwauling presently assaulted the official ears in Washington to such good end that the matter was resolved by the granting of a new post office to upper Sauk. So there were two post offices on the Sauk Prairie.

There was hardly time to take a good long breath before they were at it again with the aimless persistence of two dust motes in a sunbeam. This time it was about bridging the Wisconsin. Because it was believed that the Sauk Prairie was the gateway between the capital city, Madison, and the region north and west of the Wisconsin, the settlement on the prairie was looked upon by many visionaries as the logical site of a future city of importance. So promising, indeed, was the site regarded that investors in real estate in the vicinity included, among many others, no less a personage than Senator Daniel Webster. A bridge, therefore, was vital, but the cost of bridging the largest river in the state was no small item in the calculations and plans of the state officials. Certainly one bridge, properly located, would have served the Sauk Prairie very well. But it would have been easier at this period in their relations to unearth a herd of unicorns than unity on the Sauk Prairie.

The inhabitants of the upper prairie were confident that if they were first on the scene with a bridge, the state would come to their aid. An enterprising young fellow named Moore pushed the matter vigorously, and under his direction work was begun in the autumn of 1851. Unfortunately, the guiding motive was haste and not durability; the bridge was constructed directly on a spile foundation simply put down on the bed of the Wisconsin—at that point no staple thing, sandy and shifting; and in the next spring the first floodwaters swept virtually the entire bridge down the river. Since Moore had a lumberyard, he did not perhaps grieve too much. The bridge was replaced in the following two years, this time of wood on substantial stone piers.

So there was Prairie du Sac with a bridge, and Sauk City with none, but only a ferry. Prairie du Sac did not envy Sauk City the ferry. It was enough to try the patience of a Job, clearly, especially since the best thing Sauk City could do in a hurry was to throw up a causeway to a near-by island. A causeway, unfortunately, is not a bridge, and Sauk City had to rely upon the ferry until 1860 when that village, too, constructed a bridge across the Wisconsin. The river, meanwhile, possibly owing to convulsions of mirth at this ceaseless and inane bickering, moved some distance to the east, so that wing dams had to be put in to save the moraine ridge and throw the current back again.

It was not long before another bone of contention arose. This time is was secondary schools. Farsighted men in both villages, feeling that the quarreling and strife had gone far enough, urged the construction of one high school. Some of them, particularly the Perkins brothers of Prairie du Sac, even offered substantial sums of money in donations, and the land for the joint school. The populace rose almost as one—but not to accept the generosity of the farsighted. Oh, no—far from it. What could the Perkins brothers be thinking of? Expose our upper Sauk children to the Catholics and the Freethinkers down there? Down there they shuddered to contemplate any mixing of the liberal youth of Sauk City with the convention-bound of Prairie du Sac (and Protestants, too!). Two schools it had to be, and two schools it was. No one but the Perkins brothers gave any thought at all to the obvious advantage of one large school over two small ones.

There occurred then a brief lull, during which Sauk City put on a show of its own, enabling citizens of the upper village to point to this evidence of the natural contentiousness of the lower. Sauk City's show was a grand spectacle—a thunderous rift in the Roman Catholic congregation, a cleavage between the so-called Old Catholics, the original settlers, and an alleged Prussian element, the newer farming population, because a bumptious little priest had the effrontery to break a contract for a new church about to be built. The church had been designed by the Old Catholics and the former priest, but the new priest and the farming element thought it not orthodox enough, and the contract for its construction was broken in favor of the more orthodoxly designed structure standing today, broken with the usual arrogance of small-minded clergy who are apt to discard humility and understand "shepherd of his flock" to signify "master of his servants." In a body, the Old Catholics left the church. They had good cause. The rub, unfortunately, was that it was these Old Catholics who in the main supported the faith in Sauk City, and their defection was a body blow which must have beaded the clerical forehead when the priest was called upon to explain to his bishop. The church designed by the Old Catholics was of surprisingly modern design— simple, effective, it would have done credit to any village from coast to coast. Repercussions were not long in coming, and before the anger of the farming element had cooled, shots were fired, threats were made to ride out of town on rails some of the Old Catholics. Square-jawed old Michael Derleth, who had coldly told the pastor that he was not accustomed "to take the orders of priests, without the authority of greater intelligence, more than the authority of a turned-about collar," had his hat shot off. That was too much for the Freethinkers; they rose up to preserve law and order and ranged themselves beside the Old Catholics. The result was that many of the Old Catholics joined the Free-thinkers; those who did not, including Michael, returned to the faith as soon as the bishop moved the priest, which was sooner than the priest expected, but not soon enough to save the original plan for the church.

But being an audience did not suit Prairie du Sac for long. The bickering went merrily on. Small things for some years, then—fights between groups of Sauk City boys and Prairie du Sac boys, gossip, the essential trivia of such twin-village rivalries. When U.S. 12 was routed through Wisconsin, a delegation of Prairie du Sac's most substantial citizens made a special journey to lay before the responsible officials a proposition that the route follow a devious road east of Sauk City and the river, and come to the prairie over the upper bridge. There was really no need to route U.S. 12 through such a comparatively unimportant little town as Sauk City. U.S. 12, however, went through both towns. When re-routing was proposed, over a century after the two towns were founded, a rerouting that would leave Prairie du Sac cut off from the highway, it was only natural that no Sauk Citizen appeared at the official hearing to support the Prairie du Sac citizens in their protest against the rerouting. They have long memories in both towns, particularly for small grievances. They argued and debated about a single railroad station to serve both towns, but to no avail; the single station was placed as close as possible to the boundary between the villages, within the corporate limits of Sauk City. They approached the idea of a new joint school with some trepidation, but when the Board of Education of Sauk City in 1941 laid before that of Prairie du Sac the pro-posal to study the advantages to be gained, it was the considered opinion of the Board of Education of Prairie du Sac that "the time was not ripe" for such a move.

Admittedly, the cultural differences between the two villages were as marked as possible in the early decades of their history, and contributed no little to the rivalry between them. There was in Prairie du Sac no counterpart of the Turnverein, the Gesangverein, of the dramatic classes conducted by Mrs. Emilia Crusius, of Turner Academy, of the lectures given and the discussions held every Sunday in the Freethinkers' Hall, of the scientific activities of the Lueders men, father and son, of the intellectual gatherings at the Naffz home, of the general striving toward liberalism—a striving which has pretty well overcome bigotry even to the present day. Old Prairie du Sac was a blue-laws village; not so Sauk City. From the beginning, Sauk City was influenced toward political liberalism by men like Carl Schurz, and later, Bob La Follette; Prairie du Sac remained staunchly conservative. Educationally, Sauk City early took liberal strides—in the caliber of its teachers, in the readiness of its public school graduates to take advantages of the opportunities for further education offered by the University of Wisconsin, in the furnishing of free textbooks, a custom carried on to this day; Prairie du Sac remained conservative almost to a reactionary point, though more recently, under the able guidance of R. S. Babington, for three decades superintendent of schools there, that village has come closer to breaking the bonds of those limitations which have hampered the educational opportunities of its young people. As a consequence of the culture so manifest in Sauk City, there were those who were inclined to look down their noses at Prairie du Sac, and those who live in the past do so to this day, though, since those early years, Prairie du Sac has given to the nation such scholars as the historian, Lowell Ragatz, and the biologist, Paul Sidney Conger, to stand beside Sauk City's seven authors, scholars, poets—Count Haraszthy, F. G. J. and Herman Lueders, Marcus Bach, Mark Schorer, Madge Hahn Longly, and August Derleth—to say nothing of Sauk City's Filibert Roth of Cornell, pioneer in United States forestry development, and the famous doctors Ochsner and Governor Emanuel L. Philipp from the prairie west of the villages.

But such rivalry is doomed to ultimate defeat. In the past decade the signs of its decay have become evident despite the still manifest life it displays churlishly from time to time. For a decade, the villages have co-operated in joint Memorial Day services, following the leadership of the American Legion. In 1938, after an amazing amount of puttering and reluctance on the part of both villages, the twins astonished the rest of Wisconsin by actually getting together to put on a joint Centennial pageant and program under the leadership of Ethel Rockwell of the University of Wisconsin, and there was nothing of rivalry visible in the pageant crowds as they sat listening to the choral intonation of the "Ode to the Sauk Prairie Dead," in which Sauk City and Prairie du Sac names were inextricably linked:

This day, this year or any year,
returned to where their fathers turned the plow,
and turned last wildness under, returning, coming here
to see again new town in places old to ways
of the hepatica, wild blowing rose, aster and frost,
to think of old, old names—
the fields and burial stones that add their cost
set long in earth, in earth-green, snow-white frames—
Inama, Baxter, Schroeter, Merk—
a priest, surveyor, a new-come leader, cooper and a clerk
of schools: Quimby, Hallasz, Leland, Duerr, and Bell—

a lawyer with dog-eared musty books, a lumberman with
    brawn, tall tales, miller, printer, a farmer who knew well
how rich the soil: to ask, "Where are our fathers and the
    way they came?"—Under the loam,
under the grass, the grass-root and the fern, where we, too,
    will follow home.

Naffz, Schneller, Babington, Alban, Pohlmann, Lueders,
Obrecht, Lachmund, Ochsner, Deininger, Accola, Tripp,
Evans, Ragatz, Sprecher, Cummings, Kindschi, Kirschner,
    Philipp,
Tabor, Ferber, Kelsey, Schweppe, Morrill, Canfield, Viebahn,
    Lodde,
Johnson, Burrows, Steuber, Perkins, Noyes, Moore, Cunradi,
Haentsch, Schlungbaum, Smith, Stowell, Hahn, Wiskocil and
    Keller,
Schmidt, Clas, Glarner, Grotophorst, Clement, Spiehr and
Heller—

Where are their hands, their ways, their plows?
—Under the sky they watched, the boughs
of trees they planted, under loam,
under blossom and green blade; under sweet earth, under sweet
shade where their sons' sons' feet
shall follow—home
in the deep dust, sweet earth
that gives through them, their ancient age,
new brightness birth,
an old race, new, new days.

Just previously the villages had acted in unison, even if
under duress, to achieve a sewer system, causing that
well-known town character, Billy Ynand (the same Billy
Ynand who in 1893 was a national champion high
jumper on ice skates), to lament that it would seem the
only way Upper and Lower Sauk could get together was
underground. Though the Gesangverein is long gone,

there is in its place an excellent women's chorus, the MacDowell Club, composed of ladies from both villages. But the hope that the twin villages might become one foundered constantly against a stumbling block to further action, particularly a new joint school. Supervisor of Education Harry E. Merritt from the State Department pointed to that block in his annual report for 1940-1941, when he wrote that the utility tax from the near-by power dam above Prairie du Sac was divided thusly: "Sauk City Village received $256.11, and Prairie du Sac school district $15,751.00." A joint school would mean the sharing of this financial advantage; doubtless, were Sauk City in a position to be selfish, it would be as reluctant to share that advantage as is Prairie du Sac. However, the inexorable wheeling of time will soon force the citizens of Prairie du Sac to share their financial advantage in the utility tax with its neighboring village and town, or face ultimately the loss of the bulk of that tax by legislative action. Farsighted citizens in both villages have recognized that the utility tax is the major obstacle to joint action and the ultimate death of the century-old rivalry. Hope continues to flower, but meanwhile the bickering goes on—still the same two dust motes in the same old sunbeam.

3. EARTH HEAVY ON THE PLOW

Hercules Dousman might still be taking in furs and making a good thing of it down at Prairie du Chien, but throughout the Wisconsin River valley after 1840 the ever-increasing numbers of settlers turned to the soil, plowing up the grassy land, clearing away the forests. They found the soil good—loam and clay, in some places a red, sandy loam, though here and there was too much sand. On the whole, however, the soil was heavy on the plow, rich, alluvial, certain to repay the hard labor of turning under the heavily matted grasses of this virgin land.

Settlements sprang up rapidly along the lower Wisconsin—some to become ghost towns, like Orion, some to continue to eke out an existence on the land. The English Prairie—so named because an English trader named Lansing, and his son, were slain there by Indians in 1763—the site of an Indian village in 1827, when it was also Laurent Rolette's trading post—after serving as headquarters for a detachment of Dodge's Rangers in 1832, harbored the smelting furnace of Colonel William Hamilton, youngest son of Alexander Hamilton, who invested in the lead diggings of southwest Wisconsin. After serving as a United States land office in 1842, the English Prairie country became the site of the village of Muscoda. To Port Andrews, nine miles north, came a group of Scotch families to settle apart from the Germans and Bohemians of Muscoda. Farmers flowed into the valley of the Baraboo River north of the Sauk Prairie, and in many places along the river settlements came into existence.

With the settlers, of course, came the rugged individualists. People like Dr. Brisbane, the South Carolina abolitionist, who laid out Arena on paper in 1852. A great many abolitions exist there today; so Dr. Brisbane may be said to have left his mark. Like the eccentric Mormon who gave his name to the Pewit's Nest in the town of Baraboo. This delightful fellow was a genuine individualist, no mistake about it. True, he may have been a bit misanthropic, but the failing is common enough. In any case, he came to the region in 1843, and plainly, by that time, the Wisconsin's valley at this point was far too settled for him. He was reluctant to move on, however; the river and its shores were very beautiful here; so he compromised by building himself a workshop in a recess of solid sand rock, ten feet above a deep pool of water confined in a canyon, and formed originally by a waterfall from some distance above. Entrance could be made in two ways: through a trapdoor in the roof— necessitating a steep and difficult climb down the rock wall; or through a similar trapdoor in the floor—by means of a bridge, with a ladder attached, floating on the surface of the pool. This was manifestly about as inaccessible as a man could get to be, and how he managed to eke out a living repairing watches, clocks, guns, and farming utensils is a mystery. It is also a mystery that he should want to make his living in this way, when he had other talents. On those occasions when he appeared among his fellow men he enjoyed telling lively stories and fiddling. Indeed, he fiddled well. Writing of him in 1861, William H. Canfield, the pioneer historian of Sauk County, wrote: "He preached some for the Mormon church." What a wealth of information is inherent in that succinct line! No comment, no explanation, simply: "He preached some for the Mormon church." Perhaps he had reason for misanthropy. Since the year of his coming to the valley coincides with the year that Joseph Smith, down along the Mississippi River at Nauvoo, Illinois, had another vision confirming the sanctity of polygamy, it may well have been that this was too much for him, and, having already been chased out of Ohio and Missouri, he probably gave up and took his leave. Men with guns he could stand, but plural wives—no, sirree! There is no record of his having had a wife. What with his inclinations, no doubt he would have been depressed had he known that in future years his Pewit's, or Peewee's, Nest was destined to become almost as great an attraction for the curious as the Natural Bridge at Leland. This was, of course, before the day of commercialization, before the dollar sign left its brand on Devil's Lake and the country not far to the north—the famous Dells of the Wisconsin. As it was, when the settlers came too close to his retreat, he vanished as mysteriously as he had come.

Small wonder that settlers came early to the Baraboo valley. It was not alone the designation of Baraboo as county seat of the newly created Sauk County; it was because the movement of settlement in Wisconsin now was to the north and northwest, and Baraboo, as well as the Sauk Prairie, lay in the direct route between Chicago and the Twin Cities—though it was not for decades to come that the highways would cross the county. In 1840 Abe Wood, Eben Peck (who was the first man to build a cabin and live in Wisconsin's capital city of Madison, twenty-five miles east of the Wisconsin River, in 1837), and Wallace Rowan came to settle in Baraboo, which was named after the river, which, in turn, was named after Jean Baribault, a French trader who had traded at the mouth of the river where it emptied into the Wisconsin, and decamped at the outbreak of the Black Hawk War. So began the future county seat, in a boat-shaped valley a score of miles in length, its width varying according to the encroaching or retreating of the hill slopes.

The valley had been uninhabited for only a short time, for in that same year the United States troops removed the last of the Winnebago downriver—a removal which was memorable, for the Winnebago loved their land, and keened for the entire length of the river, making their mourning songs to ring throughout the valley of the Wisconsin. However, among the Winnebago was one Indian who was as much an individualist as any of the whites who came to the country later.

That one was a chieftain, Wakunzeekah, the Yellow
Thunder. The method of taking Yellow Thunder for
his removal was in itself disgraceful; he had been invited to Fort Winnebago to obtain provisions, but no
sooner had he come than he and those others who had
accompanied him "were put into the guardhouse, with
ball and chain, which hurt the feelings of the Indians
very much, as they had done no harm," said John T.
de La Ronde, of the American Fur Company. Yellow
Thunder wept at this disgrace, but he had all the same
a keen understanding of the whites. He had no intention of being parted from his land; and before long he
led a small party of the exiled Winnebago back to the
upper Baraboo valley on foot, and, once there, he decided to observe the white man's custom; he bought
what he considered his own land from the government,
and settled there; though later he removed to the shore
of the Wisconsin River itself, where he died. He was
therefore much publicized as a "white man's Indian,"
and no doubt, with his sensitivity, he resented that to his
dying day.

Baraboo flourished quickly. Indeed, by the middle
of the 1840's, almost every village now extant in Sauk
County had been begun, and by the same time a stage
route connected the Sauk Prairie to Madison, established by Prescott Brigham—that same Brigham who
was so great a champion for the removal of the county
seat from Prairie du Sac to Baraboo. He was also instrumental in changing the name of Baraboo to Adams, simply because he admired John Quincy Adams, but this
change did not last. His stage was as persistent as Brigham, however, because it continued in operation forty
years. The route to Baraboo followed, and then to
Reedsburg and Spring Green—the town which had
finally grown up across the river from Helena, founded

by Thomas B. Shaunce, who had been in Dan Whitney's employ for the purpose of erecting the shot tower there. And Baraboo managed quickly enough to get into the news.

Fourteen years after the first settlers came, Baraboo had a war of its own—a Whisky War, so to speak. The doughty warriors were largely ladies, moved by the spirit of temperance to get rid of the spirits of intemperance, though, of course, it was a pair of ministers who started it by fulminating against the saloons. Manifestly, the saloons of pioneer days were something to fulminate against, and the wives of many well-known citizens decided that fulminations were not enough, action was necessary. They took the offensive with a vengeance, combining cunning with violence. One of the ladies, appropriately named Martha Battles, entered the Brick Tavern and proposed to purchase the entire stock, which so overwhelmed the proprietor that before he could collect his wits and take her up by setting a price, the rest of the ladies had got in at the back door and had wreaked havoc by opening his faucets and emptying his kegs and bottles. The same ruse was effectively worked on a second tavern, but by the time the ladies reached French Pete's place and the Van Wendell saloon, word had got around, and the opposition had mustered its forces. The ladies were refused admittance to Van Wendell's by a patron who blocked their way. By this time the smell of battle, the flush of success, and the odor of the spilled whisky had had their way with the ladies and they were not to be stopped by a patron. He was promptly caught by the waistband and jerked aside, whereupon he was rendered hors de combat immediately by the unhappy occasion of losing his trousers. "His fastenings gave way," a contemporary account put it, which is a polite way of saying that his pants came down. No doubt that was not all that gave way. Undeterred, the ladies pushed on.

But the Demon Rum had the law on his side, and he could afford to take a couple of blows. The ladies had just got into fine fettle when a deputy sheriff appeared, read the riot act to them, and ordered them to disperse without delay. What the ladies said and did is not on record. Perhaps delicacy forbade putting down the facts in regard to this aspect of the Whisky War. The upshot of the matter, however, was that several of the ladies were placed under arrest, and some days later were taken down to Sauk City so that they might be given a fair and impartial trial in that place. They got it. They were ordered to pay damages to the amount of $150, and did so. Both sides claimed the victory, and there was rejoicing at the bar and in the pulpit. Whether or not the ladies paid for the gentleman's fastenings, those that "gave way," is not recorded.

There were other ladies of initiative in the Baraboo country. Mrs. Ann Garrison, for instance. This enterprising soul laid out a paper city, called Garrisonville, near Baraboo, put up a tavern, a sawmill, a pottery, a ferry, and a hop house. There was even a salted gold mine. Mrs. Garrison knew her business. She sent east and sold lots, particularly in Philadelphia; she sold a good many, but no matter how many she sold, nor how she prospered, Garrisonville remained only a paper city, lost even to memory now.

The prosperity of Baraboo was destined to be augmented by the possibilities of Devil's Lake. James S. Alban of Prairie du Sac saw the lake in 1839, before he had quite made up his mind to stay where he was; he was apparently the first white man on record to have seen it, and it was perhaps he who called it the Lake of the Hills, before the Indian name, Minnewaukan, or

Evil Spirit Lake, was known—the Indians having long ago believed that the shattered rocky walls and loose rock at the lake resulted from a titanic struggle between the thunder birds and the water monsters. John T. de La Ronde saw it in 1842 and wrote: "I went and saw the Devil's Lake, which is a little south of the village of Baraboo. The lake is surrounded by high bluffs and I could not see the sun until ten or eleven o'clock in the forenoon, and it would disappear from view about two or three o'clock, so hemmed in by bluffs is this romantic body of water. . . . I saw a quantity of tobacco that the Indians had deposited there for the Manitou. The voyageurs denominated it Devil's Lake, from the sound resembling hammering and tinkling of a bell that we hear all the time, and from the darkness of the place."

H. E. Cole, most able chronicler of the region's history, tells succinctly of the lake in his *Baraboo, Dells, and Devil's Lake Region*, when he points to the Wisconsin River's part in its formation, and to its geological history: "Geologically Devil's Lake is one of the wonders of the world. At the dawn of the earth's history there were no rivers or lakes or bluffs in the Baraboo region, the ocean or an inland sea covering all the land. At the bottom of the sea were the Archean or igneous rocks, the oldest formation known to geology. Upon these rocks the sand was piled a mile deep, which sand at a later time was changed into sandstone and still later metamorphosed into the hard quartzite which towers high in the bluffs. Resting upon the beds of sand were deposits of clay which changed to slate, limestone which became dolomite, and iron which remained in its elemental state. . . . Later there was a mountain-making movement of the earth and slowly there were created in this region peaks as lofty as those in the Alps or Rockies. The once horizontal beds of sand, clay, limestone and iron were uplifted and folded in the process, the layers at the lake being inclined about fifteen degrees as seen along the East Bluff. The Baraboo Bluffs are among the oldest formed things on the globe—older than the Rockies or Alleghanies, older than a pound of coal in the earth. . . . Following the formation of the quartzite there was a long period of erosion and a river cut a gorge through the range where the lake is now located. This river no doubt came from the north and after flowing through the Lower Narrows of the Baraboo River, swept through the gap in the south range and continued its course to the ocean. . . . In Paleozoic times the sea returned again, the tops of the bluffs stood as islands above the waves, the loose rocks were rounded on the shore, and the sandstone almost filled the gorge where there was once a river. . . . The sea retreated and a river once more cut a gorge through the range, not only at Devil's Lake but at the Lower Narrows. Geologists know the river has performed this task because in places some of the sandstone still remains, not only in the Devil's Lake gap but at higher levels on the region roundabout. . . . Next came the Glacial Epoch, when the advancing ice from the northeast came into the Baraboo region. Into this gorge, where probably once flowed the stream we now know as the Wisconsin River, the ice advanced to the terminal moraine, where the visitor descends just before reaching the lake. At the same time another tongue of cold crept into the valley between the Devil's Nose and the lake. Sand and gravel were washed into the gorge, leaving a deposit hundreds of feet thick. The well at the north end of the lake is 283 feet deep, and yet the drill stopped before it reached the bed of the ancient stream."

Nor was this the only curious feature of the county to which the settlers now came in ever-increasing numbers. The early farmers found there hundreds of Indian mounds, most of them of Winnebago origin—conical, effigy (deer, bear, lizard, turtle, eagle, swallow, frog, etc.) wall, and pyramidal—and one unique: the famed Man Mound, northeast of Baraboo, 214 feet in length and with a shoulder width of 48 feet, the only mound of its kind in the world. Fortunately, though other lesser mounds were destroyed (there were still more than six hundred counted in Sauk County alone as recently as 1905), the Man Mound was discovered and preserved by William Canfield, who surveyed the area and came upon it in the course of his work.

The settlers came from all over, and soon occupied both banks of the river. After Sauk City, Honey Creek, Merrimac, and Roxbury, there were comparatively few Germans among them, though several farmers soon put up impressive houses along the east shore between the Sauk Prairie and Portage, handsome houses of stone, with white pillars and blinds, testifying to the richness of the soil they tilled. But the majority of the settlers who came in now were English, Scotch, and Irish, perhaps many coming by the same chance that brought the Muirs. John Muir tells of their choice of a land to settle in *The Story of My Boyhood and Youth*, when he writes: "On our wavering westward way a grain-dealer in Buffalo told father that most of the wheat he handled came from Wisconsin; and this influential information finally determined my father's choice. At Milwaukee a farmer who had come in from the country near Fort Winnebago with a load of wheat agreed to haul us and our formidable load of stuff to a little town called Kingston for thirty dollars."

John Muir, more than anyone else, left a revelatory record of the lives of these early farmers. They came to wilderness—"Oh, that glorious Wisconsin wilderness!

Everything new and pure in the very prime of the spring when Nature's pulses were beating highest and mysteriously keeping time with our own! Young hearts, young leaves, flowers, animals, the winds and the streams and the sparkling lake, all wildly, gladly rejoicing together!" The settlers came rapidly. "Although in the spring of 1849 there was no other settler within a radius of four miles of our Fountain Lake farm, in three or four years almost every quarter-section of government land was taken up, mostly by enthusiastic home-seekers from Great Britain, with only here and there Yankee families from adjacent states, who had come drifting indefinitely westward in covered wagons, seeking their fortunes like winged seeds; all alike striking root and gripping the glacial drift soil as naturally as oak and hickory trees; happy and hopeful, establishing homes and making wider and wider fields in the hospitable wilderness. The axe and plough were kept very busy; cattle, horses, sheep, and pigs multiplied; barns and corncribs were filled up, and man and beast were well fed; a schoolhouse was built, which was used also for a church; and in a very short time the new country began to look like an old one.

"None of our neighbors were so excessively industrious as father," Muir goes on; "though nearly all of the Scotch, English, and Irish worked too hard, trying to make good homes and to lay up money enough for comfortable independence. Excepting small garden-patches, few of them had owned land in the old country. Here their craving land-hunger was satisfied, and they were naturally proud of their farms and tried to keep them as neat and clean and well-tilled as gardens. To accomplish this without the means for hiring help was impossible. Flowers were planted about the neatly kept log or framehouses; barnyards, granaries, etc., were kept in about as neat order as the homes, and the fences and corn-rows were rigidly straight. But every uncut weed distressed them; so also did every ungathered ear of grain, and all that was lost by birds and gophers; and this overcarefulness bred endless work and worry." But their work was not such as to forbid the social amenities. "Corduroying the swamps formed the principal part of road-making among the early settlers for many a day. At these annual road-making gatherings opportunity was offered for discussion of the news, politics, religion, war, the state of the crops, comparative advantages of the new country over the old, and so forth, but the principal opportunities, recurring every week, were the hours after Sunday church services. I remember hearing long talks on the wonderful beauty of the Indian corn; the wonderful melons, so wondrous fine for 'sloken a body on hot days'; their contempt for tomatoes, so fine to look at with their sunny colors and so disappointing in taste; the miserable cucumbers the 'Yankee bodies' ate, though tasteless as rushes; the character of the Yankees, etcetera. Then there were long discussions about the Russian war, news of which was eagerly gleaned from Greeley's *New York Tribune.* . . ."

This was their way of life in those years. There were exceptions, of course, most notable of whom were perhaps the Durwards. Head of the family who gave their name to a glen along the Wisconsin was Bernard I. Durward—professor, poet, painter. He set out one day to paint a portrait of Archbishop Henni in Milwaukee, and while there, he was converted to Catholicism. Shortly after this, he made the glen his retreat, bringing there his extraordinary family, which included Percy, another artist; Emerson, who was likewise a writer and joined the priesthood, as did another brother; Wilfred, a taxidermist, photographer, and author. The Durwards

Catholicized the glen, leaving memorials for such eminent Catholic artists of the mid-century as Aubrey De Vere, Coventry Patmore, and others; there are also memorial initials for Ruskin and the Melzls—the musicians, one of whom presumably brought to light of day the metronome to inspire the sly second movement of Beethoven's *Eighth Symphony.*

Nor did all the settlements survive; some mushroomed into life, and passed away almost unnoticed. Some, like Decorah and Okee, lived through a long bright dream, and then became settled in a rut of neglect and time lost, not quite ghost towns like Newport, but almost.

4. THE CANAL

Throughout this time, the Wisconsin remained the chief artery of traffic. True, there were stage routes, there were roads; but both were short, and designed to facilitate river traffic to points more distant from the shores. Thus, the road from Madison to Sauk City was heavily used to haul lumber which had come down the river, bound for Madison. All the way up and down the Wisconsin between Portage and Prairie du Chien there were landing places, such landings as Laws' Ferry, south of Avoca, across from Richland City, an early settlement at which was held one of the first Fourth of July celebrations in the valley—a notable affair that lasted three days. James Laws ferried men, wagons, buggies, oxen, horses, swine, *et al* across the Wisconsin, and was protected by a charter from competition for miles either way along the river. Point Independence was another such landing; this one was north of Richland City, and it is worth remembering now only because Ed Wallace of that point once got a contract for building wing dams on the river there, a work into which he plunged with great enthusiasm which was destined for quick fading, for one of his first dams succeeded in deflecting the Wisconsin so effectively that its current washed out part of Richland City, and his boom, built to stop the washing out, failed; he changed the course of the river, but had nothing more than that simple fact to show for it.

Naturally, the Fox-Wisconsin waterway was of such importance that the actual portage itself must inevitably prove increasingly onerous. As early as 1793 Laurent Barth had purchased from the Winnebago at the portage the right to transport goods over the portage. Barth was followed by Jean Lecuyer, a brother-in-law of the Winnebago chief, Decorah, and in 1803 Barth withdrew, selling his interests. Such methods of transportation as these men had to offer served very well prior to the building of Fort Winnebago, but immediately thereafter it became apparent that the logical improvement of the portage would be a canal connecting the Fox and Wisconsin rivers.

Quickly, then, the Fox-Wisconsin rivers improvement project became the topic of all conversation along the lower Wisconsin, and work on the canal itself was begun as early as 1837 with the chartering of the Portage Canal Company. The actual digging was not started until the following year. But the first fire quickly enough died down; this is so often the procedure, and, after ten thousand dollars had been spent, the company was dissolved, work was stopped, and the project temporarily abandoned.

The next move was up to the War Department, and in 1839 Captain Thomas Jefferson Cram made a preliminary survey of the Fox and Wisconsin rivers to estimate the cost of clearing a channel from Lake Michigan to the Mississippi. His report was not immediately taken up or acted upon, and it remained for the territorial delegate to Congress, Morgan L. Martin, to secure passage of an act August 8, 1846, "making a grant of land to the state, upon its admission into the union, for the improvement of the Fox River alone, and the building of a canal across the portage between the two rivers. The grant covered every odd-numbered section within three miles of the canal, the river and the lakes, en route from the portage to the mouth. When the second constitutional convention was held, this proposition on the part of congress was endorsed, and at the first session of the state legislature, the latter body passed an act, approved August 8, 1848, appointing a board of public works . . . providing for the improvement of the river." On the board, among four others, sat Hercules Dousman, who by this time was deeply interested in facilitating the passage of wheat out of Wisconsin. This was at a time when the Wisconsin farmer raised wheat to the exclusion of most other grains, when it was the dream of rural Wisconsin to become a wheat state—as, actually, Wisconsin was for a short time; the time was not far distant, however, when the depredations of the chinch bugs put an end to that dream forever.

The sale of public lands for the profit of Wisconsin proceeded apace, and work was again begun on the improvement of the Fox River channel and on the canal. This continued for slightly over two years; already by 1850 it was apparent that there would not be nearly enough money available for the project; the lands had in large part been sold, and the remainder of the land sales lagged to such an extent that by early 1851 the board of public works reported to the legislature that the work would have to stop unless they could hasten the sale of public lands. At this juncture, Morgan Martin stepped in again and proposed to the state legislature, through Governor Nelson Dewey, "to do the work from Green Bay to Lake Winnebago, except what the board of public works had finished or was already under contract for. The board had dug the canal at Portage, before there was any steam navigation possible on the lower Fox." The board, unfortunately, had fallen under the influence of members of the legislature who, with the customary lack of vision afflicting the majority of legislators in all times, demanded that money be spent in their districts, without consideration of the goal. Morgan was awarded a contract, and went to work immediately, only to run afoul of Governor Farwell the following year. Bickering of a political nature then delayed the work, and though Morgan won his battle with the governor, he had lost almost a year in his task.

The United States government came through with an additional land grant in 1854; New York capitalists (Horatio Seymour, Erastus Corning, Hiram Barney) began to invest, and in 1856 the canal was in operation. The New York investors shortly maneuvered the Fox-Wisconsin Improvement Company into such a position that, as Martin records it, "we were obliged to submit ... to a foreclosure of the bonds and sale of the whole concern to the New Yorkers. The big imported fish swallowed the little natives." Not long after, the United States appraised the assets of the company and purchased the entire improvement, including the canal. Long before, the first boat had gone through the canal; the date was May 24, 1851, and the *River Times* chronicled the event thusly: "The beautiful steamer, *John Mitchell,* near accomplished the feat of passing through the canal at this place on Saturday last. She came up as far as Main Street. As the *John Mitchell* came up the canal, the *Enterprise* came up the Wisconsin River to the head of the canal. The blustering rivalry between these inhabitants of different waters (the throat of each giving its best pull and whistle alternately) was quite exhilarating, and called out a large concourse of citizens to gaze upon the scene presented and make predictions for the future. After a short time boats and citizens withdrew, amid strains of music and the noise and confusions were over."

Predictions for the future, however, were conditioned by factors beyond the control of the men who fostered the canal and the improvement of the Fox-Wisconsin waterway. By the time the entire waterway was open to steamboats, the dream of Wisconsin as a wheat-shipping state was over. (In 1849, Wisconsin had produced four million bushels of wheat; seven years later Wisconsin was producing the second largest crop of wheat in the nation, 28,000,000 bushels; and along many of the Wisconsin's tributaries water-powered gristmills arose, flour mills were built. The dream died hard; but it died.) The dominant trend toward dairying was clearly evident, and, more important still, the railroads had begun to encroach into the state. However, the valley of the Wisconsin was to remain an important artery of traffic for some decades; by 1855, it had been crossed at only two places by the railroad—at Prairie du Chien and at that portion of the river between Portage and Kilbourn. No railroad and few roads reached into the greater north portion of the valley of the Wisconsin; they were to come.

PART FOUR

Timber!

"Your grandma was with her sister in Eau Claire that time," said grandfather. "We had your Uncle Charlie then already. She never got to see me all winter long. We went into the woods in October and in that winter they were clearing a place three miles in, piling the logs on the river bank for the spring break. We didn't come out until April—sometimes later. That job of breaking the logs—nobody wanted it. It was dangerous, to break out the pile and send it rolling down into the river. There were sixty men in the big outfit, and thirty in the little outfit. They were Canucks for the most—and Norwegians and Swedes, but there were some Germans and Irish and Scotch. Oh, everything. . . . At four o'clock in the morning the cook was almost ready with breakfast. We had fresh biscuits every morning. At that time he woke up the teamsters, and they went out and gave their horses hay and grain. Then they came back and laid down again. When cook called breakfast of biscuits and pork, fried or cooked, they fed the horses again. Oh, those horses were well taken care of; they had to do a lot of work; everybody knew it, and the teamsters most of all. . . . Nobody left camp before sunup, and everybody was back before dark. That was always the way it was. I never remember that there was a time when anybody was out after dark. . . . Sometimes the cook made prune and dried apple pies. The way grandma used to make them—you remember that. But there was nobody could make pies like

167

that cook. I kinda shined up to him and he used to hang a red handkerchief on his door so I could see it; that was his signal that he'd just finished a batch of pies and I could come over and have a piece. . . . And the men were liberal with their money; they threw it away, and when they went to town, the money was like water in their hands. They never saw a woman all that time, nor had anything to drink—they just went crazy when they hit town. . . . I was working there between the fires:— the Peshtigo and the Hinkley fires—the Peshtigo was the biggest, bigger than the Chicago fire that same year, and the Hinkley was close up to it. I was with the Badger Company then, and we were working over toward the Mississippi. That was in the early spring of '81. I remember the year because it was that time Chris Bernhardt slipped on the snow and ice and came down with his head so hard he almost killed himself. The same year the train came into Sauk City, too. Obrecht, Keysar, Tripp, and Ed Perkins went down to Mazomanie and came up on that first one. . . ."

Sac Prairie Journal: 1941

1. Dan Whitney

A QUARTER of a century before the railroads came into Wisconsin to make lumbering for a time Wisconsin's greatest industry, the Wisconsin forests had beckoned Daniel Whitney of Green Bay. In the winter of 1827-28 the rivers were still pre-eminent in facilitating travel; so it was along the rivers that any kind of woodcutting must be done. In that year Whitney negotiated permission from the Winnebago to make shingles on the Wisconsin, above the portage, which was terrain unknown to most white men before that time. With twenty-two Stockbridge Indians, his nephew and another employee as superintendents, Whitney set out in the following year under the guidance of Colonel Ebenezer Childs, who had been engaged not only to take them to their destination, but also to supply them with provisions. They came up the Fox, took the portage, and went up the Wisconsin for approximately fifty miles, passing through the beautiful Dells of the Wisconsin to the mouth of one of the Wisconsin's longest tributaries, the Yellow River. There Colonel Childs left them and went back downriver.

He had not gone far before he was stopped. This was at Fort Winnebago, whose commandant, Major David Twiggs, haled Colonel Childs before him and informed him that Whitney's men must be removed from the Winnebago land at once—apparently because any agreement with the Indians must be made by the agents of the government, who were far more skillful in being devious in their dealings with the simple, honest red men. In short, Colonel Childs was to carry no provisions to Whitney's party, and was to remove the Whitneys and their men at his earliest convenience. Colonel Childs' opinion of the military is not on record; but it is certain he had no very high opinion of Major Twiggs and his orders. "I told him [Major Twiggs]," wrote Colonel Childs many years later in his *Recollections of Wisconsin,* "that I was employed by Whitney to supply his men with provisions; and that all the Indian Agents and soldiers combined could not prevent me from fulfilling my engagements. . . . He flew into a violent passion, and told me that I would be sorry for my course, and for what I had said. I told him that I disregarded all his threats, and then left him." The colonel went back up the Wisconsin with provisions in the course of time and found that Whitney's party had made some two hundred thousand shingles.

Major Twiggs was not unaware of his going. He waited a brief time for the Indian agent from Prairie du Chien, and then sent a force from Fort Winnebago— these same soldiers who had grown so restless in inaction prior to the Black Hawk War—to deal with Whitney accordingly. They dealt with him. They seized as many of Dan Whitney's shingles as they could take back with them, and destroyed the rest, causing Whitney to lose close to two thousand dollars. No small potatoes in 1828. The major, however, had good use for the shingles; at the moment of the seizure, the soldiery lived in barracks while the construction of Fort Winnebago was being carried on—the time being the same year that Lieutenant Jefferson Davis was operating in Whitney's vicinity with troops cutting logs and floating them down to the site of the fort. Whether or not it was Jeff Davis's soldiers who dealt with Whitney is not known; it is not likely, however, that it was.

Dan Whitney was irate and chagrined. He took a little time off to send Tom Shaunce down the Wisconsin to build a shot tower for him at Helena, and then turned his eyes to the forests once more. With the Winnebago willing, there was no reason why a good man couldn't take out needed lumber. This time, having already come to an agreement with the Winnebago, he went to the War Department direct and got a permit to erect a sawmill and cut timber on the upper Wisconsin—the upper river being considered as that portion above the portage, though that portion was both middle and upper Wisconsin.

During that winter, with the help of his nephew and A. B. Sampson, he built the first mill on the Wisconsin at Whitney's Rapids, below Pointe Bas, (now Nekoosa), not far below Wisconsin Rapids. For four years he had a virtual monopoly. It was not until 1836 that Grignon and Merrill, armed with a similar War Department permit, built the second mill on the upper Wisconsin. In that same year, 1836, the Menominee ceded their lands along the Wisconsin for a distance of forty miles above Pointe Bas, a cession which was obtained specifically in response to demands by prospective lumbermen; the result of this extinguishing of the Menominee title was that the Wisconsin was thoroughly explored by enterprising lumbermen all the way up to Big Bull Falls (Wausau) before 1837.

Two years later, the government was having the first of its troubles with the lumbermen. The practice of buying a small piece of land and ruthlessly taking out the timber on all the adjoining lands, then still the property of the government—a practice to be carried to its highest peak of efficiency by the lumber barons in the coming decades—had begun almost at once, and complaints that timber was being cut where no one had authority to cut it reached the government. The problem was no small one, for by 1840 almost every eligible place on the Wisconsin as far as Big Bull Falls was occupied, and the exploration of the northern tributaries had been started. Moreover, almost every kind of timber was cut from the beginning: white, yellow, and Norway pine—choice, of course, rock and soft maple, all varieties of oak, balsam fir, white and red cedar, spruce, hemlock, ash, poplar, basswood, and hickory; though the tendency was to leave the softer woods until last. Moved by these complaints, the government sent Joshua Hathaway in February, 1839, to survey the Wisconsin River from Pointe Bas to Wausau for a distance of three miles back from the Wisconsin, a survey completed in May, 1840, and thenceforth known at the Three Mile Survey. A decade was to elapse before land farther back from the river was surveyed. Nevertheless, the Three Mile Survey brought to the shores of the upper Wisconsin ever more and more settlers, and when in 1852 the lands were brought into the market in Menasha and Mineral Point, they were bought up at a steady and gratifying rate.

Meanwhile, Dan Whitney was at last coming into the money. From his mill near what is now Plover, he sent downriver to Sauk City and thence overland to Madison the logs for the early houses in Wisconsin's capital, until the mill of Amable Grignon and Samuel Merrill near Port Edwards began to compete with him. Neither of these two early mills was ever short of help, for settlers came pouring into the upper Wisconsin valley from the time that Wisconsin's territorial status was defined in 1836, and they came in such numbers that by the middle of the forties, almost every village and town along the river had come into existence. By 1848, when Wisconsin joined the Union, the upper Wisconsin had twenty-four mills, operating forty-five saws; ten years later, there were one hundred and seven mills turning out more than one hundred million board feet a year, and already the industry was giving employment to over three thousand men.

The region into which Whitney and those who came after him entered was rich with standing pine to the amount of almost a hundred and thirty billion feet.

There was one thing Dan Whitney found out soon enough, and that was that the upper Wisconsin was a mighty crooked river. It was so crooked, in fact, with so many curves and bends and rapids, that a man simply could not for a moment think of sending logs down the river in large rafts, or lumber either. The rapids in some places, particularly above Pointe Bas, were narrow channels thirty feet in width, through which the water surged wildly over rocky bottoms at a speed which ranged from ten to twenty miles an hour; even dynamiting the rapids did not greatly affect the dangers of running them. So from the beginning, as soon as it became possible to do so, the lumbermen secured sawmills farther downstream, to expedite logs and lumber to the Mississippi and St. Louis. Since this was not usually possible, most of the logs were sent downriver to the vicinity of the portage, there made into larger rafts, and thence shipped on down into the Mississippi, either to go on to St. Louis or to be broken up along the Iowa shore and sent overland into the west.

Dan Whitney, who had engaged in transportation, in the fur trade, in the lead mining and now in lumbering, following the rise of industry along the Wisconsin River, grew to rival Dousman's position as one of the wealthiest men in the country of the Great Lakes, though he was a far cry from the lumber barons who were to rise as a result of the spoliation of the Wisconsin forests.

2. INDUSTRY NORTH

Steadily now, the pulse of industry moved upriver. The peak year of lead mining in Wisconsin was 1847, and at that time ninety per cent of the lead was shipped down the Wisconsin and Mississippi to St. Louis, the rest of it trucked overland by ox teams to Lake Michigan ports. A decade later lead production had fallen off by half, and as a result the population in those river towns which had grown with the rise of the industry began to diminish, in some cases to disappear entirely (so ended Helena, at the site of Dan Whitney's shot tower), in others to reach a static level above which even the influx of farmers to take up the remaining land seldom brought them. The census of 1870 clearly indicated the development of the upper Wisconsin in so far as settlement was concerned, the moving northward of settlers in the wake of the rising lumbering industry; for in that year Prairie du Chien, once the first city along the Wisconsin, had passed to second place with a population of 2,700, and Portage had gone to first at 3,945. Four cities of importance had come into being above Portage over a distance of something like two hundred miles— Kilbourn, Grand Rapids—which were to become Wisconsin Dells and Wisconsin Rapids respectively— Stevens Point and Wausau.

They were not alone. By 1870 even the trading post near Lac Vieux Desert was almost a decade old; in 1857 Joshua Fox had made the first settlement at Eagle River, the beginnings of Rhinelander had also been made, and at least sawmills stood at the sites of the remaining river towns which were to be founded before 1900. The northern Wisconsin River valley drew the daring and adventurous men, men like Daniel Gagen, who came to the Eagle River country at eighteen, following a short career in the copper mines of northern Michigan. He came to trap and to put up a trading post on the trail along the Wisconsin at that point, but luck did not immediately attend him; he took the pox and was nursed back to health by an Indian girl, whom he married. Despite his having gone to work in his early teens, he was well educated, largely self-educated, and he could entertain his guests by recitations from Shakespeare and English poetry. Like many another trader, he was quick to abandon his post and go into lumbering when the conversion of industry came.

The meanderings of the Wisconsin make lumbering a problem; they were almost unbelievable; for almost half its length through the heart of the forest area, the Wisconsin twists and turns to such a degree that the actual distance from Merrill to Wisconsin Dells is easily doubled by the water route. The trip upriver with saw-mill machinery was made by canoe and raft, always with great difficulty, and very often it was easier to haul the machinery north on human backs. Moreover, because of the density of the forests and the uncertainty of the ownership of the lands beyond the Three Mile Survey limits, the Wisconsin's northern tributaries were invaded almost as early as the Wisconsin itself. Once lumbering had begun, it was apparent how difficult it was to run rafts downriver; most of the logging drives offered a few hazards apart from jams at the rapids and in the narrows.

There are rapids and falls enough on the upper

Wisconsin—the Wabojewun, or Narrow, Falls just below the forks of the Wisconsin, the Grandfather Bull
Falls—where the falls are two miles in length, with three
perpendicular drops of several feet each, the Grandmother Bull Falls, the Jenny Bull Falls (Merrill), the
Big Bull Falls at Wausau, the Little Bull—and others.
Curiously, almost every rapids and falls is a Bull falls.
The French voyageurs of the American Fur Company,
going north from the portage, first heard the roaring of
the rapids, and, coming upon them, named the ripples
or ruffles "bulles" (the Canuck word for rapids), "gros
bulles," "grand-père bulles," etc., which speedily became corrupted into *bulls* by the lumbermen. Thus the
rapids and bends made inconceivably difficult any large-
scale rafting along the river, though all kinds of attempts were made to lessen the difficulties attending the
running of the rapids—the building of dams to cover
eddies, the use of life preservers (for the mortality at
some of the bulles was frightening, twenty-seven men
listed as killed in one season, forty in another, etc.),
snubbing over with rope lines; but the most successful
attempt to lessen the hazards was the employment of
standing pilots, that is, men who did nothing but pilot
rafts through the rapids. For a while, however, the dangers of the rapids and bends held back the peak of development of lumbering in the upper Wisconsin
country.

Nor did improvements in the sawmills wait upon
adequate transportation. Before the Civil War, the
"muley" and gang saws were replaced by the circular
saw, cutting a half-inch kerf, the over, and undershot
water wheels were replaced by the vertical shaft water
turbine, and both circular edging saws and mechanical
log conveyers were not far distant.

The Civil War brought a brief but beneficial scare

to the valley of the upper Wisconsin. Fearing that England, sympathetic to the Confederacy, might attack from Canada, three military roads were built into northern Wisconsin, one of them following an old canoe trail along the Wisconsin to Eagle River, and, by 1870, when these roads were completed, the railroads were pushing up into the logging camps.

Nevertheless, despite all these difficulties, the logs were run; they were not rafted until they reached the lower river, but were floated down the tributaries and down the Wisconsin, and by law were required to be marked by brands, such brands to be recorded in each district through which the logs were floated, and notice of brands to be circulated among all booming companies, so that penalties could be imposed upon anyone illegally in possession of logs belonging to others whose marks were so recorded. This method made it possible to float logs with greater freedom than might otherwise have been done.

The outfits, meanwhile, traveled by every conceivable method. For the most part bateaux were used on the tributaries, but on the Wisconsin dugouts some thirty feet in length, made from fine lumber and designed to carry sixteen men, were used almost exclusively in the boom years of the industry. The loggers themselves usually traveled along the shore, followed on the river by a wanigan—a crude shanty constructed on top of two canoes coupled together, sometimes used as a kitchen, sometimes as a supply shop for socks, gloves, tobacco, clay pipes, sometimes as a hospital, and occasionally as all three. The canoes supporting the wanigan were at least forty feet in length, holding up either a canvas superstructure with a width of six feet, or a wooden shanty eight by ten. Such travel was by no means easy. In testifying before the Interstate Commerce Commission in Madison recently, regarding the navigability of the Wisconsin, one old-timer told of making the trip from Eagle River to Rhinelander in a wanigan. "Took us twenty-one days," he said dryly, "and we tipped over twenty times. Slept almost every night in wet blankets."

Despite the railroads, however, it was only toward the close of the last century that logging left the river route for the rails; long before that time the power dams had made logging and rafting almost impossible. Between 1850 and 1885, millions of feet of sawed lumber went down the Wisconsin in cribs 12 to 20 inches deep, measuring from 16 to 32 feet, each crib containing up to 10,000 feet, and several cribs lashed together for quiet-water passages forming a "string," or "rapids piece." Sometimes as many as four strings could be lashed together to form a great raft in quiet waters; this was especially possible from the islands opposite the twin villages' boundary line at the Sauk Prairie, the last of the places where swift water made it necessary to break up the rafts, to the ultimate destination of the lumber. (Since that time the shifting channel of the Wisconsin has passed to the east of the islands and left them little more than a further abutment of land on the east edge of the Sauk Prairie.)

The market for this sawed lumber centered at St. Louis, where the seasoned buyers were located; but runs were made to Memphis, and as far as Helena, Arkansas. The great rafts often covered the Mississippi to mid-channel, where the steamboats sometimes lent assistance in moving them. The pineries-to-St. Louis trip might take only three weeks, but it might take all summer. The fluctuation of the Wisconsin accounted for the difference. It was reckoned that a good trip to the mouth of the Wisconsin from Wausau could be made in from

twelve to sixteen days; from Wausau to St. Louis took
an average time in good water of twenty-four days;
and the return trip was made by boat usually as far as
Portage, and from there by stage or on foot until the
railroads came to bring the men back by rail.

The story of lumber has been told a score of times.
With the railroads, the highways, the rivers, Wisconsin
soon became primarily a lumbering state—this was during the same decades that William Dempster Hoard was
pointing to dairying as the way from wheat raising in
the economic life of Wisconsin. Until 1910 lumbering
remained Wisconsin's first industry, and for a while the
lumbering and railroad interests completely controlled
the political and economic life not only of the Wisconsin River valley but of the entire state. The lumber
barons found their way into legislative offices even to
the United States Senate. The man who was by dint of
his own efforts to crack the control of those interests,
the late great Senator Robert Marion La Follette, born
not far from the Wisconsin in the little township of
Primrose, in Dane County, has left in his *Personal Narrative of Political Experiences* a portrait of one of the
lumber barons who became for a time Wisconsin's most
powerful man, Senator Philetus Sawyer, then leader of
the Republican party in Wisconsin.

"Sawyer was a man of striking individuality and of
much native force. He was a typical lumberman,
equipped with great physical strength and a shrewd,
active mind. He had tramped the forests, cruised timber,
slept in the snow, built saw mills—and by his own
efforts had made several million dollars. So unlearned
was he that it was jokingly said that he signed his name
'P. Sawyer' because he could not spell Philetus. He was
nevertheless a man of ability, and a shrewd counselor in
the prevailing political methods. He believed in getting

all he could for himself and his associates whenever and wherever possible. I always thought that Sawyer's methods did not violate his conscience; he regarded money as properly the chief influence in politics. Whenever it was necessary, I believe that he bought men as he bought saw-logs. He assumed that every man in politics was serving, first of all, his own personal interests—else why should he be in politics? He believed quite simply that railroad corporations and lumber companies, as benefactors of the country, should be given unlimited grants of public lands, allowed to charge all the traffic could bear, and that anything that interfered with the profits of business was akin to treason.

"I had not been long in Washington before Sawyer invited me to go with him to call on the President. I can remember just how he looked climbing into his carriage—a short, thick-set, squatty figure of a man with a big head set on square shoulders and a short neck —stubby everywhere. I remember he talked to me in a kindly, fatherly manner—very matter-of-fact—looking at me from time to time with a shrewd squint in his eye. He had no humor, but much of what has been called 'horse sense.' His talk was jerky and illiterate; he never made a speech in his life."

It was Sawyer who had La Follette, then a young congressman, put on the Committee for Indian Affairs, only to realize with some pain shortly thereafter that the bumptious young maverick who had bucked the party in Wisconsin and still got himself elected, was going to raise a hullabaloo about the way the Indian reservations, not only in Wisconsin, but elsewhere, were being robbed of timber and other natural assets. It was the beginning of a long struggle against vested interests which was to occupy La Follette's life until his untimely death in 1925.

It was not alone the advent of such courageous fighters as La Follette that the lumbermen had to fear. Almost from the beginning there had been a conflict of interests between the log drivers and the sawmill men, the latter firm in their ambition to manufacture into lumber all the pine cut from the Wisconsin forests, without interference from the former, whose interests were best served by supplying raw material to the mills along the Upper Mississippi and the lakes—an antagonism that forced upward the price of logs. There were many clashes, resembling the old fur-trade rivalries of nearly a century earlier, and this rivalry continued until the rise of Frederick Weyerhauser and his Mississippi River Logging Company, which soon dominated the declining years of the industry in Wisconsin. The lumbermen frequently collided with other interests in the state; naturally, anything which might obstruct their navigation of the already difficult Wisconsin River would certainly arouse their antagonism; so they fought the building of dams and bridges, a conflict that reached its height from 1855 to 1880 in the controversy over the Kilbourn dam.

The lumbermen were their own greatest enemies, however; the greed of the owners coupled with the carelessness of the lumberjacks brought about the rapid end of the industry and despoiled Wisconsin, as previously Michigan and the eastern states had been despoiled, of a source of income which, under regulation, would have meant untold wealth for the state for centuries to come. Public unawareness, of course, as always, played its part. In his excellent book, *Economic History of Wisconsin During the Civil War Decade*, Frederick Merk (grandson of that George Merk who came to Sauk City from Bavaria in 1854 and gave his three daughters to the teaching profession, and his only living son to lithography), comments upon the controversies which took the interest of the people of Wisconsin and left them unaware of greater issues.

"The enormous waste that was going on in logging, sawing, and marketing lumber was likewise regarded as of little moment. Every step in the transformation of the pine tree into the sawed board was marked by improvidence. The log choppers cut the trees high, wasting long stumps, while the sawyers in dividing the fallen pine into logs wasted many feet of clear timber at the tops. Young growth was given scant consideration, while windfalls that were not in prime condition were left to rot. It has been estimated that as a result of careless logging and fires not more than forty per cent of the magnificent forest that once clothed northern Wisconsin ever reached the sawmill." And the conditions under which, "The loggers removed only the choicest pine, while on the floor of the forest they left great heaps of branches and tops, known in the vernacular of the trade as 'slashings' . . . soon dry as tinder," invited the forest fires that came, such as the million-dollar fire of 1863, the northern pineries fire above Wausau in 1864 (one of the greatest), a similar conflagration four years later over an equally wide area along the upper Wisconsin and its tributaries, and the greatest forest fire in the history of the continent—the great Peshtigo fire of 1871, which burned not only priceless timber lands but villages and farms, taking more than a thousand lives—all events which were scarcely even noted in the press. Of course, Peshtigo had to compete with the Chicago fire; that it was the greater of the two did not seem to mean anything to the press, for it was only "a wilderness fire."

This shameful waste with its costly aftermath, combined with the "trespassing" of timber lands—that is, the robbing of lands—to arouse opposition to the lumber kings. ("Loggers purchased what was known as a 'big forty,' fortified by the possession of which they proceeded to strip half an adjacent township. The most common practise . . . was to purchase from the state its choice pine-lands, paying therefore, in accordance with the loose requirements of the day, only a small installment of the purchase price; then quickly to strip the lands of all their valuable pine, and when they were denuded allow them to revert to the State. In 1865 the Wisconsin Commissioners of School and University Lands reported to Governor Lewis concerning trespassing as follows: 'Quietly but actively trespassers have been stripping off this timber, sometimes merely for their own use, sometimes making small sales, and sometimes carrying on the shameful business so extensively as to cover the rivers with stolen logs, and to grow rich upon their illgotten plunder. Others, equally guilty, purchase the stolen property, and thus support and encourage the iniquity. Important corporations and prominent men in some parts of the State have been for years engaged in the traffic. Public sentiment thus becomes demoralized, and efforts for the detection and punishment of the criminals are thwarted, and even resented as unwarrantable interference with private rights. To a considerable class, including many besides those actually interested, this robbery of the children's inheritance has come by long use to seem excusable and even right.' " —Merk.) As early as 1867 the state legislature, inspired by the scholarly Increase A. Lapham, brought about an inquiry into the effects of forest destruction on the stream flow and climate of Wisconsin, resulting in passage of a totally ineffective law to encourage tree planting. The voices of other idealists and farsighted men were raised in protest from time to time, but as is all too often the case, the people, who could not sense any tangible ill effects of the highhanded rape of the forests, pursued a blind policy of complacency, so that by the time La Follette rose to battle against the lumber, railroad, and utility interests, the industrial barons, including many of the despoilers of the forests, had entrenched themselves within the ranks of the Republican party to the extent of controlling every aspect of policy.

But the end of lumbering as a major industry in the valley of the Wisconsin was in sight. As the land was stripped and the railroads moved north, settlers came to occupy the valley; with the decline of wheat raising and the rise of dairying, the flour mills along the rivers shut down and their places were taken by paper and pulp mills, particularly along the Fox River valley, though many mills flourished in the upper Wisconsin valley. When statistics of the federal government reported in 1905 that the state of Washington had produced four billion feet of lumber, more than twice as much as Wisconsin, it was clear to the lumbermen that the hell-roaring era in Wisconsin was over, and the westward migration began. By 1920 the lumbering industry had fallen to seventh place among the industries of Wisconsin, and ten years later to fourteenth. Lumbering along the Wisconsin today is like a pale revenant of a long-past time.

3. Hop Interlude

During these decades the valley of the lower Wisconsin was by no means idle. They were the scene of most of the innovations in the agriculture of Wisconsin during the Civil War, the place where first the wool and dairy industries took root, where the crop experiments were carried on. Already a certain deterioration in the quality of the soil had become noticeable, and it was vitally necessary that new crops be tried and that agriculture undergo changes from the one-crop system; so the movement away from wheat began.

But there was one brief phase of industry in the lower Wisconsin's valley which cannot be passed over. Heart of the industry was in Sauk County, and in the years immediately following the Civil War the industry boomed in Sauk County to a degree none ever has boomed since. A louse was the cause of it all. In New York, and throughout the East generally, wherever hops were grown, the hop louse invaded the fields and year after year decimated the crops, causing prices to rise. Hops had already been grown in Wisconsin at that time, but now, because of this catastrophic louse, prices of the best Wisconsin grades moved from a low of fifteen cents per pound in 1861 to sixty-five in 1865 and to seventy two years later.

The result, manifestly, was that hop growers in Sauk County and elsewhere increased manyfold, and hop growing became almost overnight the major industry along the lower Wisconsin. Profits began to range from $800 to $1,200 per acre, and by 1867, according to an estimate made by the Milwaukee *Sentinel,* three-fourths of the two million dollars paid to the hop growers of Sauk County in that year represented clear profit. The Wisconsin Agricultural Society's *Transactions* made public the results of a survey conducted in the following year: "Gathering renewed force with every new acre planted in the county of Sauk, where it may be said to have originated, and where the crop of 1865 was over half a million of pounds, it spread from neighborhood to neighborhood, and from county to county, until by 1867 it had hopped the whole State over; so completely revolutionizing the agriculture of some sections that one in passing through them found some difficulty in convincing himself that he was not really in old Kent, of England."

Against less than seven million pounds in 1867, Wisconsin produced eleven million pounds of hops in the following year. In 1867, Sauk County had 2,548 acres under hop cultivation and produced one-fifth of all the hops raised in the nation; not content with this, the enterprising hop growers of that county more than doubled their acreage, and by that time Kilbourn, then still in Sauk County, was called by the *Wisconsin Mirror* "the greatest primary hop depot in the United States—perhaps in the world."

Frederick Merk, quoting the *Wisconsin State Register*, leaves a picture of the hop pickers that lives still in the memory of many Sauk County residents. "Harvest time in the hop district was a season of unusual and picturesque animation. Far and near from the surrounding country girls and women of every class and condition, in response to the call for pickers, streamed into the hop gardens. 'The railroad companies are utterly unable to furnish cars for the accommodation of the countless throngs who daily find their way to the depots . . . to take the cars for the hop fields. Every passenger car is pressed into service, and freight and platform cars are fixed up as well as possible for the transportation of the pickers. Every train has the appearance of an excursion train, on some great gala day, loaded down as they are with the myriads of bright-faced, young girls. . . .' The girls, in addition to receiving their board, were ordinarily paid at the rate of 50 cents per ten-pound box, a rate which permitted industrious workers to earn readily from $1.75 to $2.25 a day. . . . The picking season was a time of feasting and merrymaking. Each night when darkness put an end to labor, the well-used fiddle was fetched from its case, and to its merry strains, under the mellow autumn moon the unwearied tripped the jovial steps of the hop dance."

Coincident with the expansion of the hop industry, breweries sprang up along the Wisconsin and flourished particularly in German communities like Sauk City, where a taste for lager did not need to be developed. In all the towns of Sauk County a kind of boom-headiness possessed the citizens, the immediacy of great profit seemingly making it impossible to foresee an end. A resident of Sauk City typified the lack of foresight then so common, an enterprising young fellow named Nebel; he constructed a handsome limestone building to be used for milling and/or brewing purposes on the bank of the Wisconsin two blocks south of Sauk City's bridge, and he constructed it without previously getting permission to throw a small dam across the Wisconsin at that point. After his building was ready, he made application for that permission, and, the powers being then in the midst of spirited trouble with the rivermen, the loggers and lumber runners and the owners behind them, summarily refused to permit him to construct the dam necessary to run his mill. So there was Nebel with a fine building, little capital, and nothing to do. They called it Nebel's Folly for years.

At least Nebel still had his building. It seems never to have occurred to the hop growers that the inventive Yankees—whose Wisconsin cousins were even then busy trying to invent machines to pick hops (nine such machines had been invented by Yankees in the hop region of the state in 1868)—might find some way of ridding their fields of the devastating louse. The flow of money dizzied them, and the sight of "farmers' daughters . . .

in silks and satins," purchasing pianos and visiting foreign courts, while the farmers' sons "changed overalls
for broadcloth and sported blooded horses and fancy
phaetons," was too much for even the far-sighted. On
a wide scale, they sank profits and credit in hops and
more hops on steadily increasing acreage. The time was
ripe for the crash: 1868, and plenty of the long green
on all sides, Sauk County and Wisconsin booming, and
the hop pickers beginning to be a major part of the
Wisconsin scene.

What with all the to-do in Wisconsin about hops,
it was inevitable that the louse would hear about it; in
1868, coincident with a bad growing season, the louse
moved out of the East, where the Yankees were in any
case making things hot for him, and settled in Wisconsin. At once the average yield was cut by almost
fifty per cent, the quality fell to inferior levels, the
eastern fields produced a bumper crop and glutted the
market, with the result that the bottom fell out of it.
A short span—less than a decade, of a heady, joyous,
colorful time in the valley of the lower Wisconsin.

By 1870, the boom over, hop growing returned
to its former, relatively insignificant level.

4. LUMBERJACKS AND RIVER RATS

The heyday of lumbering on the Wisconsin did
not pass without leaving its impress on the river valley.
The lumberjacks and river rats were a colorful lot. The
first men who came were Canucks—descendants of the
voyageurs and engagés—but right at their heels were
the New Englanders, Maine Staters for the most part.
Norwegians, Swedes, some Germans, Scotch, and Irish
came later.

They were rough, rugged men, lusty in living, filled with gusto, addicted to Booze, Bawds, and Battle. They fought each other individually and in outfits, they fought the mill owners, they fought the dam builders, they fought the law, and they even fought their bosses when in 1881 they carried on the "Great Sawdust War," a strike for a ten-hour day which began in the Eau Claire Lumber Company and spread to all the other mills, the men crying, "Ten hours or no sawdust!" and winning their ten-hour day demand. For brawling, the raftsmen were indistinguishable from the lumberjacks; they brawled all the way down the Wisconsin—from Wausau to Kilbourn, from Portage to Sauk City, from Lone Rock to Prairie du Chien. On at least one memorable occasion they were set upon by the indignant citizenry of Sauk City and actually outbattled, and their chagrin was so great at this that they sought to sue the village for damages, whereupon both raftsmen and legal representatives were run out of town. But this took place in the late seventies, when the days of rafting were almost over, and perhaps the boys were getting a little tired.

Spending their time as they did—all winter in the woods, working from daylight to darkness every day, subsisting almost entirely on pork, beans, hot biscuits, molasses, tea, coffee, dried apples, prunes, and plenty of seasoning, without much variety save for occasional gingerbread, beef, and codfish—in big and little outfits, it was natural that by the time of the spring drive in April the men were restless and eager to get into the towns which had sprung up along the Wisconsin and its tributaries. Booze, Bawds, and Battle were often a psychologically necessary release from the rigorous confinements of camp life. There, in the towns, the rivermen and lumberjacks, in their heavy shoes, their blue-woolen trousers, their red-woolen shirts and caps were picturesque and ominous to the peace-loving citizen. But they were welcome; they came to spend their money, and they spent it lavishly. An old ledger salvaged from one of the stores which catered to the lumberjacks was typical in its revelation of what one Sargent (a Maine Stater, perhaps?) bought before going into the woods with his outfit: "4 pr. socks, 1 pr. suspenders, 1 pr. boots, 1 Bair skin cap, 1 Buffalo robe, 2¼ yds. flannel, 1 skein of thread, 1 deck playing cards, 2 hickory shirts, 245 drams whiskey." This was in 1846, but the pattern held through to 1900—the saloons, the bordellos, and the gambling houses getting most of the money.

A few of the towns sought to control liquor and direct the spending of money by the lumberjacks. In Rhinelander—named in honor of the New Yorker, then president of the Milwaukee, Lake Shore and Western Railway—prohibition was enforced; despite being in the heart of the pineries, it was a dry town. But, Gene Shepard wrote years later: "A man who was badly in need of strong liquor, or, more correctly, who wanted it badly, could get it at the Faust Hardware Store if he exercised due discretion. He would sneak off by himself to the store, open the door under the stairs and step inside when Mrs. Faust was not looking, and draw a glass of something in the liquid form that tasted like corn juice, make a deposit of ten cents on the head of the barrel, or make his own change from what he found by the dim light of a lantern hanging on a nail, listen very quietly for customers in the store, and then step out quick and leave the premises like an honest man." Prohibition in Rhinelander, however, was not so much a matter of reform as a peculiarity of the deeds of property; under an agreement with the railroad when the town was first platted, all deeds sold contained five years' restriction prohibiting the sale of liquor on property included in the deed. But the traffic in liquor soon grew, and with it went the only experiment in Prohibition along the upper Wisconsin. In some places the harlots were run out of town, but they managed to filter back again as long as there was a demand for their services.

But it is not to be understood that, because of their frequenting of saloons, gambling houses, and bordellos, the lumberjacks and raftsmen were uncouth and uncivilized; their gusto was symptomatic only of a way of life. Both lumberjacks and raftsmen have their apologists, who protest the portraits of them without seeming to realize that there is little reason to protest; a lust for life repels only the Puritan of the old school. When the lumberjacks and raftsmen interfered with the normal life of a community, their activities were curbed quickly enough; they seldom did. They were not nearly so fraught with danger to the communities along the river as were the moneyed bandits who despoiled the forests with their aid. Dick Menefee, writing of *The Old-Time Lumberjack*, paints this portrait: "His morals were of the highest; no good woman need ever fear trusting her safety with him. He might be intoxicated; might be a veritable-looking ruffian; but he always remembered he had a mother whom he believed in. He would fight and drink and curse—and do it over and over again—but he was always ready for a long-houred day's work in the woods. . . . Being a lumberjack in those days . . . was no weak-man job. He must be a 'he-man'; must be an adept at road-making in the woods; must know all there was to know in the handling of a team, if a teamster; must know the scientific use of a saw or an axe; must know good from bad timber from a measured glance at the standing tree; must know how to load one of the huge logging sleighs and how to properly pile up the logs in a huge pile upon the bank of some stream wherein the winter's cut was later on to be transported down by water to market. He must know just how much of a flood-head in the river was needed to move the timber in the least possible time; he must know the art of 'riding' a log while it was being floated without being 'spilled' in the icy waters of early spring-time driving. . . . For all his faults, the early day lumberjack was morally and mentally a gentleman."

While they were in winter camp, however, they found methods of entertaining themselves. Stag dances, jigs, games like Shuffle the Brogue and Hot Back; they read old newspapers and magazines like the *Police Gazette*. If the men gathered for an entertainment, each one in the outfit was required to do his part; he must sing a song, tell a tale, whistle, or dance; failing to do so, he was required to donate a pound of tobacco to the "poor-box." Their games were sheer horseplay, and were almost as much fun as initiating the greenhorn in the outfit by playing the sheep game with him—one in which the greenhorn played the part of a sheep and was trussed up and let down repeatedly on a sharply pointed stick which was the scales on which was to be settled the argument in regard to the sheep's weight which was carried on interminably between two other jacks, one playing the part of a farmer, the other of a sheep buyer—or by sending him after various fantastic things, like the bean hole, the cross-all, or sending him out to hunt the dangerous sidehill gouger.

They told hilarious tales, tall and otherwise. From camp to camp went the story of Mike Murphy, who walked into a saloon at Oconto one spring, according to B. A. Claflin, who hands the tale down, and said he was leaving for South America. No more camp life for him; it was beyond his power to stand living in the Wisconsin woods any longer. "The Finlanders 've got around to talkin' English, and the Irish are chewin' snuff!" Claflin also relates the story of the floater from the Twin Cities, then at the height of their early rivalry; he had come, he said, because he found it difficult to stomach the mayor of Minneapolis, who had gone into all the public buildings and removed all the Bibles. "The dang things keep a-tellin' every little while about what St. Paul done—he done this and he done that—and never once a mention of Minneapolis!" Such anecdotes made the rounds of the camps, but they are secondary in the impress of the lumbering men on the history of the Wisconsin River valley. Pre-eminent were two factors: ballads and songs, and legends.

If, as Stewart Holbrook says, Booze, Bawds, and Battle made up the lumberjacks' trinity of entertainment, Balladry must have come to be the fourth B, particularly in upper Wisconsin and Michigan. Some of the songs they sang came from the eastern states and Canada; but, as Holbrook maintains in *Holy Old Mackinaw*, "More blown-in-the-bottle logger ballads seem to stem from Michigan and Wisconsin than elsewhere." The lumberjacks and raftsmen brought song to the river again, song to ring along the same valley where almost a century before the French songs of the voyageurs had echoed.

Such songs as the well-known and widely sung "The Jam on Gerry's Rock" and "Canaday I O" were older in origin than lumbering in the Great Lakes region, though sung lustily along the Wisconsin and Upper Mississippi and their tributaries none the less. But some —indeed, most—of the songs that were popular with the raftsmen had their origin in the Midwest. "Jack Haggerty's Flat River Girl" is typical, stemming from

the Six Lakes Michigan region. But "The Little Brown
Bulls" has a Wisconsin origin, beyond doubt, attributed
to Pat Murphy of Chippewa Falls:

Not a thing on the river McCluskey did fear
When he drew the stick o'er the big spotted steers.
They were young, quick and sound, girting eight foot and three.
Says McCluskey the Scotchman, "They're the laddies for me."
Derry down, down, down derry down.

Bull Gordon, the Yankee, on skidding was full,
As he cried, "Whoa-hush" to the little brown bulls.
Short-legged and soggy, girt six foot and nine.
Says McCluskey the Scotchman, "Too light for our pine."

It's three to the thousand our contract did call.
Our hauling was good and the timber was tall.
McCluskey he swore he'd make the day full
And skid two to one of the little brown bulls.

"Oh, no," says Bull Gordon, "that you cannot do,
Though it's well do we know you've the pets of the crew.
And mark you, my boy, you would have your hands full
If you skid one more log than the little brown bulls."

The day was appointed and soon it drew nigh,
For twenty-five dollars their fortunes to try.
Both eager and anxious that morning were found,
And scalers and judges appeared on the ground.

With a whoop and a yell came McCluskey in view,
With the big spotted steers, the pets of the crew,
Both chewing their cuds—"O boys, keep your jaws full,
For you easily can beat them, the little brown bulls."

Then out came Bull Gordon with a pipe in his jaw,
The little brown bulls with their cuds in their mouths;

And little we think, when we seen them come down,
That a hundred and forty could they jerk around.

Then up spoke McCluskey: "Come stripped to the skin.
We'll dig them a hole and tumble them in.
We'll learn the d—d Yankee to face the bold Scot.
We'll mix them a dose and feed it red hot."

Said Gordon to Stebbin, with blood in his eye,
"Today we must conquer McCluskey or die."
Then up spoke bold Kennebec, "Boy, never fear,
For you ne'er shall be beat by the big spotted steers."

The sun had gone down when the foreman did say,
"Turn out, boys, turn out; you've enough for the day.
We have scaled them and counted, each man to his team,
And it's well do we know now which one kicks the beam."

After supper was over McCluskey appeared
With the belt ready made for the big spotted steers.
To form it he'd torn up his best mackinaw.
He was bound he'd conduct it according to law.

Then up spoke the scaler, "Hold on, you, a while.
The big spotted steers are behind just one mile.
For you have a hundred and ten and no more,
And Gordon has beat you by ten and a score."

The shanty did ring, and McCluskey did swear,
He tore out by handfuls his long yellow hair.
Says he to Bull Gordon, "My colors I'll pull.
So here, take the belt for the little brown bulls."

Here's health to Bull Gordon and Kennebec John;
The biggest day's work on the river they done.
So fill up your glasses and fill them up full;
We'll drink to the health of the little brown bulls.
Derry down, down, down derry down.

Popular in various versions from coast to coast was a tragic ballad usually entitled "Come, All You Jolly Shanty Boys"; the Wisconsin River valley version of this one was called "The Shanty Boy on the Big Eau Claire," and credit for this ballad must go to one of the most interesting figures along the river in lumbering days—Billy Allen of Wausau, who wrote under the pseudonym of Shan T. Boy and who, before his death, came to be hailed as "The poet laureate of the golden age of Wisconsin lumbering." His version of this old ballad is this:

> Come, all ye jolly shanty boys, and listen to my song;
> 'Tis one I've just invented and it won't detain you long;
> 'Tis of a pretty maiden, a damsel young and fair,
> Who dearly lovèd a shanty boy upon the Big Eau Claire.

> The shanty boy was handsome, a husky lad was he;
> In summer time he labored in the mills at Mosinee,
> But when cold winter came along and blew its blasting breeze,
> He worked upon the Big Eau Claire, a chopping down pine trees.

> "He loved a milliner's daughter, he loved her long and well,
> But circumstances happened and this is what befell:
> The milliner swore the shanty boy her daughter ne'er should wed,
> But Sallie did not care a lot for all her mother said.

> So when brown autumn came along and ripened all the crops,
> She lighted out for Baraboo and went to picking hops;
> But in this occupation she found but little joy,
> For thoughts came rushing to her mind about her shanty boy.

> She took the scarlet fever, lay sick a week or two
> Within a dreary pest-house, way down in Baraboo,
> And ofttimes in her ravings she tore her auburn hair,
> As she talked about the shanty boy upon the Big Eau Claire.

When this news reached the shanty boy his vocation he did leave;
His terrible anxiety was awful to perceive.
He hid his saw in a hollow log and carried off his ax,
And hired out to pilot on a fleet of lumber-jacks.

'Twas at the Falls of Mosinee from a precipice fell he,
And put an end to his career and all his misery.
The bold Wisconsin River is rolling o'er his brow,
His friends and his companions are weeping for him now.

The milliner now is bankrupt, her shop has gone to rack;
She talks of moving some fine day down to Fond du Lac.
At night her pillow's haunted by her daughter's auburn hair
And the ghost of that young shanty boy upon the Big Eau
        Claire.

Come, all ye maids with tender hearts, and be advised by me,
Don't be too fast to fall in love with everyone you see;
The shanty boys are rowdies, as everybody knows;
They dwell far in the forest, where the mighty pine tree grows.

In stealing logs and shingle bolts and telling jokes and lies,
And playing cards and swearing, they get their exercise;
But if you will get married for comfort and for joy,
I'd have you for your husband choose an honest shanty boy.

Billy Allen very probably originated more lumber-jack ballads than anyone else in Wisconsin lumbering; he seldom wrote them down, but usually sang them as the words occurred to him; putting them down came later. At eighty-three, he told an interviewer, "I began composing my poems about 1870. Of course, I had written lots of poetry when I was a kid, but it wasn't much good. I went to the woods when I was seventeen, and as a cruiser in the Wisconsin valley, I visited a great many logging camps in the course of each winter. In each camp I sang for the boys in lumberjack style."

Among Billy Allen's shanty boy songs are "The Banks of the Little Eau Pleine," "Driving Saw Logs on the Plover," "The Hemlock That Stood by the Brook," "The Ballad of a Blowhard" and "Ye Noble Big Pine Tree." Allen's best-liked song was perhaps "The Banks of the Little Eau Pleine":

One evening last June as I rambled
    The green woods and valleys among,
The mosquitoes' notes were melodious,
    And so was the whip-poor-will's song.
The frogs in the marshes were croaking,
    The tree-toads were whistling for rain,
And partridges round me were drumming,
    On the banks of the Little Eau Pleine.

The sun in the west was declining
    And tinging the tree-tops with red.
My wandering feet bore me onward,
    Not caring whither they led.
I happened to see a young schoolma'am.
    She mourned in a sorrowful strain,
She mourned for a jolly young raftsman
    On the banks of the Little Eau Pleine.

Saying, "Alas, my dear Johnny has left me.
    I'm afraid I shall see him no more.
He's down on the lower Wisconsin,
    He's pulling a fifty-foot oar,
He went off on a fleet with Ross Gamble
    And has left me in sorrow and pain;
And 'tis over two months since he started
    From the banks of the Little Eau Pleine."

I stepped up beside this young schoolma'am,
    And thus unto her I did say,

"Why is it you're mourning so sadly
    When all nature is smiling and gay?"
She said, "It is for a young raftsman
    For whom I so sadly complain.
He has left me alone here to wander
    On the banks of the Little Eau Pleine."

"Will you please tell me what kind of clothing
    Your jolly young raftsman did wear?
For I also belong to the river,
    And perhaps I have seen him somewhere.
If to me you will plainly describe him,
    And tell me your young raftsman's name,
Perhaps I can tell you the reason
    He's not back to the Little Eau Pleine."

"His pants were made out of two mealsacks
    With a patch a foot square on each knee.
His shirt and his jacket were dyed with
    The bark of a butternut tree.
He wore a large open-faced ticker
    With almost a yard of steel chain
When he went away with Ross Gamble
    From the banks of the Little Eau Pleine.

"He wore a red sash round his middle,
    With an end hanging down at each side.
His shoes, number ten, were of cowhide,
    With heels about four inches wide.
His name it was Honest John Murphy,
    And on it there ne'er was a stain,
And he was as jolly a raftsman
    As was e'er on the Little Eau Pleine.

"He was stout and broad-shouldered and manly.
    His height was about six feet one.
His hair was inclined to be sandy,
    And his whiskers as red as the sun.

His age was somewhere about thirty,
   He neither was foolish nor vain.
He loved the bold Wisconsin river
   Was the reason he left the Eau Pleine."

"If John Murphy's the name of your raftsman,
   I used to know him very well.
But sad is the tale I must tell you:
   Your Johnny was drowned in the Dells.
They buried him 'neath a scrub Norway,
   You will never behold him again.
No stone marks the spot where your raftsman
   Sleeps far from the Little Eau Pleine."

When the schoolma'am heard this information,
   She fainted and fell as if dead.
I scooped up a hatful of water
   And poured it on top of her head.
She opened her eyes and looked wildly,
   As if she was clearly insane,
And I was afraid she would perish
   On the banks of the Little Eau Pleine.

"My curse attend you, Wisconsin!
   May your rapids and falls cease to roar.
May every tow-head and sandbar
   Be as dry as a log schoolhouse floor.
May the willows upon all your islands
   Lie down like a field of ripe grain,
For taking my jolly young raftsman
   Away from the Little Eau Pleine.

"My curses light on you, Ross Gamble,
   For taking my Johnny away.
I hope that the ague will seize you
   And shake you down into the clay.
May your lumber go down to the bottom
   And never rise to the surface again.

You had no business taking John Murphy
Away from the Little Eau Pleine.

"Now I will desert my vocation,
  I won't teach district school any more.
I will go to some place where I'll never
  Hear the squeak of a 50-foot oar.
I will go to some far, foreign country,
  To England, to France or to Spain;
But I'll never forget Johnny Murphy
  Nor the banks of the Little Eau Pleine."

There were, of course, scores of lesser known songs, or songs which had their origin elsewhere and were simply transplanted. Some have come down as they were sung; some have been lost in part; and occasionally stray verses crop up. There is, for instance, this tantalizing stanza from a song the rivermen often sang when they paused on an island near Kilbourn at the Dell House—the first frame house built on the river above Portage:

Hairlip Sal from Rowley Creek,
  She wore a number nine;
She kicked the hat off a big galoot
  To the tune of "Auld Lang Syne."

And finally, there was that staple, "The Shanty-Man's Alphabet" or "Logger's Alphabet," supposedly authored by one Bill Cross, who spent most of his time with the upstate Indians.

I

A is for axes we very well know, and
B is the boys who can use them just so.
C is the chopping we did and begin, and
D is the danger we sometimes were in.

Chorus

So merry, so merry are we,
No mortal on earth are as happy as we,
Hi derry, ho derry, hi derry down,
The shanty boys will and there's nothing goes **wrong.**

II

E is the echo that through the woods rang, and
F is the foreman that headed our gang,
G was the grindstone, our axes had ground, and
H is the handle so smooth and so round.

III

I was the iron we stamped our logs with, and
J was the jolly, jovial crew,
K was the keen edges our axes did keep, and
L was the lice that kept us from sleep.

IV

M was the moss that we stuffed up our camps,
N was the needle we mended our pants,
O was the owls that hooted at night, and
P was the pine that always fell right.

V

Q was the quarreling we did not allow, and
R was the river our logs down did flow,
S was the sled so stout and so strong, and
T was the team that could haul them along.

VI

U was the use we put our streams to, and
V was the valley we cut our roads through.
W is the woods that we leave in the spring, and
Y have sung all that I am going to sing.

The lumber camps in northern Wisconsin in their last stages of greatness could boast, too, of a blind singer, who went from place to place—still a young man in the late nineties, minus his left arm: Emery De Noyer, "The Bard of the Lumber Camps," who in his time ranged from Michigan to Minnesota, and sang the lumberjack ballads in a full-throated baritone, and with all the words, in contrast to the snatches sung by the jacks themselves. He was a Michigan man by birth, and logged in the Saginaw country until 1892, after which he came to Wisconsin, where the heaviest logging in the country was being done along the upper Wisconsin River.

The best of the lumberjack songs have been gathered together by Franz Rickaby and published in *Ballads and Songs of the Shanty Boy*. There are still others turning up from time to time, but the old-timers are passing swiftly now, and many versions of the songs are destined to pass with them.

5. TALL TALES

"The Paul Bunyan legend had its origin in the Papineau Rebellion of 1837," asserts James Stevens positively in his *Paul Bunyan*. So Bunyan came down into the Maine woods from Canada, and into the Great Lakes lumber camps from Maine. He came complete with Babe, the Blue Ox, Johnny Inkslinger, and most of the animals of his legendary world: the axhandle hound, the flittericks, the gumberoo, the tote-road shagamaw, the goofus bird, and many another. But, though he came into the lumber camps of Wisconsin and moved on to the west coast, he went west with a few additional tall tales to his credit, such as the formation of the lakes in the now-famed vacation land of northern Wisconsin in Paul's footprints, and the embellishments of the Round River drive story.

The lumberjack's Paul Bunyan had his raftsman's counterpart in Whiskey Jack, who was of Wisconsin birth, a mythical character of the Wisconsin River in the decades before the coming of the railroads. "The Whiskey Jack yarns had their origin," writes Charles E. Brown, director of the Wisconsin Historical Museum, in his *Whiskey Jack Yarns,* "in the adventures of particularly strong and daring pilots and raftsmen."

"Whiskey Jack . . . was over seven feet tall and a Samson in power. In a brawl he was never bested by any man on the river or on its banks. He licked all of the other fighting raft pilots, all of the town bullies, and all of the wild Indians along both the Wisconsin and Mississippi rivers. . . . In seasons of low water, if his raft ran aground on a sandbar, Whiskey Jack thought nothing at all of picking up the raft, crib by crib, and carrying it into the deeper water beyond." Clearly, as Brown puts it, "Whiskey Jack was the raftsman's Paul Bunyan."

Whiskey Jack's exploits were not as numerous as Paul's. Not all were feats of strength. Whiskey Jack was cunning as well. When on one occasion Jack's raft was tied up at Richland City and the crew were thirsty, and yet were without money with which to buy drinks, it was a clever ruse that brought them all drinks at the cost of a bundle of laths. One of the raftsmen took along a bundle of laths and bartered it for drinks; the tavernkeeper was willing; when the raftsman left, he dropped the bundle outside. The next raftsman to come in carried the same bundle in, and so it went until all had been served at the price of one bundle of laths.

Perhaps the best of Whiskey Jack's adventures illustrates that he was not made of the same stuff as Paul

Bunyan. This is the story of Whiskey Jack and the blue racer, which Jack encountered when he went on foot back to the sawmills at Stevens Point. He met up with a monstrous blue racer when he was in a state of fortification by virtue of "snake juice" drunk at various taverns. Jack maintained that for a liquored man to meet a blue racer was bound to be fatal, for the snake was poisonous to a man with whisky inside him. Jack lit out along the river's banks, and the blue racer took after him. At the Sauk Prairie Jack swam the river; so did the blue racer. At Merrimac, Jack swam the Wisconsin again; so did the blue racer. At the Dells Jack crossed the river once more, and the snake followed him. All the way up to Stevens Point Jack tried to shake off the persistent blue racer; he even took to leaping from bank to bank—he hadn't wanted to do this at first because he was such a modest fellow; but the snake leaped, too. Finally, at the Point, his lumberjacks saved his life; they came running with cant hooks and pike poles and beat the blue racer to death. It measured twenty-seven feet.

But the real Wisconsin River lumberjack tales are those of E. S. (Gene) Shepard. Gene Shepard was a Wisconsin man, and a riverman; he was born at Fort Howard at the mouth of the Fox, and he spent most of his life on or near the rivers, dying at last at the Pines, his beautiful home at the confluence of the Pelican and Wisconsin rivers. He was a lettered man, a born naturalist and raconteur. It was Shepard who took up the Paul Bunyan legends to augment and embellish them. And it was Shepard who brought the hodag to life.

Late in the last decade of the last century, Gene Shepard came out of the north woods and announced that he had discovered a prehistoric monster, and, after great effort and incalculable danger, had ensnared it.

It would soon be put on exhibition, he promised, and, true to his promise, so it was. It was indeed fearsome to look upon: a bovine creature, with six large spines on the ridge of its back, two blinking eyes, and a wide, toothy mouth, which, with its large eyes, the ridged back and long, thick, saurian tail gave it a ferocious appearance. Shepard exhibited it that year at county fairs at Wausau and Antigo, keeping it in a dimly lit tent, where each time it moved it emitted unearthly groans, its eyes leered, its nostrils blew forth flames. Shepard's pleasant conceit spread from one end of the country to another, and on the heels of the publicity won by the hodag came eastern writers and scientists, including a representative of the Smithsonian Institution, to examine Gene Shepard's monster, about which he had been having a lot of fun, lecturing with great gravity on the habits of the beast, habits which were peculiar, to put it mildly. "It will eat nothing but white bulldogs, and then only on Sundays.... It never lies down, but just leans up against the trunks of trees, and at such times, it can only be captured by cutting deeply into the trunks of its favorite trees."

The coming of a scientific expedition finally forced Shepard to admit that the hodag was nothing more than a hoax; its body had been expertly shaped by a wood carver; he had fashioned the spines along its back from bull's horns, and the hodag's eyebrows from bear's claws, while the claws on its paws were nothing more than steel spikes. The hoax had been carefully covered with oxhides to serve as the hodag's skin, and Shepard had brought Rhinelander and the valley of the Wisconsin into the news in such a way as to bring to the area thousands of curious tourists, even going so far as to circulate picture postcards of the hodag in black and white and in color, and, moreover, of a party of friends assembled, armed with axes and pitchforks, to hunt hodags!

The hodag came to an untimely end in a fire at Ballard Lake a few years later. It was not the only one of Gene Shepard's hoaxes and practical jokes; but it was certainly the most famous. Before Shepard had finished with his hoax, he had circulated a thrilling story of its capture—how he had blocked the entrance to its cave with rocks, and then chloroformed it by means of a sponge attached to a long pole, how he had then tied it securely and brought it to Rhinelander. Subsequently, Shepard claimed to have captured a female hodag with "thirteen eggs": all of these, he maintained, hatched out, and he was on the verge of training the hodag's young for exhibition of the creatures when he was forced to reveal the hodag as a hoax. In his book, *The Hodag*, Luke Kearney enters into the spirit of Shepard's hoax and tells a slightly different version of the capture of the prehistoric beast: "How to capture the hodag was a real man-sized job, and none realized it more fully than the heroic Mr. Shepard. He ordered a crew of men to dig a large pit, several miles from the point where he had first sighted the animal. This huge excavation, which was fifty feet in diameter and thirty feet deep, was covered with poles thrown across the opening. The trap was successfully hidden by limbs and grass, laid carefully across the poles. ... Because the hodag relished beef on the hoof more than any other food, the ox was to serve mankind in a new way for scientific futurity. The hero led the ox through the dense forest until he came in sight of the monster. Then came a growl so deep, loud and sepulchral, that it fairly shook the earth, causing a vibration so great that it started a great shower of leaves and limbs from the giant trees. The ox became frantic, but his brave leader steered him along the blazed trail with greater force than before. On they went, toward the pit, while traveling towards them was the hodag, bent upon capturing his prey! Though the beast's powerful legs were short, he covered the ground with unbelievable swiftness, tearing out trees and the heavy growth of underbrush and leaving in his wake, great gashes in the earth itself. At intervals, one could hear an indescribable growl and with each breath, the beast emitted an odor that baffled description! Finally, only one hundred yards separated the great animal from his prey, then forty, and then twenty yards. At the crucial moment, one could hear the rasping teeth of the pursuing beast coming together as he opened and closed his ugly jaws. . . . The leader directed the ox in such a manner that he avoided the pit, but the impetus of the great hodag carried him forward over the mass of branches and grass, which covered the trap. In he crashed, emitting a roar that could be heard for miles, as he struggled to extricate himself. Friendly hands led the hero away, and the ox, with tongue hanging from his mouth, was rewarded with a good bed and plenty to eat that night."

When, later, Shepard was the proprietor of a summer resort, he appeared one day with a scented moss, which could be taken up only before dawn, since the sun's rays wafted away the delicate perfume. His lady guests were up early next day, and went out to fill their boxes with the plants; they had shipped them all over the country before they discovered that Shepard had been the sole person responsible for the aromatic moss; he had simply gone out in the night and sprinkled a little ordinary perfume on the first mossy bank to which he came. Moreover, he put his hoaxes to good practical use, as in the case of his string- and spring-controlled rubber muskellunge, which he caused to break water at his resort whenever the guests began to grow restless about the poor fishing. A demonstration by the giant muskie was usually a guarantee of renewed reservations. He was a frothing horror before any agent, particularly book agents. Literally. He began by listening attentively to any agent; then suddenly, by means of a pellet designed to produce foam out of mixing with saliva, he would begin to froth at the mouth and, moaning horribly, he would fall to the ground; he never failed to be amused by the terror of the agent.

In his *Badger Saints and Sinners*, Fred Holmes recounts one of Shepard's most dramatic exploits: "Shepard once gave Governor John J. Blaine a nerveracking hour. When the executive visited Rhinelander in 1920, an uncouth, slouched individual passed through the train searching for the Governor, boldly voicing that he intended to assassinate him. But the Governor was not to be found. After an interval, Shepard appeared to inquire if any one had seen his 'insane brother,' who had that day escaped from an asylum.

"Hours passed and the incident was almost forgotten. Just before Blaine's speech of the evening, the same 'insane man' reappeared in the audience and demanded that he be given an opportunity to speak with the Governor. Secretary of State Merlin Hull and others protested, fearing an act of violence. But Blaine, learning of the demand, courageously consented.

" 'The railroad commissions have fooled about the dam on my property long enough,' shouted the distraught individual. I've got you now and something must be done.'

" 'If you will come to my hotel in the morning I will go with you to the dam site and find out how to proceed,' the Governor remonstrated in an attempt to soothe the disturber.

"That promise quieted the irate visitor. Satisfied, he left the meeting.

"Sufficient time was to elapse for 'Gene' Shepard to shed his disguise. Returning to the gathering he approached the Governor. This time he was smiling.

" 'Well, John,' he remarked jovially, shaking hands, 'do you now feel the same way about that dam as when I was insane?' "

It was natural that Paul Bunyan would appeal to Shepard's sense of humor and imagination. He added to the Bunyan legend the story of the sidehill gouger, "whose right leg was only one-third as long as his left, so he had to go clear around the mountain to get home." He added to his book about the hodag the tale of the *Round River Drive,* not his own, but from the pen of Douglas E. Malloch, who published it in the *American Lumberman.*

> Paul Bunion and his fightin' crew,
> In '64 or '5 or '2
> They started out to find the pines
> Without much thought of section lines,
> So west by north, they made their way
> One hundred miles, until one day
> They found good timber logging land,
> With roarin' water close at hand.
>
> .   .   .   .   .   .
>
> Now near the camp, there was a spring
> That used to steam like everything.
> One day, the tote team brought supplies
> Had on a load of mammoth size,
> A load of beans. Just on the road
> Beside the spring, he ditched his load,
> And all those beans, the bloomin' mess,
> Fell in the spring,—ten tons, I guess.

He came to camp, expecting he
Would get from Bunyan the G. B.
But Joe the cook, a French Canuck,
Said, "Paul, I teenk it is ze luck—
Zem spreng is hot, so Paul pardon,
And we will have ze grand bouillon!"

To prove the teamster not at fault,
Joe took some pepper, pork and salt,
A right proportion each of these
And threw them in among the beans—
And got enough and good soup too,
To last the whole long winter through.
The rest of us were kind of glad
He spilt the beans, when soup we had—
Except the flunkeys; they were mad
Because each day, they had to tramp
Three miles and tote the soup to camp.

. . . . . . o

This stove of Joe's, it was a rig
For cookin' grub. It was so big
It took a solid cord of wood
To git a fire goin' good.
The flunkeys cleaned three forties bare
Each week, to keep a fire in there.
That stove's dimensions, south to north,
From east to west and so forth,
I don't remember just exact,
And do not like to state a fact,
Unless I know that fact is true
For I would hate deceivin' you.
But I remember once, that Joe,
Put in a mammoth batch of dough
And then he thought, (at least he tried)
To take it out the other side.

But when he went to walk around
The stove, (it was so far) he found
That long before the bend he turned
The bread not only baked, but burned.
We had two young coons for flunkeys, Sam
And Tom. Joe used to strap a ham
On each foot of both of them,
When we had pancakes each A. M.
They'd skate around the stove lids for
An hour or so and maybe more,
And grease 'em for him. But one day,
Old Pink-Eye Martin, (anyway
He could not see so very good)
Old Pink-eye, he misunderstood
Which was the bakin' powder can.
And in the dough, eight fingers ran
Of powder,—blastin' powder, black—
Those niggers never did come back—
They touched a cake, a flash, and poof!
Went Sam and Tommie through the roof.
We hunted for a month or so
But never found 'em—that you know,
Was the winter of the black snow.

We put one hundred million feet
On skids that winter. Hard to beat,
You say it was? It was some crew.
We took it off one forty, too.
A hundred million feet, we skid—
That forty was a pyramid;
It ran up sky-ward to a peak—
To see the top would take a week.
The top of it, it seems to me,
Was as far as twenty men could see.
But down below, the stuff we slides
For there was trees on all four sides.

o   .   .   .   .   .   o

At last, a hundred million in,
'Twas time for drivin' to begin.
We broke out rollways in a rush
And started through the rain and slush
To drive the hundred million down
Until we reached some sawmill town.
We didn't know the river's name,
Nor where to someone's mill it came,
But figured that, without a doubt,
To some good town, 'twould fetch us out,
If we observed the usual plan
And drove the way the current ran.
Well, after we had driven for
At least two weeks and maybe more,
We came upon a pyramid
That looked just like our old forty did.
Some two weeks more and then we passed
A camp that looked just like the last.
Two weeks again and then another, too,
That looked like our camp, came into view.

Then Bunyan called us all ashore
And held a council—as of war.
He said with all this lumbering
Our logs would never fetch a thing.
The next day after, Silver Jim,
He had his wits scared out of him;
For while he's breakin' of a jam
He comes upon remains of Sam.
The coon who'd made the great ascent
And through the cook house ceilin' went
When Pink-eye grabbed the fatal tin
And put the blastin' powder in.

And then we realized at last
That every camp that we had passed
Was ours. Yes, it was then we found
That the river we was on was round.

And though we'd driven for many a mile
We'd drove in a circle all the while!
And that's the truth as I'm alive,
About the great Round River drive.

Today the hodag has joined the hoopsnake and the hidebehind in Paul Bunyan's private menagerie, and the lumberjacks, old men now, have added a couple of spines of their own to its prehistoric backbone. It remains Wisconsin's most famous hoax, but it was by no means the only hoax to arouse interest in the river valley and its environs. The *Rusk County Journal* of Ladysmith, west of the Wisconsin River, was the source of some prime hoaxes, attributed to a mythical newspaper, the *Rusk County Lyre,* ostensibly to increase circulation. Of them, only one concerned the valley, but that one was a feat of the imagination. It was nothing less than an assertion that two woodsmen had discovered in a hollow tree the body of Pierre D'Artagnan, a "lost" member of the Marquette-Jolliet voyage of discovery; the body had been petrified by the tree's sap, and not only was the body there, but also a slip of paper conveniently containing an account of the expedition. M. D. Hinshaw, the editor, and Edward Richardson, the publisher of that now defunct paper, were either permitting someone to waste his talents on the staff, or were themselves wasting talent. The story, which appeared early in 1926, was picked up first by the Prairie du Chien *Courier,* whose colorful, old-school editor, Henry Howe, knew a good circulation builder when he saw one; then by the Muscoda *Progressive,* probably for a similar reason, and then by newspapers throughout the state. A page-one story. Within thirty days the hoax had a national circulation, and shortly thereafter it attracted the attention of curious scholars—all of

which is an object lesson in the gullibility of Homo
sapiens. A few moments of cogent thought somewhere
along the line might have blown up the story, which is
told in toto in Curtis MacDougall's *Hoaxes*, together
with an abbreviated history of the hodag. As it was,
however, it required a specially prepared release by the
Historical Society of Wisconsin to explode the hoax.
Dr. Joseph Schafer, then the society's superintendent,
wrote dryly that the sap of a tree with its mineral matter could not take the place of the cell content of the
human body. In any case, clothing and the convenient
slip of paper could not have withstood the ravages of
time. It was a good story while it lasted, but it lacked
the staying power of Shepard's hodag.

6. THE OLD MEN REMEMBER

In 1937 the Interstate Commerce Commission at
Madison began to take testimony in regard to the
navigability of the Wisconsin River in the Tomahawk
Dam Case, and the old men of the river came in, to
remember the lusty days of their early years. They told
in their own words of their experiences; they gave from
memory instructions in regard to building a raft ("You
use three grub planks in the bottom, which answer the
purpose of runways. Takes three grub planks two by
ten inches, sixteen feet long, with holes bored in each
end, ten inches from the end, and one board immediately in the middle of the plank. Get three of those
planks, and lay them at equal distances, about seven
feet, six inches apart. On that you put the tie board,
one by six, with holes bored similar to the ones in the
grub plank"—Gustave Giese) ; about running the rapids
("Took one rapids piece at a time, took it five or six

miles, and then went back after a second piece. One time on a fourth piece the bowman dropped an oar and struck a rock and broke the blade off. We were up against it; so planks were grabbed, what they could get, to hold it. There were four men on an oar, and each man grabbed a plank, put it up against the grub, next to the house there, which they wanted to go, and tried to get it downstream, but they struck the rock with the corner square, and our raft turned around, pretty near across, and broke the raft in two; and half went through and half stayed on the rock. All but one man were taken off in a skiff—he was left on the rock, a line was thrown from the next piece; he fastened the line to the raft, and, when the next piece came along, threw the line out and snapped it, gave it a jerk, and fetched the piece off . . . "—Ralph Saveski) ; about the eddies and the still water ("The Crooked Drive rapids above Biron were bad, shallow and very bad. . . . Then below there was the eddy and below that was a still piece of water, between there and Big Island, and rafts laid up after going through Biron dam and rapids to repair the pieces. The rapids below Biron were bad enough, too. Why, there was a fall of about a hundred feet in Wood County. And then Grand Rapids! The river was tortuous, the rocks rugged, impossible to navigate or even go over with a raft without artificial help, so they built little wing dams . . . "—Theodore Brazeau) ; the place names ("They called Lone Rock the Devil's Elbow because of the turn just to the north. All the way down they had their landmarks—Sugar Loaf rock across from the Sauk Prairie, the Bogus Bluff down near Muscoda, and so on . . ."—George Hager) ; the little incidents that remained in memory ("Most beautiful thing I ever saw, it was. Near that place where the voyageurs put their names on the rocks at the Dells. Notch Rock. We were coming through there at about fifteen miles an hour, when I looked up and saw a deer balance on the edge of the rock and then jump twenty feet into the river; he came up, snorted, and swam across to the other side. There were three dogs after him, but they had to stop on the rock; they wouldn't jump. I can still see that deer there against the clouds and the trees, the way he came down, he didn't seem the least afraid ... "—George Hager). Pages of testimony are there—the memories of a half century of life along the Wisconsin River valley in the heyday of lumbering.

PART FIVE

The River Tamed

Our navigable streams and rivers, like our streets and highways, are open to the free use of the people of the state. No one can acquire ownership in these waters. If the public, through legislation, grants franchises, surrendering the use of any of its navigable waters to individuals or corporations, it is entitled to a reasonable consideration therefor. This it may not choose to take as a money consideration, but the state cannot do less than recognize the rights of the public, in making reasonable reservations at the time it confers the grants. The franchises so taken in many cases, grant rights of great and rapidly increasing value. The vast amount of power which these waters produce is a resource of a public nature, in the advantage and benefit of which the public should participate.

Modern industrial development is making rapid progress. Already these water powers are extensively employed to generate electricity. The transmission of this power over considerable distances is successfully accomplished with little loss. It will, in the near future, be more widely distributed at a constantly diminishing cost. In manufacturing, in electric lighting in cities and towns and in the country, in operating street and interurban cars for the transportation of passengers and freight, and in furnishing motive power for the factory and the farm, electricity will eventually become of great importance in the industrial life of our commonwealth.

It is, therefore, quite apparent that these water powers are no longer to be regarded simply as of local importance. They are of industrial and commercial interest to every community in the state. While this is becoming more manifest year by year, it is probably true that we do not, as yet, approximately estimate the ultimate value of these water powers to the people of Wisconsin.

It must, therefore, be apparent that this subject, broadly considered, is of profound interest to the people of this commonwealth. If the policy of the state with respect to these franchises ought to be changed at all, it certainly ought to be changed now. Reserving the right to amend or repeal is not enough. When rich and powerful companies, availing themselves of these grants, acting in concert, seek to resist amendment or repeal, their influence will prove a very serious obstacle. Economic conditions are rapidly changing in this state and in the country. A legislative policy which grants franchises without substantial conditions amply protecting the public, and securing to it reasonable benefits in return, is neither right nor just, and ought no longer to be tolerated. The capital already invested, industries already established, may in a few years, find themselves quite at the mercy of power companies in combined control of the water power of the state.

Such investigations as I have been able to make of the subject plainly indicate that many of the grants to construct dams heretofore passed by the legislature, have been secured purely for speculative purposes. In such cases no improvements whatever have been made. The grants have been held awaiting opportunities to sell the same with large profit to the holders, who have not invested a dollar for the benefit of the state, or its industrial development. It is obvious that those franchises may be gathered up, and consolidated with others which have been granted where improvements have been made, and prices advanced until the state, municipalities, and the public will be compelled to pay an exorbitant rate for the power upon which we are likely to grow more and more dependent as time passes.

It is submitted to your honorable body that the time has come to give this subject the careful consideration which its great importance demands. I believe that the state should encourage the development of its natural resources, including its water power system, in so far as it may properly do so; but the obligation rests upon those charged with the responsibility and clothed with authority, to encourage this development under such conditions as will justly and fairly protect the public right in these great natural advantages.

—Governor Robert M. La Follette,
Message to the Legislature, April 12, 1905

1. Power

THE first dam on the Wisconsin River was put up as early as 1840 at Wausau for milling purposes. It was George Stevens, who gave his name to Stevens Point, who bought the first water-power site on the Wisconsin in what is now Wausau, and he bought his site at a public sale fully a dozen years before the area was surveyed by the federal government. It was only natural that some of the early lumbermen would come to the conclusion that the rapids and falls of the upper Wisconsin could be utilized for power, and the Big Bull Falls impressed Stevens as ideal; the river at that point descended gradually past the highest point in Wisconsin, Rib Hill—the closest approach to anything resembling a mountain in the valley of the Wisconsin, the water was swift, the site ideal for a dam. So George Stevens built it.

His was only the first of many dams along the Wisconsin. All the early dams were required to make allowance for the lumbering industry, and some of them accordingly did not reach all the way across the river, leaving space for rafts; those that did, included a slide for the rafts. Naturally, the raftsmen bitterly opposed the dams, though they were not as difficult to run as the rapids. "We ran down the centre of the river, until within twenty rods of the dam," Ceylon Childs Lincoln wrote years after in *Wisconsin River Rafting*. "There the current drew off to the right and came in between two piers, about thirty feet apart; between these piers was the slide, constructed of long logs (called fingers) fastened with chains to the dam; on either side of the slide, the water dropped about fifteen feet. (When a dam extended across the river, it was necessary to leave a gap at one point in its crest, from which an incline or *slide* was built down stream. It was often a dangerous operation to conduct a raft safely over such a slide, for at the bottom it would duck under water, and the men be washed off. To prevent this, an apron was sometimes constructed at the foot of the slide, comprised of logs fastened to its lower edge, whose other ends floated free.) Below the dam, the river boiled and rolled into whitecaps. If one was fortunate enough to make the slide properly, he could make his landing in the right place; otherwise, there was great danger of *saddlebagging* (running the raft squarely against a rock or any other obstruction, so that a considerable portion lay off on either side) one of the piers and breaking to pieces. ..."

Some of the dams, however, caused trouble without end. Lincoln, in listing "the dangerous places" for raftsmen on the Wisconsin, put down "Big and Little Bull Falls, Stevens Point dam, Conant Rapids (with Shaurette Rapids, are from two to three miles long), Grand Rapids, Clinton's big and little dams, Whitney Rapids, the Dells, and Kilbourn dam." No dam along the river, however, gave the raftsmen the trouble that Kilbourn dam did. The Kilbourn dam was constructed at a narrow place not far from the site of the present power dam at Wisconsin Dells; it stood just at the end of the long and arduous Dells run, and its position was such that running it was to the raftsmen an unwarranted climax to their already great difficulties. The issue was

soon joined, and remained joined for almost two decades—a kind of undeclared war between the raftsmen
and the dam owners, culminating in the final destruction of the dam by three hundred irate raftsmen. Wisconsin Dells legend has it that one of Kilbourn's citizens, Joe Bailey, defied the raftsmen successfully on
more than one occasion, but, though it might have been
like him to have done so—he was an old lumberjack
himself, and later distinguished himself in the Civil War
when, as Lieutenant Colonel Joseph Bailey of the Fourth
Wisconsin, he used his lumberjack knowledge to construct a dam and create a lift to save the Union fleet
when low water stranded it in the Louisiana Red River
campaign—history offers no corroboration of the Dells
legend.

Early water rights were comparatively simple. A
mill might be given just sufficient water rights to operate "a run of burrs or stones," or a "miner's inch" and a
"horse power." At Wausau, George Stevens's dam continued in operation until shortly after the turn of the
century, when the dam was reconstructed and a power-
house put up some distance from the old site. Following
Stevens came a score of others; the Jackson Mill dam
was put up at Stevens Point six years after Stevens's
first; Henry Merrell constructed a dam at the Little
Bull Falls (Mosinee) just before mid-century, and the
Port Edwards dam was authorized by the legislature in
1853, "not to exceed six feet in height." By 1870, 33,700
horsepower by means of water wheels were developed in
Wisconsin, most of it along the Wisconsin and its tributaries, and the overwhelming majority of the wheels
and steam engines being used by the lumbering industry
and only a few of them for rag-paper mill use. After
that year, wood-pulp mills and the railroads fingering
north brought about a quickening of dam construction

on the Wisconsin, and, after the turn of the century, with the conversion of the important dams to electricity and the rise of the great public utilities, out of almost two hundred dams the number of great hydroelectric dams on the Wisconsin came to twenty-five, ranging from Rhinelander to the Sauk Prairie.

The change, however, did not come about without difficulty. When the lumbering and grain-milling industries declined and the water power devoted to them began to be used in the generation of hydroelectric power, the electric utility industry soon learned that, unlike the lumbering, paper, and milling industries, it could not adapt its load to the fluctuations of the Wisconsin. As a result of extensive lumbering operations in the upper Wisconsin valley, the river had by this time begun to fluctuate widely in its flow; the slow, steady rise of the river in the spring gave way to rapidly rising floodwaters; the river's blue gave way for this period to the muddy brown of silt-thickened water; the sand bars, which had always shifted, now made radical movements, appearing sometimes almost overnight and, again, in another night vanishing to reappear farther downstream. The effect of rapidly rising and diminishing flow could be disastrous, and, in certain cases of extremely heavy rainfall, it was.

Improvement of the Wisconsin's flow seemed not only advisable, but necessary, and the obvious means of improvement must be a reservoir system. By 1907, therefore, the power owners along the Wisconsin sponsored a law authorizing the Wisconsin Valley Improvement Company "to construct and operate ... a reservoir system ... and to charge each of the power users semi-annual tolls for the use of storage water." There were already storage reservoirs waiting to be used—they were the old log-driving dams. Uncertainty about the weather had long ago taught the logger that it was wise to build a dam to store water and so make possible the spring drive by creating an artificial flood in place of the river's normal spring rise, should that rise fail to take place. Most of these dams were on the tributaries to the Wisconsin, with the longest reservoir on the Big Eau Pleine north of Knowlton. They were speedily investigated.

C. B. Stewart in 1911 reported that the old log-driving dams could very easily be used to reduce spring floods by storing as much floodwater as possible and releasing it in the summer months to maintain a more consistent river level in that period when the Wisconsin's average flow diminished. Thereupon, within a comparatively short time, twenty storage dams were put into use—not without opposition from summer residents who had come in to build along the upper Wisconsin and its tributaries. But the Wisconsin Valley Improvement Company forged ahead, not content with twenty reservoirs, to construct a system of reservoirs capable of storing something more than sixteen billion cubic feet. Moreover, the reservoir law of 1907 was followed by the legislature's delegating its powers in regard to water-power laws to the Railroad Commission, later the Public Service Commission of Wisconsin, the laws of 1911, 1913, and 1915 directing "that this commission set bench marks to record the levels of water maintained, measure stream flow, pass on the safety of hydraulic structures, and authorize the construction of all dams on navigable streams." At the same time the United States Geological Survey began to construct the seven gauging stations now on the Wisconsin, and the larger number on its tributaries, to maintain stream-flow records. And in 1914, the commission itself undertook a comprehensive survey of the water powers in Wisconsin, a survey augmented annually by lesser surveys and investigations, and the annual inspections of the larger dams. By 1930, water power furnished almost fifty per cent of the electricity developed in Wisconsin.

The rise of the utilities was not made without constant struggle, struggle that is still going on and must ultimately resolve itself against the private owners—the demand for public ownership. The struggle was heralded by the rise of a politician who was something more than just a politician.

2. OLD BOB

The late great Senator Robert M. La Follette did not begin the struggle against "corporate wealth," but he was first to make the people of Wisconsin conscious of it. He was tireless in his battle against trusts, monopolies, corporations, wealth, and all the aspects of existence which stood for the power of wealth and industry against the individual and the society. They called him a radical, a Socialist, a Communist, a "Red," with all the fury of the ultraconservative determined to frighten the little man by raising a bugaboo to destroy the little man's faith in the only leaders who can help him and his kind; he was at the least, a mild kind of radical, rather a liberal; and all his reforms—the reforms for which he fought so bitterly and was fought so mercilessly—the federal income and inheritance taxes, the abolition of injunctions in labor disputes, the laws against child labor, the seaman's act, taxation of war profits, the killing of water, oil, and coal grabs, the eight-hour law for government employees, the regulation of telegraph and telephone rates, among others—

all these are today looked upon as conservative by the very forces which fought him.

When he wrote his autobiography in 1913, he pointed out a vital fact of which few people were conscious, a fact that the attack on Pearl Harbor brought home to hundreds of thousands of Americans, when he wrote: "We are slow to realize that democracy is a life; and involves continual struggle. It is only as those of every generation who love democracy resist with all their might the encroachments of its enemies that the ideals of representative government can even be nearly approximated." He had realized this almost from the beginning of his career.

He was born in 1855 in a log cabin not far from the Wisconsin River, on a farm in Dane County. His people had come into Wisconsin through the Ohio valley from the eastern mountain country. Unable to attend high school, the boy nevertheless, by dint of his own efforts, entered the preparatory department of the University of Wisconsin, where he recited his lessons in the evening, since he taught country school near Madison by day, and rode back and forth on his horse. He had no thought of political life; he wanted to be an actor. It was Lawrence Barrett who told him he was too short of stature to be a good tragedian, and La Follette turned to law.

If he was too short to be an effective tragedian, he was no less dynamic; there was about his appearance a vitality and freshness, a restless drive and stubborn determination which never failed to impress those with whom he came in contact. Within a year of his study of law, La Follette entered politics by being elected district attorney of Dane County over the opposition of the Republican boss of the county. Young La Follette was too much for the organization. When they found out he was going to run for the office of district attorney, the boss told him tartly that he was fooling away his time and wasting his money, that he had better find himself a job, for he had not learned the first lesson in politics. "I can tell you who the next district attorney of Dane County will be—and it won't be La Follette!"

But it *was* La Follette; he won by the simple expedient of going beyond the bounds of the organization, taking to a horse and buggy, and going direct to the people. He had two assets which were destined to make him inevitably the best-loved of all public servants of Wisconsin—one was a wonderful quality of sympathy, which included the ability to put himself into the shoes of others, not just superficially, but down under; the other was an almost infallible memory. The story of the La Crosse livery-stable keeper is typical. When first he came to La Crosse, the chairman of the committee sent to meet him was a livery-stable owner. When, years later, nationally famous then, La Follette returned to La Crosse to speak and was met by a new committee, he saw standing on the platform the chairman of that earlier committee. He turned, excused himself, hailed the livery-stable owner as an old friend and with him, he followed the committee. By such simple means, La Follette built up the only "machine" he ever had: not a machine of ward heelers and vote racketeers, but a following of devoted men who would do anything for him.

Four years after that initial victory over an organized political machine, he was in Congress, the youngest member of the forty-ninth session of that body. In 1900 he became the governor of Wisconsin, and in January, six years later, he began to serve Wisconsin as United States senator for a period just short of two decades, in the course of which he ran as a candidate for president of the United States to poll five million votes against Coolidge and Davis in 1924.

He had not entered the political scene in Wisconsin without adequate reason; his was no happenstance choice. As a boy, he had been impressed by the Granger movement, strong enough in Wisconsin to bring about the election of Governor Taylor in 1874. At this time, the railroads and the lumber interests virtually ran rampant, and one of the first acts of the new governor and his legislature was the institution of a law regulating the railroads and establishing the railroad commission. What happened as a result of this action opened the young La Follette's eyes. He tells about it in his *A Personal Narrative of Political Experiences:*

"It was then, indeed, that the railroads began to dominate politics for the first time in this country. They saw that they must either accept control by the state or control the state. They adopted the latter course; they began right there to corrupt Wisconsin—indeed to corrupt all the states of the Middle West.... On April 28, 1874, Alexander Mitchell, President of the Chicago, Milwaukee and St. Paul Railroad Company, wrote a letter to Governor Taylor in which he asserted directly that his company would disregard the state law....

" 'Being fully conscious that the enforcement of this law will ruin the property of the company, and feeling assured of the correctness of the opinions of the eminent counsel who have examined the question, the directors feel compelled to disregard the provisions of the law so far as it fixes a tariff of rates for the company until the courts have finally passed upon the question of its validity.'

"A more brazen defiance of law could scarcely be conceived. The railroads looked to the courts for final protection, but the law which they thus defied was not

only sustained by the Supreme Court of Wisconsin, but
by the Supreme Court of the United States. But the
railroads did not intend to submit to control, courts or
no courts, and by fallacious argument, by threats, by
bribery, by political manipulation, they were able to
force the legislature to repeal the law which the Supreme Court had sustained. By that assault upon free
government in Wisconsin and in other middle western
states the reasonable control of corporations was delayed in this country for many years. . . . From that moment in the seventies—excepting . . . for a period of
two years when . . . William D. Hoard [was] governor
. . . until my fight was finally successful, Wisconsin was
a corrupted state, governed not by the people but by a
group of private and corporate interests."

The ghost of John Jacob Astor rose once more over
the Wisconsin River valley. Astor may have been dead
for decades, but his methods were not. La Follette rose
to fight the "new and dark power," to which Chief
Justice Edward G. Ryan had pointed in an address to
the graduating class of the University of Wisconsin in
1873. He began by fighting the petty party bosses, and
he was joined by incorruptible legislators—a minority—
led by Assemblyman A. R. Hall, a Dunn County farmer.
He did not always win his campaigns; he met with repeated defeats in three gubernatorial campaigns before
he was elected governor of Wisconsin. For a while the
Republican party, controlled by the "private and corporate interests," tolerated him, but the break came in
1891, when La Follette, as congressman, would not
wrongfully serve Senator Sawyer by influencing an impending court decision in a state treasury case which
involved Sawyer. From the party to which he had for a
time been affiliated, La Follette learned the value of an
organization; with energetic system, he organized his

own support, and by 1900 the people so jeeringly called "half-breeds" or "feeble-minded" because they stood behind him, held the balance of power in Wisconsin.

In 1897, at Fern Dell near Wisconsin Dells, La Follette "opened the fight against corporate power" in Wisconsin. Two decades later, he spoke from the floor of the United States Senate to say: "I would condemn and take way from them such of their holdings as would be called raw material—or natural resources. I would have the Government take back the title to its iron ore and coal and copper and timber and the other natural products. Then I would maintain such an absolute control of the production and the prices of those basic products, either by a strict leasing system or by actual Government operation, or both, that every manufacturer, small as well as large, should have an equal opportunity to get the raw material at the same price. I would do that for the purpose of restoring competitive conditions at the very foundation of all manufactured productions.

"I would apply the same method to all others who own the great primary products that may be called, in a general way, the resources of nature. I would have the Government hold the title to and maintain the absolute control of all these primary products. I would try, perhaps, operating them under a strong leasing system, under which the Government should control prices.

"But I would introduce a limited amount of Government operation in various lines of production, to the end that we might have a measure, a standard of fair production cost and fair selling price. I would try that as an initial proceeding for the ultimate achievement of industrial freedom.

"That may be temporizing, but I would try that to give the old theory of individual initiative its fair chance, and if that experiment failed, then I would go after Government operation of all those basic essentials, absolutely; and in the meantime I would not hesitate at all about Government control and ownership of all transportation and all lines of communication—everything of that character.

"I expect to stand here and make a fight alone for Government ownership and control of the railroads. I am for Government ownership of railroads and every other public utility—every one—and I propose to show on this floor that where it has ever been given a fair chance in any part of the world that it has been successful. I am going to show that the 'cards were stacked' on Government operation here in this country during the war period by those who were interested and that it was not possible for Government operation to make a fair showing."

He fought the railroad interests, the lumber barons, the utilities. Burning before him he saw always the prophetic words of Chief Justice Ryan: "Money, as a political influence, is essentially corrupt; is one of the most dangerous to free institutions; by far the most dangerous to the free and just administration of the law. An aristocracy of money is essentially the coarsest and rudest, the most ignoble and demoralizing, of all aristocracies. Here it comes, a competitor for social ascendancy. It is entitled to fear, if not to respect. The question will arise, and arise in your day, though perhaps not fully in mine, which shall rule—wealth or man; which shall lead—money or intellect; who shall fill public stations—educated and patriotic freemen or the feudal serfs of corporate capital." His thesis he put first always: "The will of the people shall be the law of the land."

He won victories, many of them, victories which

time made secure. But he was not to escape without wounds. The interests of "corporate wealth" fought him at every turn, and when, in 1917, La Follette was one of "that little group of willful men" who opposed entrance of the United States into the First World War, he was the object of vitriol and hatred—but neither was strong enough to bring about his defeat at the hands of the people whom he had served, though the condemnation was so great that he recognized it in a letter to Justice Kerwin of the Wisconsin Supreme Court when he asked, "But is it the people who are making this raid? Is it not that element directly or indirectly connected with interests which for twenty-five years have denounced me for reasons which we pretty well understood at the time?"

He could not expect that his victories could be won without cost. He could not filibuster for six days, for instance, and expect to show no strain; he could not carry on a strenuous campaign for the presidency, meeting the most vicious kind of opposition, without showing the marks. His campaign had hardly been lost when in June, 1925, he died, his heart failing him.

But his struggle did not die with him. Years before, he was in the habit of referring to his gubernatorial terms by saying, "When we were governor." It was not the editorial "we"; his reference was first and foremost to his able, devoted wife, Belle Case La Follette, who had come out of the Sauk Prairie country; and later it was to the La Follette family, that extraordinary family which dominated the political life of Wisconsin for more than half a century. Belle Case La Follette followed him six years later; behind them, Old Bob and Belle left to fight for public ownership of the utilities against the corporate interests, two sons: Young Bob, who took his place in the Senate to become exemplary of the highest type of public servant, in his unshakable incorruptibility, his sincerity, his intelligent study of national problems; and Phil, the dynamic, impulsive younger son, who more even than Young Bob had inherited his father's eloquence, and served three terms as governor. Old Bob's "we" has become a reality in the years since his untimely death.

The fight goes on, and the signs point to only one possible conclusion, and that is in victory for Old Bob's beliefs: the men in Washington today, the men who lead throughout the democratic world are no longer only the men and the servants of wealth. It would have been a strange feeling for Old Bob to find himself voting with the majority of his colleagues for the Tennessee Valley Authority and so instituting a law to put into effect nationally one of his oldest dreams.

3. BADGER ORDNANCE

It was the availability of hydroelectric power that determined in large part the role of the lower Wisconsin River valley in the Second World War. One day in late October of 1941, the Swiss, German and Yankee farmers who settled the upper Sauk Prairie and the country around Merrimac a century before were startled to hear from their radios the voice of an announcer saying that a great new industry was coming to the Sauk Prairie, specifically to the upper prairie and Merrimac, the picturesque little ferry village on the prairie's far northeastern rim. That evening there was excitement on the streets of Merrimac, Baraboo, and the twin villages to the south, in the agricultural communities from Portage to the mouth of the Wisconsin, and on the streets newsboys flashed headlines from the Madison papers: "$65,000,000 Powder Plant To Be Built Near Merrimac!" There were those who looked upon the story as a hoax, but it was soon patent that it was, as A. O. Barton put it, "one of those realities which become more deadly with each passing moment."

It was not at first evident that war had come to the Wisconsin River valley; the wider implications were not apparent—the meaning of industrialization of a region which had been agricultural for a century to be accomplished in the shortest possible time. Only a few of the readers of those evening papers on that first night understood what it meant. "I don't like it at all," said the harness maker at Sauk City. "That's going to do things to all of us here—things we aren't going to like." And the way he looked around at the old walls of his ancient harness shop told more than any words he might yet have spoken. Other businessmen, visioning quick profits in increased business, were not chary about hailing the new industry, shrugging away the threat of a social upheaval, of bombings. But the farmers waited with bated breath, uncertain, apprehensive.

The estimated cost of the proposed plant rose sharply—from sixty-five million to a hundred, from a hundred million to a hundred and thirty—and it was described in the press as "the greatest powder plant in the world." It was to be in operation by the first of January, 1943—a manifest absurdity, replied the towns along the Wisconsin south of Portage. Then abruptly the site of the proposed plant, being built for the Hercules Powder Company by the War Department, was moved southward, squarely upon the fertile soil of the upper Sauk Prairie, away from the sandier soil of the Merrimac area. Announcement of that change was made at a regional meeting called in Baraboo one night in November.

Reaction was immediate. There was no longer any question about how the farmers felt. They organized hastily under the leadership of rugged Garth Premo, chairman of Sumpter Township, and a stream of protests began to flow to Washington. To the War Department wrote one irate military man to point out that the Badger Ordnance Plant, lying along the Wisconsin just above the dam at Prairie du Sac, with Devil's Lake behind it, and the Four Lakes of Madison not far away to the southeast, would make an ideal target for enemy bombers. Doubtless Undersecretary of War Patterson was much harassed. To the president went even more letters, as well as to Wisconsin's senators and congressmen, letters from Wisconsin's humble and well-known people alike, all of whom knew and loved the Sauk Prairie country. All demanded to know why it was necessary to use the fertile soil of the upper prairie instead of more sandy soil in Adams County, not far away. "In the course of defense, sacrifices of all kinds must be expected of us, as individuals and as social units. No American worthy of the name expects to escape his duty in defense or conflict. A powder plant . . . on some of the most fertile land in southern Wisconsin does not seem to most of us here on the Sauk Prairie so vitally necessary that it should strip this predominantly agricultural country of a large part of its most arable land." Letter writers deplored "the spoliation of some of the most beautiful country in Wisconsin . . . its beautiful earth, its villages and people, some of whom represent a fourth generation on this land, in this village."

The press in Wisconsin took up the cause. There were pictures of Swain Mather holding his sheepskin deed, signed by President Polk, of the tree-shaded houses of the Kindschis, the Premos, many another; and there were the things the farmers said. "I'll never find a place

again like this home. I was born here."—"What are
you going to do about it? You've got to go, that's all."
—"A fellow has to be cheerful, I guess, but it's a pretty
hard blow. I told my three boys I would buy them a
farm somewhere if I could get one. But it'll be hard to
find a place like this again."—"A little while ago they
called us to a meeting at the schoolhouse and told us
we should produce more on the farms for the defense
program. If they take this good land, we'll have to
move to poorer land where we can't produce as much."
—"We quit plowing when we heard about the ap-
praisers being around here. We haven't spread our lime
and we don't know whether to shred our corn."

But protests notwithstanding, the plan for the
Badger Ordnance Plant moved steadily, inexorably forward. Without exception, the large-circulation papers
in Wisconsin questioned the wisdom of erecting the
powder plant on the fertile Sauk Prairie. Why not the
Adams County barrens? they demanded. The state office
of the AAA dryly added its protest by pointing to the
production record of the land about to be condemned
and appropriated; it ranked among the highest in Wisconsin. Wisconsin educators, writers, university deans
joined in the clamor.

For a brief time there was hope among the opposition. Army Ordnance announced from Washington
that the site had not definitely been picked, which was
interpreted as the opening of a door to save Army face.
At this, the businessmen rose up in alarm, and began to
write and wire protests against the opposition, and very
shortly a Democratic politician announced that Wisconsin would not lose the powder plant, and intimated
that he had brought about this boon. He made a fine
target for the press, particularly Madison's *Capital
Times,* edited by fighting William T. Evjue, a river-

towner from Merrill and an old-time Progressive Republican, now New Deal Democrat, who had added his personal protest to those of the farmers. (It was Evjue who lifted his telephone one day to hear: "Mr. Evjue? This is Franklin D. Roosevelt calling." "Yeah?" jeered Bill. "This is the King of England answering." It *was* the President.)

The attack on Pearl Harbor ended all but one phase of dissension. The farmers ceased to fight for their land, but asked only a fair price. This they did not immediately get. They were given no information about appraisals, and in many cases they were offered prices which were below the prices they had paid for the land, and made no allowance either for improvements made or for the circumstances of the sale. A committee of the Sauk Prairie farmers' organization waited upon a non-military aide in his Baraboo office to protest against the prices offered, and were bluntly told that they had been living too high, that they did not need such things as plumbing and furnaces. "Get a stove, warm your backs, then turn around and warm your bellies!" All this much to the embarrassment of the more tactful military officers on the scene.

The land hearings in the summer of 1942 generally resulted in the offering of increased prices paid for the condemned land and buildings. Farmers came armed with many photographs of their fine homes and their beautiful lands, vexing the government's attorneys, who had no evidence with which to counter claims. Piqued by Swain Mather's telling photographs, resulting in a substantially increased payment to Mather, a government attorney brought out the fact that Mather owned another farm some distance away from the homestead; in the hope of making a point to score against Mather, the attorney inquired what he did with it.

"I pasture my dry cattle there," replied Mather.

"And how far is it from your home place?"

Mather told him.

"And do you mean to tell this court that you went up there and back every day just to milk those cows?"

Adjustments began to be made, with and without benefit of counsel, and presently, into the valley of the Wisconsin, to the paw of land once occupied by the Sauk, the land to which Count Haraszthy had come with his dream of vast-spreading vineyards in 1841, came army engineers and the first workmen. The Northwestern Railroad extended a spur from Merrimac south; the Chicago, Milwaukee, St. Paul & Pacific pushed up from Sauk City—just after the amusing and now dated argument about retaining a station at Prairie du Sac—through Prairie du Sac along its old rail bed, and beyond, fingering across the upper prairie into the fertile land reaching to the base of the Baraboo bluffs. Houses, barns, sheds came down, were sold, moved elsewhere; the trek of farmers began, away from the Sauk Prairie, away from century-old homesteads, away from the Wisconsin River valley which had nurtured them and theirs for more than ten decades. And even as they moved away, to the Sauk Prairie came men and women from Kentucky, Louisiana, and Virginia, from Oregon and North Dakota, from New York and Pennsylvania and Maryland, and in the villages the lean, hard western talk mingled with the slow, disarmingly lazy drawl of people from the south, coming to work in this midwestern land and bringing to it a different culture, a different way of life—people who were not the riff-raff and poor whites the valley had at first feared might come, but fine, sturdy Americans, white and black, many of them bringing their families and doubling the population of the area within a few months in the spring of 1942, and quickly making their mark upon the countryside in the insidious manner in which their idioms were in part assimilated into the speech patterns of the people of the valley. So the towns along the Wisconsin—Portage, Prairie du Sac, Sauk City, Mazomanie—as well as those inland in the Sauk Prairie area, prepared to become boom towns, in anticipation of the influx of workmen to a number five times their population.

But beyond their anticipation rises a grim fear: that the end of the war may bring to an end the activities of the powder plant—the duPont interests being largely on the Atlantic seaboard, and the Sauk Prairie far from their center of distribution—and the boom towns along the Wisconsin of the 1940's may become the ghost towns of the 1950's.

4. An End to Waste

It was *Time,* first among national newsmagazines, which early in 1942 focused the attention of America on the Marathon Paper Mills of Rothschild on the upper Wisconsin. Among the reforms sought consistently and tirelessly by the late Senator La Follette and others was legislation to halt the pollution of Wisconsin waters. In this, the paper mills were the worst offenders, pouring hundreds of thousands of tons of waste into the streams of Wisconsin, fouling the water, destroying all life. The reformers were fought for decades; the vested interests as a matter of principle invariably stand to fight anything which may temporarily cut down their percentage of profit—just as today the billboard inter-

ests in Wisconsin and elsewhere fight all efforts to remove these blots on the beautiful landscape. But at last
public awareness was aroused, legislation was passed, and
a time limit was set for the mills, time in which to find
some substitute for dumping waste into the Wisconsin
and other rivers in the state. The expiration of that time
limit is near.

Marathon Paper Mills faced the issue squarely by
calling upon Chemical Engineer Guy C. Howard in
1927 and putting before him the problem of finding a
profitable use for waste lignin, tons upon tons of which
had been dumped into the Wisconsin. The results of
fifteen years of research were announced early this year
when *Time* paid tribute to the company and its engineer: "Highly enterprising is Marathon Paper Mills of
Rothschild, Wis., makers of food containers and chemicals. ... Today, after 15 years of research costing some
$2,000,000, Marathon adds lime to its waste liquors,
precipitates out calcium lignin sulfonate ..."

This in turn, through the scientific experiments of
Guy Howard, could be turned into a variety of products. Vanillin, for instance: this is the flavor constituent
of vanilla, and already this discovery had been put to
practical use, for in 1941 approximately fifty per cent
of American vanillin was synthesized from American
lignin, and used by great manufacturers—General
Foods, Hershey, National Biscuit—as well as the Army
and the Navy. The precipitate likewise produced tan-
ning chemicals to take the place of tanbarks, which have
become increasingly difficult to procure as a result of the
war, which has cut into imports, and the gradual extinc-
tion of the native chestnut, which was a major source
of tanbarks. True, within the past few years an injec-
tion treatment has been discovered to halt the chestnut
blight, so that perhaps this magnificent tree will once

again spread its beautiful limbs over the American landscape as in Audubon's time; but it is doubtful that it
will ever again be used to supply tanbark, since the tan-
ning chemicals derived from the lignin precipitate is
more efficient, and hence, less expensive. From the precipitate, too, come cement-dispersing and water-soften-
ing agents, and plastics in molding powders and lamin-
ated sheets, which are used in a wide variety of objects,
ranging from tabletops to aeroplane doors. These plastic sheets are lighter than aluminum, almost by half,
one-fifth as heavy as steel, and yet equally as strong
as steel. Indeed, the plastic created from the paper mill's
waste is vital in this time of war, for it can be used
almost in toto for military purposes, as parts for everything from insulators to tanks and ships.

Nor did this aspect of Guy Howard's precipitate
escape the attention of the military of the nation at war.
Said *Time:* "Lignin plastics are the cheapest plastics yet
devised; at 5¢ per pound for the powder they cost only
one-third to one-fourth the cost of most synthetic
resins. But today they have a still greater advantage—
they require as little as two or three per cent phenol
(carbolic acid), a chief component of the commonest
plastics and now a badly needed, priorities-listed ingre-
dient. Furthermore, lignin molding powders can be
mixed to 'extend' phenol plastics by 100%, synthetic
rubber for many uses by 100 to 500%. This aspect of
lignin was . . . under intensive study by the U. S.
Army and Navy."

As early as 1905, Jacob Robeson, a pioneer industrial student of lignin, developed a process of removing
lignin from pulp waste by evaporation. The Robeson
process and the precipitation method of the Marathon
Paper Mills indicate a future which will perhaps witness
the end not only of pollution but of waste, a future that

goes beyond even the greatest hopes of Old Bob La Follette—that agitator and rebel, that radical whose passionate fire threatened the foundations of capital. The aging liberals who were young with La Follette could read the saga of Marathon Paper Mills and smile bleakly.

PART SIX

Vacationland

THE rustic gave me the impression that he was well traveled—at least within the boundaries of Wisconsin; so I inquired of him whether he had ever visited the Dells. He cocked an eye at me and grinned.

"I was there," he said flatly. "I seen 'em—but I tell you I had a mighty hard time finding my way. Went up this summer for the first time. You'd think a place like that would be the easiest place in the world to find. Well, sir, it ain't; not by a damn sight! I hardly got past Baraboo on the road than I come to a big sign tellin' me I was comin' to the Dells. Well, I got ready. Then there come another big sign, sayin' about the same thing. By and by, another. Then there was a rash of little signs advertisin' cabins, hotels, bars, trips, and such like that I got myself all wore out just gettin' ready to see the Dells. First thing I knew I come to an Indian house. It stuck out like a sore thumb. Nothing like it ever in Wisconsin when the Indians hung around here; bet my bottom dollar on it! It was a southwest Indian's home; one of them Arizona Indians would be right at home in it. But no Winnebago or Sauk or Chippewa ever laid eyes on a house like that in Wisconsin before the whites stole the land from 'em. Well, I got around that all right—just gagged a little, you might say—got over the bridge and into the town. Wisconsin Dells, they call it now; used to be Kilbourn. I liked that better; a man knew what he was talkin' about when he said Kilbourn; now he's got to explain whether it's the town or the scenery he means. But you have to admit the people sure turn out to treat you right. I took the boat trips, the upper dells and the lower, and in the evening I took in the Indian show at Stand Rock. Didn't know which was the best—the show or the audience. Had a lot of smart city fellers in the audience; every little while they hollered 'How!' at the Indians, as if they had their girls to the Zoo. The Indians did a fine job when they sang the real Indian songs and did the Indian dances, but when they got around to puttin' on pretty spotlights and standin' up on rocks singin' stuff like the Indian Love Call and Pale Moon, the air got thick, even despite the fact I knew it was a sop to the city fellers who thought those tunes were the real Indian songs. Yes, sir, I seen the Dells. I might even go again. But if I do, I'll go by boat; they ain't got around to puttin' up all those signs along the river yet; might be nobody thought of it."

—*Through Wisconsin on a Bicycle*

1. The Dells of the Wisconsin

THE DELLS can be regarded as an industry without comparable competition. Even the Land-O-Lakes country across northern Wisconsin, including the basin of the upper Wisconsin, does not compare with it. No more picturesque region exists along the long, meandering course of the river, and tourists have been made to realize this, for, with the decline of lumbering and milling, and the stabilizing of dairying, the upper and middle Wisconsin found in the tourist trade a new source of income. Typical of the Wisconsin River towns now existing largely on the tourist trade is Wisconsin Dells; it differs from more northern towns only in that it is still agricultural in background, so that, while many of its places of business simply do not function during the winter months, it can exist as an agricultural community during those months.

Because of the difficulty of running the gorges and narrows at the Dells both before and after the dam was constructed, few of the early travelers had time to observe much of the beautiful rock formation, the heavily wooded islands, the ravines, glens, and gulches, the canyons and bluffs, and, by the time the commercial possibilities of the Dells became manifest, virtually all the river front on both sides of the Upper and Lower Dells was in the control of two families: the Crandalls and Uphams—and it is doubtless due to this fact that the hideous advertisements along the roadsides approaching Wisconsin Dells do not have counterparts and accompanying hot-dog stands, curio shops, and similar establishments perched cunningly among the rocks of the gorges and canyons along the shore. These are limited almost exclusively to the town itself, and such buildings as there are along the Wisconsin: private homes and resort hotels—are not garish, not displeasing to the eye, not inharmonious on the whole with the setting.

The Winnebago had a name for the Dells of the Wisconsin; they called it Neehahkecoonaherah—the place where the rocks strike together. And the Chippewa had a legend about it: a tale that the serpent whose contortions and writhings had formed the bed of the Wisconsin had encountered a great body of rock at this place, and thrusting his head into a crack, burst the rock asunder, and pushed his way tortuously through, thus shaping the gorges and rocky canyons of the seven mile lap which the early French explorers called the *Dalles,* or the narrow, rocky part of the river. Above and below this length the river's banks are chiefly of low, sloping sand; the sandstone rocks of the Dells are thus unique along the Wisconsin.

It is estimated that it took something like thirty thousand years for the Wisconsin to cut its way through the sandstone of the Potsdam or Eau Claire formation and form the Dells, not always working in the same areas, however, since it is manifest that the Wisconsin changed its channel three times; the two abandoned channels are clearly visible today. Because the process of hardening the sand into sandstone when the area of the Dells was lifted was not uniform, and because the layers of sand were slanted into position (cross-bedding, according to the geologists), the rock formations at the Dells excite the curiosity of visitors to an unusual degree, and it does not require much imagination to recognize the figures and objects to which guides draw the attention of tourists—on the Upper Dells the jaws, the alligator, chimney rock, Black Hawk's head, the frog's head, the navy yard (or steamboat rocks), devil's jug, the palisades, the toadstool, hornet's nest, devil's bathtub, visor ledge, elephant's back, stand rock, and the devil's anvil; on the Lower Dells the bear's cave, pulpit rock, the hawk's bill, the sugar bowl, inkstand, and others. There is even a Paul Bunyan legend connected with the Dells, to the effect that Paul lay down to rest there, and his head made the sugar bowl, while his heels hollowed out two lesser spots named Paul Bunyan's Heels. It is the hydroelectric dam that divides the Upper and Lower Dells; there is still prevalent among some of the older residents a tendency to date time from the construction of the dam, as in the South, "Before the War!" so that it is not uncommon to be shown the beauty of the rock formations, the caves and canyons and gulches, and be told in conclusion, "But you should have seen them before the dam went in!"

The Wisconsin is not unique in having dells, but they are clearly unique on the Wisconsin; of all the tourist trade along the river valley, a great majority visits at the Dells. Nor are the rocky shores of the river the only attraction Wisconsin Dells has to offer tourists; there are many others—Black Hawk Island, for instance, now a part of the University of Wisconsin's Agriculture Department's forest preserve, once the site of the Dell House, and once supporting the first bridge across the Wisconsin, put up in 1850, washed out seventeen years later; Camp Wawbeek, one-time estate of Horace Upham, close to five hundred acres crowned by a castle-like home on a hill, now controlled by the Wisconsin Association for the Disabled; the rock upon which Jean

Guyot, one of the earliest voyàgeurs, wrote his name in large letters, visible from afar up or down the river; the spot half a mile from the river where Schuyler Gates, builder of that first bridge across the river, was murdered one night in the autumn of 1869, as a result of which a well-known desperado, Pat Wildrick, was hanged to a tree near Portage—one of the few recorded lynchings in Wisconsin. Gates and his wife had been moving down the Wisconsin and were encamped on the bank of the river when Wildrick attacked them, robbing them of almost three thousand dollars, and injuring his wife; Wildrick's jail sentence as a result of Gates's testimony was thought to have inspired him and/or his accomplices to remove Gates, who was an important witness against him in a second trial to be held after he had broken jail. Wildrick was taken from the Columbia County jail at Portage and lynched, an act which put a quick end of the activities of desperadoes who had begun to make their depredations felt along the Wisconsin in the vicinity of Portage and Kilbourn.

Nor are these all the "points of interest" to which attention is drawn. Since 1941, the citizens of Wisconsin Dells can put their tongues in their cheeks and point to the spot where Wisconsin's Governor Julius P. Heil appeared and made one of the local Indians not only a "colonel"—a business in which the governor has so distinguished himself that he threatens to rival Kentucky's famed colonel makers—but also an "honorary white man," "a paleface"—an act which ought properly to have been accompanied by a rumbling as of thunder, to signify the turning over in their graves of all the Indians fallen victim to the rapacity of the white man, with his speeches of brotherhood, so akin to the governor's words in honor to the grandson of old Yellow Thunder. There is the legendary rock from which Julia Le Morn threw herself in suicide because of unrequited love; doubtless more than a score of rivers have such rocks, and they are common enough on the lakes. There are the Indian mounds. Mounds abound up and down the Wisconsin River valley, but seldom with the variety of those at Wisconsin Dells, in the vicinity of which are effigy, conical, linear, and oval mounds of many kinds, including a bird memorial in the Bennett group having a wing spread of almost three hundred feet, and a singularly fine water spirit mound 174 feet in length. There is the grave of Belle Boyd, whose stone bears this simple inscription:

One Flag   *One Country*
MARIE ISABEL HIGH
"Belle Boyd"
Confederate Spy
Born May 9, 1843
Died June 11, 1900

in memory of the notorious spy who, while on a stage tour, was taken ill at Kilbourn and died there one night in June, 1900—a West Virginia girl whose story is a dramatic episode in the annals of the Confederacy. Not far away is the grave of a son of John Brown. And there is Newport.

Wherever the tide of settlement has followed industry, has been passed by the railroads and the highways, there are ghost towns. Fully half a dozen ghost towns rose up and vanished along the shores of the Wisconsin. Newport, just across the river and below Wisconsin Dells, along the Lower Dells, came into being in 1849, experienced a few years of rapid prosperity, and then collapsed suddenly and bitterly, all within ten years. Its first settler, coincidentally, was that same Joe

Bailey who saved the Red River Expedition. The town was at first named Dell Creek, but when it was platted in 1852 it was renamed Newport to signify the coming of steamboats as far north as the Dells. The thriving settlement came to have a population of two thousand within three years, largely because of the promise that the new Milwaukee and La Crosse Railroad would come through the town and cross the river at that place. But something happened.

In his *Newport: Its Rise and Fall*, E. C. Dixon reveals that the attention of the railroad officials turned from Newport to Kilbourn across the river. "It is one of the traditions of the Shute family, long one of the most prominent in this region, that the site of the Kilbourn bridge was surveyed at night by the use of lanterns in the year 1856 by William Boardman Shute and Colonel J. B. Vliet." It was left to a canny Vermonter, Alanson Holley, a printer intending to begin a newspaper, to draw the proper conclusions from the activities of the various interests, and erect a building on the site of Kilbourn, and announce that it was this site and not Newport which would be the important settlement on the Wisconsin at this point. Mr. Holley was right; the bridge was located at Kilbourn, and as soon as this fact was incontrovertibly established, the citizens of Newport began to leave the town—some for Kilbourn, others for Baraboo and Reedsburg, growing up along the railroad line—and they left to such an extent that by 1858 almost the entire population of Newport had gone, and today only the hollows that were cellars and the lilacs growing there remain to give mute evidence of the town which once stood on the bank of the Wisconsin along the Lower Dells.

When Captain Wood put a motor on a barge and spent his Sundays taking people up the Dells as far as

Arch Cove, then called Paradise, he unwittingly began a business which has grown to support hundreds of people in the summer months: the business of catering to tourists. By 1875 J. J. Brown had printed a second edition of his guidebook to the Dells, and by this time, too, Henry H. Bennett had begun to photograph the beauty of the Dells; he was an earnest young photographer who had taken photographs during the Civil War, and had had the foresight to realize that the lumbering industry would soon be an aspect of history and preserved all the romance of rafting in a series of admirable photographs. The Dells of the Wisconsin soon needed no artificial advertising. For a while there was a strong movement on foot to create a state park at the Dells, the legislature passed the bill, but Governor Emanuel L. Philipp, who had reached the governor's chair from the Sauk Prairie, not far below the Dells, chose to exercise his veto, and the movement failed.

From that time on, the tourist trade grew into the first industry of Wisconsin Dells, whose rocky river shores, thanks in great part to the strictures of the Crandalls and the Uphams, remain free of those aspects of commercialization which blot the roads leading to the city. Even the hotels and tourist camps on property not under the control of the two families have preserved the becoming air of careless dignity, free of most of the tawdriness of flamboyant commercialism.

2. THE CAVES

As lumbering declined throughout the valley of the upper Wisconsin and the railroads reached all the towns, tourists began to flow into the region from the south. The tourist trade throughout Wisconsin is com-

paratively recent; despite such early appreciation of the
Dells of the Wisconsin as the Bennett photographs and
the guidebook by J. J. Brown, the tourist trade is a
twentieth century product, spread not by the railroads
so much as by the automobile. To dairying, the growing
of apples, blueberries, cherries, and cranberries, the
upper Wisconsin River valley resident could add the
tourist trade soon after the turn of the century,
though the trade began to boom only after the First
World War. To the towns and resorts along the Wisconsin as well as to the many lakes in the northern part
of the state came vacationists in steadily increasing numbers. Resorts sprang up first along the lakes backed up
behind the dams, and gradually spread down the Wisconsin toward the river's mouth.

As in all areas catering to tourist trade, every aspect
of water and land was soon utilized to interest the vacationists, most of whom came up from the city areas of
Milwaukee and Chicago—from the latter city to such
an extent that one bumptious Chicago publisher, with
his customary effrontery, claimed all of Wisconsin's
tourist country, which includes the entire valley of the
Wisconsin, as "Chicagoland." Within the past decade
the lower Wisconsin River valley began to make its
bid for a share of the trade flowing through the state.
Lacking dam-formed lakes and dells, the people of the
lower Wisconsin valley turned to the hills through which
the river flows to the Mississippi, the hills which are so
close together on opposite sides of the river that the
valley of the Wisconsin from the Sauk Prairie down is
seldom more than eight miles wide. They figured the
hills might offer something. They were right. There were
caves in the hills, and unusual caves, miniature Mam-
moths and Carlsbads.

The first of them to be opened to the public was

Eagle Cave near Muscoda. The existence of the cave had been known since 1849, when a farmer named Peter Kinder chased a bear into the cave—that is the story told by the guides despite its suspicious resemblance to the story of the brown bear that led a hunter to Kentucky's Mammoth Cave. Despite a kind of inappropriate labeling of onyx formations in the cave—Boston Teapot, Casa Loma, for instance—it draws tourists. The cave measures fourteen hundred yards on all levels, and gives every evidence that there are still further openings to be discovered and utilized. Moreover, its walls are interesting—not for the scrawled *Jesus Saves* which appears in large letters on the face of one of the rocks, but for the casual records: names and dates—put down decades ago and bearing mute testimony today of candlelight visits by the farmers in the vicinity—the adventures of Sundays, perhaps.

The second of the caves was discovered far more recently. In the summer of 1939 a contractor, engaged to supply crushed rock for the highways of Dane County, leased the Brigham quarry at Blue Mounds, southeast of the Sauk Prairie country of the Wisconsin River valley. A well driller, hoping to break loose a year's supply of rock with one blast, drilled eight six-inch holes for dynamite beyond the top of the quarry, which was of limestone and had been in operation since 1903. The blast loosed more than a year's supply of rock, and when the smoke had cleared away, the yawning mouth of the Cave of the Mounds lay exposed. "After more than 300 years of exploration and discovery in Wisconsin," trumpeted the Milwaukee *Journal,* "one of the most remarkable natural phenomena in the state wasn't found until August 4, 1939, at 11:30 in the morning!"

The cave revealed unusual limestone formations,

and some onyx. Stalactites and stalagmites abound. The Cave of the Mounds, as it was promptly christened, was so well advertised that in its first year it drew almost sixty thousand visitors. The press covered the cavern and described it fully—and repeatedly. Stressing the feeling of being in a "vast, cool, subterranean cathedral," the Milwaukee *Journal* added that "grotesque towers and pinnacles rise twenty feet above the floor like a ridge of medieval statuary." And " 'Crystal Cascade' is a glistening onyx falls, a series of black and white striped ribbons of stone. The distinct coloration is almost unique—the only other known example is in Iceland."

The two caves are not far from each other, though on opposite banks of the Wisconsin. Eagle Cave (for what reason so named is unknown) is closer to the river itself, being less than three miles from the Wisconsin; Cave of the Mounds lies at the far edge of the valley, where it meets the old lead-mining region. Each draws a steadily increasing amount of tourists from year to year into the lower Wisconsin River valley, vying in popularity with the old houses—the Indian Agency House at Portage, the house whose erection was described by Juliette Kinzie in her *Wau-Bun,* and the Villa Louis at Prairie du Chien, the mansion of the old Northwest Territory's first millionaire.

3. VILLA LOUIS

The Villa Louis—as the home of Hercules Dousman is now called—is actually the remodeling of 1872: a house superimposed upon another, with something of that older house's atmosphere remaining as well as a part of the house itself. That same Jane Fisher Rolette, King

Joe's young wife, who became the wife of Hercules Dousman after Rolette's death, rebuilt the house on the mound where once the old Fort Shelby had stood, and later the first Fort Crawford.

For some time after the death of the second generation of Dousmans in Wisconsin—Hercules and Jane had had but one child, a son, who in turn, though dying young in 1886, had left five children—the house was either left untenanted or rented. Perhaps it was the leasing of the house to a small-time racketeer during the Prohibition era, and the subsequent discovery that the tenant had rifled the attic trunks of valuable papers which began to turn up in various museums and archives to which they had been sold, that caused the Dousmans to present the house to the city of Prairie du Chien, "not . . . as a Museum in which to collect historical relics of the County and State . . . but as an historical home in which 'nothing shall be placed except historical books, documents and furniture pertaining solely to the Dousman family, and associations relating thereto,' " wrote Mrs. Virginia Dousman Bigelow in the preface to her *History of Villa Louis*.

The city of Prairie du Chien has not made the most of its ownership of Villa Louis, but it has made a good thing out of it, nevertheless. Moreover, events conspired in their favor, for the Villa Louis had hardly been thrown open to the public when the remaining foundations of the forts were unearthed, together with many relics of centuries gone by, and, through the energy of the Reverend Leland Cooper, a museum was erected in connection with the forts on the Dousman estate, so that the show place soon began to attract more comers than any other tourist haven south of the Dells. The city wisely avoided bad taste in commercialization, and managed, by means of opening pageants and celebrations, every May to enlist the aid of the press in publicizing the site to the best advantage.

The terms of the bequest were strictly adhered to, but the family connections were wide enough to allow latitude. They included the effects of Brigadier General Samuel Davis Sturgis, father of Nina Sturgis Dousman, old Hercules's daughter-in-law; he had "made an enviable record in the Indian, Mexican, and Civil Wars." They included also Lieutenant James Garland Sturgis, his son, who was one of the soldiers killed in the battle of the Little Big Horn, that unnecessary bloodletting brought about by General Custer's inability to make up his mind to obey orders. Nor are the Villa Louis and the museum, now augmented by historical dioramas and paintings by Cal Peters, the only buildings on the site; the estate has all the appurtenances of the home of a rich man in the Midwest in the latter half of the past century—an icehouse, stables, a laundry, and even a spacious office in a separate building—this belonging still to Hercules Dousman's day.

Undoubtedly a large part of the success of the Villa Louis as an addition to the tourist attractions in the Wisconsin River valley was due to the guide and caretaker who first introduced the house to the public— a voluble, imaginative, garrulous fellow: the late Charlie Minney. And it was precisely because Minney did not adhere to the familiar pattern of guide lingo that he contributed so much to its success as a tourist attraction; for he allowed his imagination free rein, giving forth stories of romance or horror in such a way that his listeners were never quite certain that they were not true —like the shuddersome tale of the spot in the tunic of the portrait of Lieutenant Sturgis in the lower hall, the place above the heart which turned the color of blood under certain psychic conditions, or the grotesque expansion of the story of the rifled trunks and the strange doings that went on at Villa Louis in the days of Prohibition. He could invent a story about any aspect of the estate without blinking an eye, from the construction of the walls to the Audubon folios, and his imagination was equaled only by his volubility. There is no record, however, of his distorting history; he simply added color to it. Before the bad heart of which he constantly complained took him off in the course of last spring, Charlie Minney had woven enough legend about the Villa Louis to be assured that some of it would adhere to the dignified old building long past his own time, and would continue to bring to Prairie du Chien an increasingly large share of the tourist trade, for it was apparent that, though the restored Fort Crawford, the old French Cemetery, the Brisbois graves high on the bluffs, and various lesser facets of the old town might appeal to many travelers, it was the Villa Louis which was certain to become, as it did, the focal point of attraction.

4. STRANGERS IN THE VALLEY

Today the tourist trade sustains uncounted thousands in employment from the source of the Wisconsin to its mouth. The tourists come as strangers, return again and again, become summer residents, many of them. They come to the Dells, to the caves, the Villa Louis; they come to take their leisure at the resorts along the lakes; they are duly shown all the places at which Marquette paused—some of them marked, some not—until it must seem to those who have traveled in the East, that Marquette must have stopped in as many places along the Wisconsin, in the circumstances, as Washington did along the Atlantic seaboard. They are

shown the rafters' bugaboos—red rock, boneyard eddy
—a catchall for drowned bodies from above; the rapids
and falls of the upper Wisconsin—the Little Bull, the
Jenny Bull, the Big Bull; they are shown Rib Mountain
—winter sport center of Wisconsin and drawing an
ever-increasing number of winter sport enthusiasts—
and the Blue Mound, the two highest in Wisconsin; they
are shown the home of Zona Gale, Taliesin, the Indian
Agency House at Portage, the Ruggles house near Ridge-
way, Little Norway at Mt. Horeb, the old shot tower
near Spring Green, and the cemetery, all that remains of
Helena; they are escorted through the state parks, from
Interstate along the St. Croix to Wyalusing at the mouth
of the Wisconsin; they are led to the trout streams and
the Indian reservations, and the young people, strangers
and natives alike, spend their evenings at countless halls
from the headwaters of the Wisconsin to the Chateau
at Devil's Lake, jitterbugging to blues and boogie-
woogie, learning to know fellow Americans from every
corner of America, broadening perspectives. Steadily,
inexorably, the valley of the Wisconsin is becoming the
heart of a new industry, the tourist trade, which already
ranks in many places along the river above the agricultural and dairy pursuits of the inhabitants to make of
Wisconsin one of the nation's great vacationlands.

PART SEVEN

River Men and Lore

SOFT-WALKER, the quiet one, paused on the trail and smelled the air. The east wind blew gently, not enough to dispel the cloying odor of locust blooms and the thick sweet fragrance of wild crab-apple that grew in the lowlands like pink clouds over all the prairie. There was something more, and the Sac's nostrils isolated it from the fragrance all around him: it was the smell of smoke. He stood for a moment in the early June dawn and marked its direction on the wind. It came from the east, along the river there; having ascertained this to his satisfaction, he set out silently through the underbrush toward an eminence not far to westward, and, mounting this, looked out upon the expanse of green that rolled away to the broad river's edge and the hills beyond.

All about him rose the growing sounds of breaking day: incessant warbling and crying of birds, insect stridulations deep in undergrowth, furtive flutterings and rustlings, the cries of animals: but from among them came the sound of human voices, faint and far. And he saw the thin curls of smoke rising from the river's shore. He could not understand who might be there, whether friend or foe, but in a moment had begun to move in that direction to settle his doubts. He went soundlessly among the trees, going so effortlessly that even a fox, lying in wait for grouse but three feet from his path, did not move, the water thrush and redstarts along the sloughs were not disturbed, and a prothonotary warbler's golden yellow throat did not cease trembling to its song at the passing of his near-naked red-brown body. In this manner he approached the place where the fire was, and at last, with the caution of his race, he found himself looking upon seven men, white and strangely clad, and he watched in curious amazement.

Some of them were making ready their canoes; one was putting out the fire whose smoke had spoken to Soft-Walker's nostrils in the wind. Another sat making signs upon a paper on his knees, but, not satisfied with what he had done, crumpled it and threw it into the wind, and wrote anew. The last of them had fixed to a tree there a crude board, upon which were other markings carved with a knife. There were in the legends of the Sac's white men in black habits, similar to those worn by two of these men; but of the others, who were differently garbed, there was nothing. Soft-Walker listened to the strange language they spoke, seeking vainly for some familiar word, some sound he might come upon to know; but he heard none.

Alarmed at their number, he took care not to show himself, but waited there until they had gone in their canoes down the river. After they had passed from sight of the prairie at that place, he came out of the underbrush and took up the paper crushed and thrown away, flattened it out, and looked upon it with suspicion, his eyes held by the strange markings there . . .

Ce Meskousing est très-large, son lit est sablonneux avec grand' nombre d'écueils qui entravent la navigation. On recontre partout des îlots couverts de lianes et de vignes, et le long de ses rives on voit des terres fertiles semées de bois, de savanes, de coteaux. On y trouve des chênes, des noyers, des tulipiers, et une autre espèce d'arbre aux branches armées de longues épines. Point de petit gibier ni de poisson, mais des cerfs et des élans en grand' nombre . . .

He turned from it to the board fixed to the tree, and with one quick motion, tore it away. But the markings it bore likewise meant nothing to him.

Jolliet—Marquette: juin 1673

He felt a faint disappointment, but knowing these for trophies, he had no hesitation about taking them with him. He turned and vanished into the undergrowth again; and traveled for many days along the trail to the Sac village in the north whence he had come.

—*Wind Over Wisconsin*

1. Canvas, Print, and Stories Handed Down

Despite its length and the extent of its drainage system, the Wisconsin has not loomed large in the work of its creative artists. Painters reached the Wisconsin earlier than writers, apart from those chroniclers of travels; most of these artists were in the employment of the government—men like Samuel Seymour, who traveled up the Wisconsin some distance from the mouth; he was an aide to Major S. M. Long when Long was on an expedition to explore the headwaters of the Mississippi and Minnesota rivers; like James Otto Lewis, who was commissioned in that same year, 1823, to make portraits of Wisconsin Indians. Lewis had the good fortune to be at Prairie du Chien in 1825 during the great council meeting of the various tribes, and, as a result, he was able to send to the government a score of Indian heads; to this number, he added later. Seth Eastman came to Wisconsin in 1829 on military duty; he was attached to the company at Fort Crawford, and while there Eastman made many paintings and sketches of the Indians, both individually and in social units.

Of all the early artists, perhaps George Catlin, who took the Fox-Wisconsin waterway route in 1835, beginning at Prairie du Chien, where he painted Wabasha's band, left the most to posterity. He had set out with the grandiose plan "of procuring portraits of distinguished Indians of both sexes in each tribe, painted in native cos-

272

tume, accompanied with pictures of villages, domestic
habits, games, mysteries, religious ceremonies" throughout the United States. Of the more than five hundred
pieces left by him, many were painted along the Wisconsin and Fox rivers.

Later there were other painters—Bernard Isaac
Durward of the famed glen east of Baraboo, just below
Portage; he began as a portrait painter, but at the glen
soon turned to depicting the familiar scenes among
which he lived, making his inks from the berries which
abounded there, and his drawing pens from quills. With
George J. Robertson, a Milwaukee painter, he made an
effort to form a Wisconsin Academy of Fine Arts, but
this came to nothing. His son Charles, likewise a painter,
devoted himself almost exclusively to religious subjects.

No one who left any mark painted the Wisconsin
between the time of the Durwards and the present.
Today, John Steuart Curry, one of the leading American regionalists in art, has begun to paint Wisconsin
River scenes; since his coming to the University of Wisconsin five years ago as resident artist, Mr. Curry has
given much of his attention to rural Wisconsin scenes,
and, apart from the illustrations for this book, he has
begun work on a large oil of the Sauk Prairie country.
But only one artist of significance lives on the Wisconsin today, and he is the wood engraver, Frank Utpatel,
making his home in Mazomanie. He has for some time
concerned himself with the cutting into wood of scenes
along the river, of rural scenes, most of them for use
as book illustrations, the best of which appear in my
Village Year: A Sac Prairie Journal and *Atmosphere of
Houses,* and Alan Devoe's *Lives Around Us.* His work
has a strong regional flavor and a marked individuality.

The Wisconsin has figured little more in literature.
The best presentations of life in a Wisconsin River vil-

lage will be found in Zona Gale's *Birth*, and my *Village Year*. *Birth*, undoubtedly the best of Zona Gale's novels, has seldom been equaled for the fidelity of its portrait of midwestern village life. *Village Year* is a day-by-day account of life in Sac Prairie: a journal covering three years. Village life along the Wisconsin has also figured very largely in Zona Gale's *Bridal Pond*, *Yellow Gentians and Blue*, *Faint Perfume*, *Miss Lulu Bett*, *When I Was a Little Girl*, *Portage, Wisconsin and Other Essays*, *Magna*, and the *Friendship Village* series; Karlton Kelm's *The Cherry Bed*; Mark Schorer's *A House Too Old*; Eleanor Green's *The Hill*; Margery Latimer's *We Are Incredible, Nellie Bloom and Other Stories, This Is My Body*, and *Guardian Angel and Other Stories*; and my *Country Growth, Evening in Spring*, and *Still Is the Summer Night*. One of the best presentations of rural life along the river is George V. Martin's charming (cult-of-simplicity) *For Our Vines Have Tender Grapes*, set among the Swedish settlers in the Stevens Point country. The river itself has been portrayed perhaps most largely in Zona Gale's *Papa La Fleur*, and in my *Bright Journey* (the Dousman story), *Wind Over Wisconsin* (the story of the Black Hawk War), *Sweet Genevieve*, and *Restless Is the River* (the story of Count Haraszthy). There is something of the fur trade and the history of that period in the Prairie du Chien area in *The Untamed Wilderness* and *Richard Haddon*, by W. S. Hoffman, still resident at the meeting place of the rivers, where he is librarian of Campion College, which is also the home of a genial Latin scholar and poet, Father A. J. Geyser. Only Laura Sherry has preserved in *Old Prairie du Chien* something of the French-Canadian dialect in verse; apart from this single volume, the writings of Billy Allen before mentioned, and scattered verse in my own *Selected Poems*, there is comparatively little river poetry. Curiously enough, there is no lumbering novel with its setting in the Wisconsin River valley. There are, however, lumbering novels with a Wisconsin setting—books like Edna Ferber's *Come and Get It*, Leslie E. Schlytter's *The Tall Brothers*, and Merlin Ames's teen-age story, *Canthook Country*, and lumbering is touched upon in the writings of Waldemar Agar of Eau Claire.

Apart from the various chronicles referred to previously—the *Jesuit Relations*, Carver's *Travels Through the Interior Parts of North America*, Marryat's *A Diary in America*, Black Hawk's *Autobiography*, and *Wau-Bun*—some of the best descriptions of the river appear in Reuben Gold Thwaites's *Down Historic Waterways*. Thwaites canoed from Portage to the mouth of the Wisconsin and filled his book with amusing and observing details: of the sand bars—"A noted engineer has playfully said that the Wisconsin can never be regulated, 'until the bottom is lathed and plastered'; and another officially reported, over fifteen years ago, that nothing short of a continuous canal along the bank, from Portage to Prairie du Chien, will suffice to meet the expectations of those who favor the government improvement of this impossible highway"; of the wing dams—"In the neighborhood of Portage, the wing dams —composed of mattresses of willow boughs, weighted with stone,—are in a reasonable degree of preservation and in places appear to be of some avail in contracting the channel. But elsewhere down the river, they are generally mere hindrances"; of the shores—"The valley of the Wisconsin is . . . flanked on either side, below the Portage, by an undulating range of imposing bluffs, from one hundred and fifty to three hundred and fifty feet in height. They are heavily wooded, as a rule, although there is much variety,—pleasant grass-grown slopes; naked, water-washed escarpments, rising sheer above the stream; terraced hills, with eroded faces, ascending in a regular succession of benches to the cliff-like tops; steep uplands, either covered with a dense and regular growth of forest, or shattered by fire or tornado. The ravines and pocket-fields between the bluffs are often of exceeding beauty, especially when occupied by a modest little village,—or better, by some small settler, whose outlet to the country beyond the edge of his mountain basin may be seen threading the woodlands which tower above him, or zig-zagging through a neighboring pass, worn deep by some impatient spring torrent in a hurry to reach the river level. Between these ranges stretches a wide expanse of bottoms, either bog or sand plain, over all of which the river flows at high water, and through which the swift current twists and bounds like a serpent in agony, constantly cutting out new channels and filling up the old, obeying laws of its own, ever defying the calculations of pilots and engineers." In description, Thwaites excelled; he was also a superb historical editor, but as an historian, he was not always as accurate as he might have been; though in justice to him, it should be admitted that his errors were trivial. After Thwaites, some of the most readable accounts of the river were written by Ernest L. Meyer in his column, *Making Light of the Times,* in the *Capital Times* of Madison, on the frequent occasions of his vacations on the Wisconsin or along its shores.

The history and lore of the Wisconsin have scarcely been tapped by the writers living within the boundaries of the state. Except for a prose treatment of the Red Bird incident in *Bright Journey* and a lesser dramatic presentation by Pearl Richards, only William Ellery Leonard has utilized the incident to best advantage in his drama, *Red Bird*. But, though the better-known writers have not turned to the background of the river, many less known have transcribed legends of the Wisconsin, notably Charles E. and Dorothy Moulding Brown, Fred L. Holmes, and A. O. Barton.

The legends begin with Indian tales—such as the story of the Potawatomi who wanted to cross the river. The Indian walked up and down the bank in an effort to find a fording place; but he could not. When he paused to consider his plight, he heard a small voice speaking, asking him what he wished; he answered that he wanted to cross the river, whereupon the voice replied, "You need only step into the water and walk across it as if it were ice; then come back." The Potawatomi did as he had been told, and discovered that he could cross the river. Returning to the place from which he had set out, he was told, "I will always help you in this—when you want to walk on the water, do so." The most exhaustive search failed to reveal the source of the voice, but once in his village, he learned from the old men that it was a spider who had spoken to him. "If you had looked down," they told him, "you could have seen him and his web-bridge across the river. The spider's promise means that you will become a great hunter, because no stream will stop you in the hunt." So it was. There are, of course, countless legends and tales about the formation of the river itself, about certain outstanding features in the river valley.

The legends of Indians were followed by those of the Cornish miners, the Cousin Jack stories, following the course of history. The French voyageurs brought with them stories of the wendigo and the loup-garou, but these legends passed with the voyageurs. The Cousin Jack stories, however, were more anecdotal, being short and amusing. So too were the tales of pioneer life which have been handed down—like the tale of Farmer

Thomas, the postmaster of his locality, who distributed the mail from his hat, where he kept it until called for, thus keeping the first portable post office in Wisconsin; or that of trader Rowan's wife, whose dark skin and place of origin so confused an interlocutor that he assumed she was an Indian, many of the early fur traders having married Indian or half-breed women, and inquired of her politely, on an occasion when he took dinner at the Rowan home, from which tribe she came. "Goll darn it!" she replied explosively. "I don't belong to no tribe. I'm from Injianner!"

Two legends of the Wisconsin in the Lone Rock region are dubious both as legend and as history, being just a little more than legend and not quite history. The first is the story of the "treasure boat." The Wisconsin has no ghost ships, unless it might be the sunken treasure boat. The story has it that a boat moving upstream from Fort Crawford with pay for the soldiers at Fort Winnebago had to put in along the rocky bluff across from the tall finger of rock which the raftsmen later used as a landmark, in order to escape a storm; but at the moment of their reaching the farther side of the Wisconsin, a slide of rock took place and buried the boat. "No trace has been found until recently," averred one of the settlers last summer, "when engineers making soundings for the new bridge site, struck timbers well in the sand in about the middle of the river."

If the story of the sunken treasure boat leans toward legend, that of Bogus Bluff leans toward history. Steve Fogo of the Richland Center *Republican Observer* managed to blow the story of Bogus Bluff up sufficiently to merit several columns in his paper. Around Bogus Bluff in the town of Orion has sprung up a really remarkable rigmarole of legend and fact. There is, for instance, the account which is purported to have appeared in print in the Vienna (Austria) *Courier* of a cave near the bluff in which abounded the bones of prehistoric animals, and the skeletons of a vanished race. One S. von W., supposedly the author of the account, wrote: "Fragments of rock were everywhere, amongst them the bones of prehistoric animals. Here and there were also fragments of antlers of deer and elk. . . . I cannot describe the horror I felt. The bottom of the cave was covered with skeletons of a vanished race. Skulls were everywhere. Here perished a tribe; very near, I could say, a nation. Their belongings were scattered among the bones. Battle axes of stone, ancient pottery, whole and in fragments, flint arrows, and spears, broken and whole, everywhere . . ." This one has the rich odor of a hoax, but it is at least colorful and imaginative.

Then there are the legends of buried treasure, but these, of course, abound in every like locality not only in the Wisconsin River valley; the treasure, curiously enough, is supposed to have been taken off another of the boats carrying soldiers' pay up to Fort Winnebago by a band of desperadoes who had to leave the treasure hidden somewhere on Bogus Bluff while they made good their escape.

But it is the counterfeiters who lend something of authority to the fascination of Bogus Bluff. There were counterfeiters, apparently. Dr. Bertha Reynolds—incidentally, one of the earliest "lady M. D.'s" to practice in the Wisconsin River valley (She told Einar Hammer, a local correspondent bent on getting a birthday story for the *Wisconsin State Journal* from her this spring, that she was put to the test by circumstances almost as soon as she reached Lone Rock to practice. "I wasn't too qualified," she said, "and when this call came—one of my first—in the middle of the night, that a farm woman was in trouble, I hurried there, thinking to find some slight illness. Instead, I found that a husband had attacked his wife with an ax in a drunken brawl, and the son had taken the ax to the father and nearly scalped him!'')—remembers the firm depositions of older residents to the effect that flares were often seen on the bluff at night. "They appeared for a time, and then for nights there would be nothing at all; then they would appear again," said Mrs. Ellsworth. "They said Blue Mound was one of the distributing points of the counterfeit money, but most of the money went down the Wisconsin and was sold or traded out." The counterfeiter was a man named Ellis; he was duly caught, though he had got rid of his plates by the time the law laid hands on him. Legend has doubtless multiplied many times the number and variety of his exploits from the cave in Bogus Bluff where he and his companions made their headquarters for part of the time before their capture in near-by Boscobel.

The variety of the stories handed down is infinite. The majority of them belong to the time of the lumberjack and raftsman, but there is no part of the river valley without its favorite lore. There are tales of place names—like the naming of Helena and Arena for two "beautiful Indian maidens," who appeared near Hayworth's Landing in the vicinity to beg for protection and shelter, saying they were Winnebago who had escaped from a band of Sioux; and innumerable tales of doughty pioneers, like Count Haraszthy, or Dick Shay—whose adventures smack strongly of the tall variety. Shay was apparently a colorful character, and clearly a man of great determination to permit nothing to get into his way, particularly not such a trivial thing as a tributary to the Wisconsin. He had put his oxen out to graze one day and next morning discovered them on the far side of the deep stream running through his land. There were no bridges, and the water was deeper than Shay was high, but, nothing daunted, Shay walked across underwater, and, with his oxen in tow, returned by the same direct route. It was the same Dick Shay who, on the occasion of being rescued from under a load of bolts, said, "I prayed to the Lord and I prayed to the Devil, and Dan Parkhurst happened to come along and he helped me more than either of them."

Nor are the legends of the Wisconsin River valley confined to the distant past; each decade adds to them. And every passing decade adds new names to the men and women of the valley, those who have made more than a fleeting impression upon the social units of which they are a part.

2. A BIBLE IN THE ROOM

On a night in late September of 1898 a pair of traveling salesmen got together in the Hotel Boscobel, and shortly they were joined by a third in Room 19. Boscobel was not then blessed by juke-boxes to keep alive the early hours of the morning, and the gentlemen, who were sober, God-fearing men, were that night concerned with the state of men's souls, particularly of those who, like themselves, needed to be much away from home and friends. Were all such travelers prey to loneliness and often unhappiness? they wondered. Neither John H. Nicholson nor Samuel E. Hill could say; they suspected they were. So did W. J. Knights. They had themselves known loneliness, and discouragement, sometimes even despair; the lot of the traveling salesman was not an easy one in those days at the turn of the century.

They had had, however, one common solace: the Bible.

And presently one of them suggested that it would be a fine thing if Bibles were made available to those who traveled and stayed in strange places—a Bible in every room in every hotel in America!

It was not impossible, they were convinced. But how to accomplish such a plan?

For a long while they talked on that September night, past midnight into the morning. By the time the early hours wheeled around, they were as one in their determination to bring about at least a beginning in their plan to put a Bible in every hotel room in America! And there was a way to do it—by organization.

Before they separated for what remained of that night, they had laid the foundation for what was to become The Gideons, the Christian Commercial Travelers Association of America—"OUR SLOGAN: 'And they stood every man in His place around about the camp' —*Judges 7:21.* OUR PURPOSE: A Gideon Bible in each guest room of every hotel in America.—With the hope that many may be brought to know the love of Christ which passeth knowledge. You should read it to be wise, believe it to be safe, and practice it to be holy."

On the way downriver in the summer of 1941, I stopped at the Hotel Boscobel, and, above the desk, saw the large acknowledgment: "This tablet commemorates the meeting of John H. Nicholson and Samuel E. Hill, the latter part of September, 1898, in Room 19 of this Hotel, who with W. J. Knights, were instrumental under God's guidance in the organization of The Gideons. . . ." I followed a bellboy up the stairs, along a narrow L-shaped hall, at the apex of which I was put into a room; it was only when I turned to close the door that I saw I had been given Room 19. There was a plate on the door: "The Original Gideon Room," and on the bureau, certainly, a Gideon Bible. I turned to it, wondering how many thousands of travelers had assuaged their loneliness and troubles by fulfilling the dream shared by those three pioneers in this room almost half a century before.

The familiar Gideon instructions were there: "Good news: If you are in trouble, real Psalm 34." (*Judge thou, O Lord, them that wrong me: overthrow them that fight against me. Take hold of arms and shield: and rise up to help me. Bring out the sword, and shut up the way against them that persecute me: say to my soul: I am thy salvation . . .*) "If trade is poor, read Psalm 37." (*Rebuke me not, O Lord, in thy indignation; nor chastise me in thy wrath. For thy arrows are fastened in me: and thy hand hath been strong upon me . . .*) "If very prosperous, 1 Cor. 10:12." (*Wherefore he that thinketh himself to stand, let him take heed lest he fall.*) "If you are lonesome and discouraged, read Psalms 23 and 27." (*The earth is the Lord's and the fulness thereof: the world, and all they that dwell therein. For he hath founded it upon the seas; and hath prepared it upon the rivers. . . . Unto thee will I cry, O Lord: O my God, be not thou silent to me: lest if thou be silent to me, I become like them that go down into the pit. . . .*)

A hot, uncomfortable room in July; it must have been pleasant enough on that September night. Across the street a dance was in progress, and later a juke-box assaulted the night until after two o'clock in the morning, entertaining the proprietor of the establishment in a loud commanding voice through the open door, while he idly swept the walk before his place of business. There was nothing of this on that September night in 1898, nothing to get between three men and their God in the corner room of the hotel to which coincidence so common in life had brought them: three men with something on their minds, come together fortuitously to the place where Providence had willed that they work out their plan to assuage the loneliness and discouragement of their fellow men.

3. BIRD-BILL KNOTTER

At eighteen, John Appleby did a man's work on his stepfather's southern Wisconsin farm. But few of his chores tired him as much as bending to bind grain, and his back made painful complaint when he sat one night to rest and watch his mother spinning, his eyes following her fleet fingers, engaged in tying the broken strands at her wheel. If only there might be something which could bind grain as easily! he thought. Thereupon he took out his knife, and from an apple bough, carved a bird-bill knotter which was destined to be the model of an invention which made practical the growing and cutting of the great grainfields of the twentieth century: the grain binder.

The year was 1858, and some time was yet to elapse before young Appleby's dream of a grain binder took more tangible form. The Civil War came between, but Appleby was soon back from the front, at work in Mazomanie. He had not forgotten his grain binder, however, and was soon contriving a wire contraption to gather into bundles the spears of grain severed by Cyrus McCormick's machine. On August 9, 1870, Appleby was ready to demonstrate his grain binder on the farm of C. W. Hazeltine, on the bank of the Wisconsin just north of Mazomanie; he had the confidence of his backer, the local Dr. Bishop, and he had the interest of a young University of Wisconsin student who had come to write an account of the demonstration for the *Wisconsin State Journal;* he was the same William E. Huntington who was later to become president of Boston University.

The experiment was also watched eagerly by neighboring farmers and by manufacturers' representatives. The grain that year was heavy, and, as a result, the wire contrivance Appleby had invented missed several bundles; but most of the bundles were bound, and Dr. Bishop said prophetically, "If it binds one, it can be made to bind all." So it was, and the manufacturers adopted it. Soon, however, the farmers were complaining that pieces of wire in their horses' stomachs brought about the death of their animals and did other harm to milling and farming, and interest in Appleby's contrivance diminished.

But four years later Appleby was back, nothing daunted by the misfortunes of his 1870 invention. This time he had fashioned his wooden bird-bill knotter into a twine binder, and it was soon apparent that he had at last hit upon the right medium for binding grain. Reminiscing about his invention a half century later, Appleby said, "The task remained of mounting the binder in such a manner as to take the cut grain and bind it by the use of power applied from the wheels of the harvester. This took more thinking and planning than the making of the knotter itself. I hit upon the frame, planned elevators to carry the grain to the binder, packers to keep the bundling in shape, and butter to form the square base of the bundle. The needle was so shaped as to compress the bundle before tying. The tripping device gauged the size of the sheaf, and all parts received power from one gear wheel. This took a tremendous deal of planning, but, after I had seen the needs of the entire scheme, I set myself to carrying them out, and little real change has been made to this day except in the way of small improvements."

The first machine was given its trial in a ryefield near Beloit. It did not miss a bundle. Within a year of that trial in 1877, William Deering, the manufacturer of farm machinery, secured the right to use Appleby's patents. In a single year, Deering sold approximately three thousand twine harvesters, and within four years more the McCormicks paid $35,000 to Appleby for manufacturing rights to his invention.

Within the decade the produce of John Appleby's teen-age dream had revolutionized the grain binding of the world, as it does today, little changed from that first wooden bird-bill knotter which he had manipulated with his hands to tie a knot resembling the nimbly tied granny knot his mother had tied in the broken strand at her spinning wheel.

4. THE PROPHET JENKIN

Those who know him know he was a great man— a sort of Old Testament prophet, whose archaic and virile English was in the best Saxon tradition, whose best sermons were close to literature. Jenkin Lloyd Jones. To say of him that he was a Chicago divine of some fame, that he founded the Abraham Lincoln Center, etc., is not to say enough, and tells virtually nothing about him as a man.

He spent his boyhood and his summers after that along the Wisconsin in the vicinity of what is now Tower Hill State Park, land which he bought for his own in 1890. The preface to his *An Artilleryman's*

Diary, written in 1913 when he was seventy, gives something of the man's flavor. He writes of himself:

"I am one of the multitude of 'hyphenated' Americans, born across the water but reared under the flag. I am a Cambro-American, proud of both designations, and with abundant heart, loyalty, and perhaps too much head pride in both. Introduced to this word in Llandyssul, Cardiganshire, Wales, November 14, 1843, I celebrated my first anniversary by landing at Castle Garden, in New York City. My parents were sturdy 'come-outers' who, after the manner called 'heresy,' even among Protestants, worshipped the God of their fathers. They came from what in orthodox parlance was known as the 'Smwtyn Du' the heretical 'black-spot' in Wales. I am the third Jenkin Jones to preach that liberal interpretation of Christianity generally known as Unitarianism. The first Jenkin Jones preached his first heretical sermon in his mother's garden way back in 1726, ninety-three years before Channing preached his Baltimore sermon (1819), from which latter event American Unitarianism generally dates its beginning. . . . May, 1845, found us in the then territory of Wisconsin. The broad, fertile, and hospitable open Prairie country in southern Wisconsin was visited and shunned as a desert land, 'a country so poor that it would not grow a horse-switch.' And so, three 'forties' of government land were entered in the heavy woods of Rock River valley, forty miles west of Milwaukee, midway between Oconomowoc and Watertown, which then were pioneer villages. The land was bought at $1.25 an acre, then were purchased a yoke of oxen and two cows; and when these were paid for, there remained one gold sovereign ($5) to start life with—father, mother, and six children. . . . In 1856, my thirteenth year, the family began to realize that they had chosen a hard place in which to make a home. . . . In 1855 we moved to a farm of 400 acres in Sauk County. . . . Here I worked on the farm in the summer time, and during the winter time grew with the growing village school in Spring Green."

He spent from 1862 to the end of the Civil War in service, and kept a diary which is prosaic enough save for occasional, unexpected flashes of Jones's individuality. After his war years, he went into farming and spent a winter teaching at Arena. "During one year there was an honest attempt to accept the path apparently laid out for me—that of an honest, hard-working farmer. And then the hunger for books, the blind push on thought lines, the half-unrecognized leanings towards another career, broke beyond control, and I left the farm." He left for study at the Theological Seminary at Meadville, Pennsylvania: four years of it, and then, moved by that fire which was to burn in him to the end of his life, he took a pastorate which led after a decade to thirty-two years in the pulpit of All Souls Church, Chicago. For thirty-two years, too, he edited *Unity*—"a weekly independent religious magazine, devoted to 'Freedom, Fellowship, and Character in Religion.'" Only toward the end of the century did he turn back to Wisconsin. "In 1890 I secured possession of a tract of land which was once the site of the prosperous early Wisconsin village of Helena. . . . There in connection with the little farm adjoining, I have found vacation rest and renewal for the last twenty years."

He was an intense, earnest, zealous man, a big man physically as well as mentally, with commanding, brooding eyes, a sensuous but determined mouth, and heavy, curved brows. To his head of thick hair he later added a majestic, flowing beard, which made him look more than ever a prophet. Even at rest he could not be inactive; at Tower Hill he initiated the Tower Hill chautauqua, intent upon educating the people who lived about him as well as those who came from Chicago in his wake. The Tower Hill Pleasure Company began as a summer resort specifically for ministers, teachers, and other professional workers in the fields of religion and education, and it was for this group that Jenkin Lloyd Jones maintained his "summer assembly and institute."

He wrote on one occasion that the soldier of the Civil War he had been "continued his contentions for freedom, justice, and union." So he did, and his sincerity, his militancy, his eloquence in his sermons caused him to loom large for almost fifty years in the history of the valley and of a state rapidly becoming known from coast to coast for liberalism of a stamp exemplified by such men as Robert M. La Follette and Jenkin Lloyd Jones.

5. Frontiersman in History

"Up to our own day American history has been in a large degree the history of the colonization of the Great West. The existence of an area of free land, its continuous recession, and the advance of American settlement westward explain American development. Behind institutions, behind constitutional forms and modifications, lie the vital forces that call these organs into life and shape them to meet changing conditions." So wrote Frederick Jackson Turner in his *The Significance of the Frontier in American History*, read before the American Historical Association at the World's Fair historical congress in Chicago, July, 1893. He was on the threshold of a great career as an historian who was to become the author of such important studies as *The Frontier in American History, The Significance of Sections in American History,* and others.

He was born in the Portage country—Portage, which gave to Wisconsin many an illustrious son and daughter, from the gentle, well-loved Zona Gale, who became famous as an author and a leader of women in her native state, to colorful Dan Grady, an old-school lawyer—though he is matched in near-by Baraboo by such able men as the senior James H. Hill and Judge Henry J. Bohn, who, as district attorney of Sauk County, matched wits two decades ago with a pair of the most brutal murderers ever to shed blood in the Wisconsin's valley, despite all threats of vengeance, saw them to prison, and today rises up in righteous wrath whenever a misguided effort is made to parole those two vicious men, who escaped a well-earned death sentence only because no death sentence can be imposed in Wisconsin. From Portage came John Muir, Margery Latimer, Eleanor Green, Karlton and William Eulberg Kelm, and others less widely known.

Doubtless, Turner's childhood and youth along the Wisconsin, representing an experience in frontier living, helped shape his future; he was familiar with the culture of the frontier, and had played a part in its social life when he entered the University of Wisconsin to take his first degree there in 1884. He learned other aspects of life at first hand in a year as a reporter on the staff of the *Wisconsin State Journal,* but journalism was not for him. As a tutor in rhetoric and oratory, he went back to the university to prepare for teaching. The ideals of his youth had become the convictions of his young manhood: a deep respect and reverence for science and the scientific method, a profound belief in democracy. While he taught rhetoric, he studied history.

Soon he was teaching history, assisting William F. Allen in the department, and in 1888 he took his Master's in history.

Before the awarding of that degree, Turner had swung from the emphasis on narrative in history to the study of history in relation to social evolution. In his third year as a teacher, the university offered students Turner's new course for juniors and seniors in history: "American history. Treated more largely from the genetic standpoint than the preceding; developed by topics. Twice a week for one year." So read the *Catalogue of the University of Wisconsin, 1887-1888.* A year later Turner had written the most comprehensive account of the subject in *The Character and Influence of the Indian Trade in Wisconsin,* and his treatment of the subject was in full accordance with his clearly indicated course, marking his awareness of social and economic influences: "The Indian village became the trading post, the trading post became the city. . . . In a word, the fur trade closed its mission by becoming the pathfinder for agriculture and manufacturing civilization."

After a year at Johns Hopkins, he came back to an assistant professorship. He had been taught by men like Richard T. Ely (soon to join him at Wisconsin), Woodrow Wilson, and Albion Small. Herbert B. Adams had been his adviser in his thesis, which was that brilliant study of the fur trade in Wisconsin. He came back to Wisconsin convinced more than ever of the overemphasis placed on the Atlantic seaboard in the study of American history, determined that the West and the South should reserve their rightful share of attention. To that end he, as well as Woodrow Wilson and other young historians, bent his efforts. But more than that:

Turner felt the need of a sociological point of view of history in the Mississippi Valley.

"Economic history finds here a rich harvest. In this rise of a new industrial world, the economic conditions of not only the older states of our own country, but even of Europe, have received important modifications. To this valley, also, have come migrations from the Old World such as can be compared only with the great Wandering of the Peoples—the Völkerwanderung—of the Middle Ages." It was in the West, Turner maintained, that we had "the almost unique spectacle of heterogeneous peoples, in a new land, forming self-governed communities, peacefully as regards each other, drafting constitutions and growing into states of a federal union." The occasion for his statements was a review of Theodore Roosevelt's *The Winning of the West*, written for the *Dial* in August, 1889.

Turner's direction was thus clear, and he did not waver from it. He pursued his studies of the Middle West in this direction and soon began to study the current of American history from its beginning to his own time from a similar perspective. When he died a decade ago, he died a great teacher and a great historian, and he left behind him a school he may be said to have founded, a school of historiography, which has had a permanent influence on the study of American history throughout the nation.

6. BIG TOP

Wisconsin has been called the cradle of circuses, and not without reason. Out of Delavan operated the Mabie Brothers' Circus; from Janesville, Burr Robinson's; from Watertown, Seibel Brothers; from Evansville, the circus of George ("Popcorn") Hall; from Wonewoc, Dode Fisk; from Baraboo, the Gollmar Brothers' Circus; from Portage, that of Orton Brothers; from Burlington, of Stranders; and Whitewater, of Wintermute Brothers. There were others, and they were the source of many circus yarns, the best of which have been collected by Dorothy Moulding Brown in *Wisconsin Circus Lore*.

But the Baraboo valley gave rise to the most famous of them all when the five sons of the Baraboo harness maker, August Ringling, turned away from the trade for "devil's employment" in a circus. The five boys—Al, Otto, Charles, John, and Alf—formed their own company; their beginnings were uncertain; they had to contend with opposition at home and the circumstances of the rough country in which they lived. But on November 27, 1882, the Ringling Brothers Classic and Comic Concert Company put on a performance at Mazomanie. Not until two years later, on May 19, 1884, did the Yankee Robinson and Ringling Brothers Double Shows Circus and Caravan perform at Baraboo, which was to remain the winter headquarters of the "Greatest Show on Earth"—the earlier Barnum claim—until 1919, when the circus became the Ringling Brothers and Barnum & Bailey Circus—indeed the greatest show of its kind on the globe!

The "Greatest Show on Earth" began with that Mazomanie performance by the Ringling Brothers Classic and Comic Concert Company. "I was never again to be as uneasy as on this first appearance," said Al Ringling later. "We had gone far enough from Baraboo so that no one would know us. On the afternoon of the day of the show we paraded the streets. People lined the sidewalks to listen to the music. There were fifty-nine paid admissions at the performance—sufficient to meet the hotel expenses and have a little left over." Only three of the brothers took part in this first show— Al in blackface, Alf at the drums, and Charles at the trombone. Their menagerie consisted of not more than four horses, a monkey, and a hyena billed as a "grave-robbing man eater." With it, they moved from Mazo-manie to other Wisconsin towns, and then into Iowa and Dakota territory, and back to Wisconsin. Sometimes they met their expenses, sometimes they did not. The story is told that on one occasion they had to leave with-out paying their expenses, but later, having met with success, sent back a handsome check in appreciation of the hotelkeeper's tolerance. They went with old Au-gust's doubts strong at their heels. He did not like their choice of a career; he did not believe in the possibility of its success; he was convinced that show people were of necessity "instruments of the devil." He predicted their failure, saying that they might come back to work in the harness shop when they tired of tramping around, the shop would always be open to them.

But old August was wrong. They came back from that first season wearing new clothes and with a profit of $300, which, much to August's embarrassment, was more than the harness shop had earned in the same period. Filled with confidence, the Ringling Brothers prepared to launch their circus. No longer afraid to contend with the people who knew them, they put up a tent forty-five by ninety feet in the old jailyard at Baraboo on that May day in 1884, and, featuring a menagerie consisting of a monkey and a hyena, they performed. That first Baraboo showing—the first time they had dared to call their show a "circus"—was a suc-cess, financially and otherwise, of sufficient magnitude to encourage the Ringlings to transport their exhibits and troupers by means of farm horses and lumber wagons from town to town in the Wisconsin River valley and beyond, and to bring about the establishment of the winter quarters of the circus along the river south of Baraboo—a section long called Ringlingville.

By 1888 the circus boasted two elephants as well as a band and many new acts. But new acts were added every year, and tent space had doubled in less than five years. All five of the brothers were devoting all their time to the circus now—Al as director, John to route the show, Alf as press agent, Otto and Charles to perform and play. By this time, too, Al had married, and his wife, who had a genius for details, was proving her value to the circus. They went up and down the state, and ranged far beyond Wisconsin. Because of the persistence with which they drove away grafters and circus hangers-on, their show soon had the reputation of being the most courteous and cleanest show of them all. By the end of that first decade, representing seven years of the Ringling Brothers Circus, the brothers were realizing as much as $15,000 profit annually.

Moreover, the brothers worked smoothly together, without argument of any kind. There was never a written agreement among them; they began to work as a team, and continued to work that way "without a scrap of paper" to certify and legalize their teamwork. By 1890, the Ringling Brothers Circus had become a railroad show of eighteen cars, featuring "two giant hippopotami, the leviathans of biblical lore, the stupendous river horses of antiquity." Two years later the Ringlings and Barnum & Bailey engaged in a battle of billboards in Milwaukee, the opening gun in an undeclared war between the two circuses. But the latter circus, for years pre-eminent, was on the way out, and in 1908 it passed into control of the Ringlings, to be operated thenceforth under their management until 1919, when it was absorbed into the Ringling Brothers Circus. Barnum & Bailey's was not the only circus the Ringling Brothers bought, however; they vanquished competition wherever they encountered it, until theirs became so great an enterprise that they employed 1,600 people and operated at a cost of $12,000 a day.

Shrewd, canny showmen, the Ringlings never passed a season without innovations, such as their pageants of history, begun in 1891 with *The Fall of Rome,* and carried on by *Jerusalem and the Crusades, Solomon and the Queen of Sheba, Joan of Arc, Cinderella,* and many another, Biblical and historical. They spared no expense to make theirs the most lavish of spectacles, their music was of the best, they stressed pomp and heraldry, and gave particular attention to the popular circus parades until they discontinued them after the 1922 season. Writing in the *Wisconsin State Journal* June 25, 1904, Amos P. Wilder, its editor, watching a barefoot boy with a handful of water lilies entranced by the parade, put down a memorable description of the Ringling Brothers Circus as the boy must have seen it:

"But as the magnificence of the parade grew on him, the boy forgot all else. The trumpeters came first. The season . . . early, the costumes . . . fresh, the colors undimmed. The paint on the great wagons glistened in the sunshine. . . .

"The boy forgot his home, his lilies; he was in wonderland. Then came a huge, lumbering, glorious chariot, from the top of which musicians poured out strains of triumph and marvel that made the air heavy and rich with sweetness. Twenty-four great Norman horses—six parallel of four each—dragged this splendor! Jim Hill's Northwest had been searched to make up this show of horseflesh; and as the heavy metal trappings flopped on their stolid forms, the barefoot boy thought of stories of Arabia and the field of honor. . . .

"It was then that the boy, whose life had been a dreary round of potato field and pasture lots and dreams —after chores were done—fairly looked into heaven. The pattering hoofs of six fine-lined, aristocratic, black horses hastened toward him. In the next car one of the six male lions, with whom a keeper was caged, gave a low, sullen growl as he sneaked into his corner under a threat; but the boy heard it not. Further down the parade the steam organ was pouring out 'Home, Sweet Home' in real harmonies (no mere steam calliope); but all this was sealed to the boy. The big, black horses bore six beautiful women. . . . Their long, vari-colored robes hung nearly to the ground, and in their hats and poise and long gloves lingered the life of knighthood in flower; and the delicate blacks lifted their hoofs in dainty fashion and tossed flecks of foam from their sensitive mouths, and their thin nostrils showed red in impatience and half-formed fear.

"It was a graceful scene even to the old folks who looked on and could see beneath the tinsel and paint the weariness and the grind of the daily round. The sextette were now hard on the lad. He could see the perspiration on the glistening necks of the horses and hear the russet leather harness creak. And oh! Paradise! he could look up into the faces of the fairy creatures, who ruled their impatient steeds so carelessly.

"An inspiration struck the lad. Holding out his dripping lilies, he ran eagerly along the side of the cavalcade. Some of the women threw a glance at the boy, but that was all. It's a dreary round, the circus business, and it's Madison today and Janesville tomorrow! The boy was about to give up his dream, when one of the women saw him and smiled. Perhaps she had somewhere

a nine-year-old boy herself, or perhaps on some Nebraska farm, where she was early clever with horses and thus fixed her destiny—perhaps under a mound lies some brother who died long before she joined the Ringlings, and who, had he lived—well, the threads of a human life are strangely twisted.

"The woman seemed scarcely to draw the reins, but the princely black was thrown back on his haunches, and as she leaned, the picture of grace, to take a lily, she smiled again, and said 'Thank you, my boy,' and a strange thrill went through us who looked on, as when a mob falls back to let a baby's funeral pass, or some other firm note of sweet human nature is struck to remind a despondent world how near to grandeur is our dust."

Only once after 1918 did the Ringling Brothers Circus return to the valley of the Baraboo River where it had come into existence, and that was for its golden jubilee in 1933—a spectacle that drew almost fifty thousand people to the valley, far more than could be admitted to the two performances, and brought to the valley also a national gathering of the Circus Fans Association. Of the brothers in 1933, only John was left, and he was to survive only three years, dying as head not only of Ringling Brothers and Barnum & Bailey, but also of Sells-Floto, Hagenbeck-Wallace, John Robinson, Sparks, and Al G. Barnes shows. The circus today is still the "Greatest Show on Earth," a monument to the persistence of the five sons of the old German harness maker of Baraboo. And only late this spring, President Franklin D. Roosevelt took a few moments from his burden of war to send congratulations to John and Henry Ringling North, the two grandsons of the Ringlings, the two boys who rescued the "Greatest Show on Earth" when it was close to failure not many years ago.

7. THE SHINING BROW

"If I were suffered to apply the word 'genius' to only one living American, I would save it for Frank Lloyd Wright." So said Alexander Woollcott a decade ago, and, since Woollcott is not overly given to superlatives, the owner of Taliesin on the shores of the Wisconsin just below Tower Hill, across the river from Spring Green, had every right to be proud of that accolade. This kind of adulation was sweet wine for a man who had for decades endured the gall of being jeered and hooted at for his revolutionary ideas, a man whose architectural concepts were far in advance of their time. Today *prairie architecture, functional architecture, Usonia* are synonymous with Frank Lloyd Wright, as the architect's name is synonymous with Wisconsin.

He was born not far from the Wisconsin River, in Richland Center, in June, 1869, a grandson of that same Welsh hatter and preacher who had fathered Jenkin Lloyd Jones. His own father was a preacher when he was not a teacher of music. Frank was born into a family of preachers and teachers, and he was a preacher himself, differing only in that he preached a new gospel of architecture. When he went to Chicago to join Dankmar Adler and Louis Henry Sullivan in their architects' office there—"A muggy day in late spring in eighteen eighty-seven a tall youngster of eighteen with fine eyes and a handsome arrogant way of carrying his head arrived in Chicago with seven dollars left in his pocket from buying his ticket from Madison with some cash he'd got by pawning Plutarch's *Lives,* a Gibbon's *Decline and Fall of the Roman Empire* and an old fur-collared coat," wrote John Dos Passos in *U. S. A.*—he was already a rebel against the traditional in architecture which was ruled by the traditions of the past, the details borrowed from the Greek and Roman, the Byzantine and Gothic. There was as yet no Modern Architecture, but Frank Lloyd Wright was determined to remedy that lack.

He had had little training in architecture. He had read Viollet-le-Duc, he had left behind him an unfinished course in engineering at the University of Wisconsin. But he had something more valuable than either: a quotation from Thoreau: "True—there are architects, so-called—in this country, and I have heard of one, at least, possessed with the idea of making architectural ornaments have a core of truth, a necessity, and hence a beauty, as if it were a revelation to him. A sentimental reformer in architecture, he began at the cornice, not at the foundation. What reasonable man ever supposed that ornament was something outward and in the skin merely—that the tortoise got its spotted shell, or the shell-fish its mother-of-pearl tints by such a contrast as the inhabitants of Broadway got their Trinity Church. ... The man seemed to me to lean over the cornice and whisper his half-truths to the rude occupants who really knew it better than he. What architectural beauty I see I know has grown from within outward—out of the necessities and character of the indweller, and whatever additional beauty of this kind is destined to be produced will be preceded by a like unconscious beauty of life."

Habit dies hard. For years Frank Lloyd Wright's preachings fell on deaf ears. A few Oak Park men had the courage to let him build suburban dwellings for them—the first buildings of their kind in America, not strictly the first breaking away from the European traditions, for Sullivan had already accomplished that before the advent of Wright. He called his style *prairie*

architecture, and in 1893, when he left Adler and Sullivan after six years with them, to begin independent
practice, he built the Winslow house, his first building.
In an address before the University Guild in Evanston
the following year he stressed the importance of utility,
simplicity, beauty. "Do not think that simplicity means
something like the side of a barn, but rather something
with graceful sense of beauty in its utility from which
discord and all that is meaningless has been eliminated.
Do not imagine that repose means taking it easy for
the sake of a rest, but rather taking it easily because
perfectly adjusted in relation to the whole, in absolute
poise, leaving nothing but a feeling of quiet satisfaction
with its sense of completeness. These...qualities...
are there only when *integrity* is there, when your work
is *honest, true to itself...*"

He worked at first in wood and stucco, but he could
not confine himself to any one medium; he was eager to
experiment, and soon he was building houses of poured
concrete, of concrete blocks and slabs, of stone, all designed to be functional, with later emphasis upon the
harmony of relation to their setting. This was no far
cry from his prairie houses, whose low roofs, horizontal
lines, window groupings, and open treatment of in-
teriors distinguished them from the work of his contemporaries. His ideas were all radical; they became
practical, one after another. In his own country he remained a prophet without honor, but there was no
diminishing in the authority with which he spoke and
lectured. In 1902 he said: "I believe the time not so far
distant when the 'American home' will, generally, be
owned by the man who paid for it; owned in this sense:
it will belong to its site and to the country, as a matter
of course. Naturally, in the light of a finer consideration for the modern opportunity, will grow a more

practicable truth and beauty. An American home will be the product of our own time, spiritually, as well as physically. And it will be respected the world over, because of its integrity...." In 1908 he wrote in the *Architectural Record:* "I believe that only when one individual forms the concept of the various projects and also determines the character of every detail in the sum total, even to the size and shape of the pieces of glass in the windows, the arrangement and profile of the most insignificant of the architectural members, will that unity be secured which is the soul of the individual work of art." By 1914, in the same magazine, he recognized the existence of opposition, largely blind and unintelligent, to his theories, when he wrote: "Nowhere even now; save in Europe, with some few notable exceptions in this country; has the organic character of the work been fairly recognized and valued; the character that is perhaps the only feature of lasting vital consequence."

America was complacent, settled, satisfied with the grotesques of the 1880's and 1890's. Europe had long been teeming with unrest and rebellion against architectural tradition and eagerly embraced the theses of Frank Lloyd Wright. It was true, as he wrote, that in Europe the principles of organic architecture were appreciated, understood, adopted, that neophytes and disciples rose up there to put his theories into practice, sometimes as he postulated them, sometimes with modifications. In 1915 he left for Japan, where he spent three years directing the construction of Tokyo's Imperial Hotel, designed to withstand earthquakes and constructed on paired central concrete supports and cantilevered floors, in a special construction Wright himself compared to the balancing of a tray on a waiter's fingers. Architectural eyebrows went up, and the Imperial Hotel had been completed only three years before it was given its supreme test; in 1923 it was one of the few buildings left standing after the disastrous earthquake of that year, and the wires of the world carried the information that the building, erected by "the American architect, Frank Lloyd Wright," had withstood the onslaught.

And who was Frank Lloyd Wright? asked the man in the street, who knew Wright only as the center of many a lurid and sensational news story—for Wright's private life had been a stormy one, his marital troubles were a godsend to the yellow press, his divorces, his women, and the horrible tragedy of 1914, the first destruction of Taliesin. In 1911 Wright had come into possession of two hundred acres crowning the hills south of Tower Hill, a wooded tract along the Wisconsin, once the home of Richard Lloyd Jones, his grandfather. There he built Taliesin—from the Welsh, meaning: Shining Brow. Of the hill upon which he built his home, Wright wrote in his *Autobiography* that it was one of his favorite places when he was a boy, "for pasque flowers grew there in March sun while snow still streaked the hillsides." The first Taliesin was destroyed by a Barbados Negro, a servant of the house, who had run amuck; but the firing of Taliesin was not the worst aspect of the tragedy, for before setting the house afire, the Negro had killed the woman who had taken refuge there, her two children, an apprentice, the son of a carpenter working there, the gardener, and another workman: seven people in all. It was after this tragedy and its scarehead-chronicling in the press that Wright left for Japan.

So the people of America discovered Frank Lloyd Wright, the architect. Much to the embarrassment of many of them, they had to read about him in German, they had to hear his praises sung by foreigners who had only a polite tolerance for the names of those most Americans considered the great in architecture.

Taliesin was rebuilt, and ten years later fire once more destroyed it. In 1925-1926 the third Taliesin was built, the house which *Time* early in 1938 described thus: "Facing southwest over this valley a big, long house folds around the summit of one hill, its roof lines parallel to the line of ridges, its masonry the same red-yellow sandstone that crops out in ledges along the stream. Under the snow the house melts easily into the landscape." The third Taliesin was a good example of Usonian architecture, said Wright—that is, of architecture indigenous to the locality, a completely American type. It is so much a part of its setting, as it is meant to be, that strangers can miss it completely in passing by.

After the earthquake of 1923, Wright began to take his rightful position on the roster of America's great in architecture, and his followers began to change the face of the United States with buildings grown from the theories of Wright—the rugged, functional essentials, simply and beautifully created for utility. His sons had begun to follow in his footsteps, and his buildings increased in number, more than two hundred of them by the present decade. His plans for the future included a city of the coming day, Broadacre City, the Usonian city of the future, to be founded on his philosophy: "It is easy to realize how the complexity of crude utilitarian construction in the mechanical infancy of our growth, like the crude scaffolding for some noble building, did violence to the landscape. . . . The crude purpose of pioneering days has been accomplished. The scaffolding may be taken down and the true work, the culture of a civilization, may appear."

The enormous influence of Wright in Europe has not had its counterpart in America, and yet he is already hailed by many as the architectural genius of the century. In his seventies now, he works to perfect plans for Usonia—no Utopian conception, but a strictly practical concept—both at Taliesin, and at Taliesin West, constructed within the last decade on Maricopa Mesa west of Phoenix, Arizona; he summers with the men and women of his apprentices in training, his Taliesin Fellowship, established in 1933, at the home along the Wisconsin; he winters in the Southwest. In 1932 Wright saw published the first draft of his famed *Autobiography*. It might have been supposed that this marked an ending to the period of his greatest activity, but leonine Frank Lloyd Wright, like John Brown's body, went marching on. In the decade since 1932 he has constructed or begun constructing some of the most notable projects of his career—the S. C. Johnson Administration Building in Racine, Wisconsin; the sixteen buildings of the Florida Southern College in Lakeland; the Suntop Homes for the Tod Company of Ardmore, Pennsylvania; the Community Church of Kansas City, Missouri; the experimental low-cost Herbert Jacobs house in Madison—a far cry from the quaint Romeo and Juliet tower which swayed so in the wind, and was put up for his aunts, who were conducting the Hillside Home School, now a part of Taliesin, housing the Taliesin Theatre. In the past decade, too, he has mellowed; the defiance, the chip-on-shoulder cockiness has been tempered by time and adulation; he could take with a sardonic grin the doubts expressed about the heating pipes in the floor of the Jacobs house, the incredulity of the Public Service Commission about the hollow tapered piers, reinforced by tissues of expanded metal lath and supporting only their own lily-pad tops for the Johnson building, their credulity holding up a building permit for six months.

Frank Lloyd Wright carries on; his work will be carried on long after he is gone. He will never be anything but restless, wherever he may be. If age has mellowed him, and his fame has tempered his ire at the slowness of America to accept the things he preached, he has lost none of his fire.

"Here on this low hill in Southern Wisconsin, life and work are synonymous terms. In retrospect is the vast panorama of life as human experiences; tapestry shot through with threads of gold as light gleams whenever truth was touched, wherever love rose worthy of noble self-hood, whenever life rose higher because of death ..."

8. PEOPLE OF THE VALLEY

There are others who have left their mark on the valley of the Wisconsin—men like Neal Brown, the Wausau author; fighting Bill Evjue, Merrill-born river boy who became editor of the *Capital Times* and helped fight La Follette's battles; Robert E. Pinkerton, who spent his boyhood in the Arena country along the Wisconsin before becoming one of the most entertaining of the writers of light fiction with a far north setting; Muscoda-born Joseph Schafer, long superintendent of the State Historical Society of Wisconsin and devoted to history of Wisconsin and the Pacific Coast in various books; Emanuel L. Philipp, who came from a Sauk Prairie farm to become Wisconsin's governor; Baraboo-born Stuart Palmer, who created the popular Hildegarde Withers to add to the roster of the best sleuths of fiction; Governor and later Senator John J. Blaine, of Boscobel, a La Follette Progressive-Republican who was largely instrumental in ridding America of Prohibition;

Prairie du Chien's Michael Spettel, who, when in the employ of philanthropist John Lawler of that city, designed for Lawler's building in 1874 the first pontoon railroad bridge ever to cross an American river, a bridge that still serves the railroad on the Mississippi at Prairie du Chien; Mary Waterstreet, the Spring Green monologist, whose repertoire is familiar from coast to coast; Mary Katherine Reely, likewise Spring Green born, author of juveniles; H. E. Cole of Baraboo, assiduous in his devotion to local history, and the author of several scholarly books; and Baraboo's Trimpeys, Bert, the antique collector, a picturesque, transplanted Yankee with his flowing tie and white goatee, and Alice Kent Trimpey, owner of one of the finest collections of dolls in the country.

And there are the thousands of people who have led their quiet lives—not lives of quiet desperation, though there are these, too, buried under headstones in innumerable Spoon River cemeteries—people like the Wiswalls, local educators, like the local historian, Dr. P. L. Scanlan, like Josephine Merk, teacher, librarian, school board clerk at Sauk City, one of a family of teachers, giving of herself her entire life to combat bigotry and further the cause of liberal education, the kind of woman who has her counterpart in many a community, the kind of citizen who is the marrow in the backbone of democracy.

There are those who lead prosaic, humdrum lives by choice, and those who lead a dramatic existence by accident. The Wisconsin River valley abounds in characters—like the old, unknown gentleman encountered one day fishing from a virtual throne in a rowboat, a cleverly constructed chair in the center of the boat, fishing contentedly from a perch that by all the laws of balance ought to have precipitated him into the river.

There are others. Men like the late politician-poet J. R. Henderson, who came out of the Mount Horeb country and went down in the hearts of his constituents for a book of poems, *Thoughts at Random,* of which the first stanza of "Little Joe" is typical:

> It was February, and we had a thaw;
> The wind from the east blew cold and raw,
>   Two years ago,
> And fever with its deadly paw
> Laid hold of Little Joe.

And Harry Lathrop of Bridgeport.

My journal of a trip downriver in 1941 reveals this record of our landing at Bridgeport: "I found among those on shore a thin, slight figure of a man, nattily wearing a visored cap and pince-nez, with an iron grey moustache and modified Van Dyke beard. He looked down at me as I mounted the bank and introduced himself as Harry Lathrop. 'I said August Derleth wouldn't go past here without stopping to say hello to me,' he said cheerfully, quite obviously happy that we had paused. He was eighty-five; the village storekeeper had told me; he confirmed it. Moreover, it developed that he had been the first railroad station agent in Sauk City. 'That was in 1881,' he remembered. 'I wrote many a waybill for those stations. Later on, I was the first one in Prairie du Sac.' He was garrulous, and wanted to know whether I had ever heard the story of Ben Ochsner's bass. I said I had not, whereupon he told how Ben had gone fishing one day, had caught a sand sturgeon, which in turn had been devoured on the hook by a sand pike, and this had been eaten by a four-pound bass. He sold the bass for twenty-five cents, three fish in one.... He took me into his house there on the river

bank: a simple, almost severely furnished place, with
gadgets and whatnots of shells et al much in evidence,
and displayed some of his hobbies—making bows and
arrows, playing the flute, keeping bees. In fact, he still
had twelve hives of them; at one time he had had forty.
'And when I went abroad that time, I took my time
and visited as many beekeepers as I could find.' It
emerged finally that he did a little writing himself, and,
when I had walked down the station platform briefly,
he went into the station and reappeared with two paper-
bound volumes, both slim. He had inscribed *The Yankee
Abroad*, and explained that everyone called him 'The
Yankee.' The book was a record of the letters he had
sent back from his trip abroad. The other, however,
was a collection of his poems, entitled *Memories of the
Wisconsin and Other Poems*, and dated 1903; this one
was filled with orthodox poems typical of his time, with
some photographs of the Wisconsin River country. I
opened the book to page nine, facing a photograph of a
'Shaded Road at Honey Creek Bluff on the Wisconsin,'
a road that resembled the Ferry Bluff road. His first
poem was his title poem:

'We crossed from off the river front,
    And climbed to that old tower;
'Twas 'Mac and I out on a hunt
    For wine that evening hour.

'Our boat was moored upon the beach,
    As up the mount we went,
The vineyard gate at last to reach,
    Good cheer an interest lent.

'For Kehl, the owner, kindly gave,
    Of grapes to eat our fill,

And showed the cellars where they save
    The vintage of the hill.

'Great rows of casks all placed with care,
    The cellar ranged along,
Containing wine so old and rare—
    I taste it in my song.

'When we had tasted this and that,
    And our departure made,
We sauntered down upon the flat,
    As night began to shade.

.   .   .   .

'Above the dells the fleets were tied,
Each crib detached to safely ride;
As through the gorge they singly shoot,
And down the rapids swiftly scoot;
Then reaching quieter waters still,
With joy the boatman's heart would thrill,
And onward swept by rippling tide,
Reach stiller waters deep and wide.
So might we strive with tongue and pen,
To teach the duller ears of men,
The poem written by the wave,
Where rock and bar and beaches lave;
From source to mouth its course along,
A poem sweet, a nature song.
I love the river's pebbly side,
The islands where the streams divide;
I love in memory's fondest dream
To visit rock and hill and stream;
Return to every well known place,
And well remembered steps retrace
Where oft we hunted, fished and played,
In child-like freedom safely strayed.
At Honey Creek, the lovely port,
Our camping place, and once resort,

The water lillies stoop to drink
The limpid waters by the brink,
Where overhanging trees and flowers,
Great mossy rocks and shady bowers,
Where ferns and copse-wood all combined,
With vines and creepers all entwined,
Exclude from out their deeper shade,
The steps of wanderer through the glade.
Assembled there for health and rest,
Each angler tried to do his best;
And proudly were his trophies shown
At evening hour when day had flown.' "

Varying in degree of self-expression, of articulation, there are doubtless many more men like Harry Lathrop along the Wisconsin. And perhaps there are undiscovered men like Earl Sugden of Yuba, the self-taught artist-farmer, who does incredibly realistic portraits and landscapes in colored sand in bottles! And not alone that, but has taught himself to write poems in Latin as well as English, and paints creditably well also.

There was Jennie O'Neil Potter, who was born and grew up in the hamlet of Patch Grove, in Crawford County, a place so small that, as Mrs. Potter said, "when a baby is born someone has to move out and give the child a chance to grow." Left a young farm widow on stony acreage, Mrs. Potter, a member of a family of which all the members were inventive and able, turned to her one talent, dramatic reading, and turned to it with such determination, such assiduity, that within a few years she was a favorite in New York, and soon after entertained the crowned heads of Europe. She was one of the toasts of the Chicago World's Fair in 1893; her untimely death came soon after. Famous as she became, she never made any secret of her birthplace; *Patch Grove, Wisconsin* was written in her hand on hotel registers all over the world. She returned to Patch Grove after she had become famous, and performed there under the impulsive management of her brother, who said he knew how to advertise, and proved it by filling the hall by means of such a simple but novel expedient as plastering posters advertising Jennie O'Neil Potter on the backs of hogs! "I would rather have faced all the critics in the world . . . My heart beat almost to suffocation as I went out on that plain little stage, where as a child I had stood many a time to speak my pieces. Many of the women had spread my bread and butter with jam and said, 'Now run away like a good little girl, and get out from under foot.' Many of the men had trotted me on their knees and given me rides on their loads of hay," she told later. Death ended her career at its height.

And there are all those men and women who go about their work day after day, conscientious, living from day to day, often totally unaware of the natural beauty of the land in which they live. Small lives. Perhaps. But they too, all those who are doing their work in life as well as they can, are playing their part in the history of the Wisconsin River valley, building the strength of democracy, as did those countless thousands who went before them.

PART EIGHT

This Is the Wisconsin

Fades now, the night
to one star bright
in haze of heaven:
                    star
of morning, Venus, poets' star.
In east comes dawn afar.
Over the rim
of earth, the dim,
the fog-hung trees, the river
and the water's height,
Wisconsin at the flood: retreating night.

Still on the stream
where moving vapors hold the gleam
of dawn, the ghosts of yesterday
move past: canoes, piroques, showboats: play
of voices from the rafts, oars, sound
of music, dip of paddles
at landing: shrouded in dawn.
under the vapors ceaselessly surging, deep in
    mist.

Winneconne, Ellen Hardy,
The Blue Mound

Under the passing night,
under the haze,
under the fog of white,
the yesterdays
long gone.

                    Now
winks and disappears, the morning star: under
    the bough
of oak upon the hill, the sun:
briefly, dark and day are one.
Vapor and fog, the endless sea
of white drives ceaselessly
along the stream; the light
of sun marks out hill and tree, each leaf bright
to leaf—gone voice and song,
gone with the long, the slow
sun creeping: dip of paddle, shout,
creak of oar and grinding logs of rafts turned
    sharp about
among the islands: gone to the heart's dark
    deeps,
gone with the vapor rising.
                    Pale fog creeps
up bank and tree, the early lark sings in his
    song
their magic names again: the *Winneconne* and
    the long
Blue Mound, the *Ellen Hardy:* Portage, Prairie
    du Chien and down,
New Orleans, hill passed and passing slope,
    prairie and wood and town.

                    Winneconne, Ellen Hardy,
                    The Blue Mound

Gone, gone
to linger, linger, linger long,
gone in the mists of dawn
from dark earth rising to the poplars' windy
  sound, lark song.

> *Winneconne, Ellen Hardy,*
> *The Blue Mound*
>   *—The Poplars' Windy Sound*

THERE is something about running water that has an enduring magic for a man. I know that I have never been able to pass a brook without the urge to construct a dam across it, to make a waterfall or a rapids; and in spring I yield to the impulse as often as possible. A brook or small river is an intimate thing; strangely, perhaps because of its many beautiful islands and its heavily wooded shores in those regions away from the power dams, the Wisconsin is an intimate river, though it is not a small river in any sense of the word. Its meandering course makes it flow leisurely; its valley divides easily into small, neighborly segments; and all its tributaries are beautiful streams, flowing through agricultural country that is still largely wooded. Making its winding way from sparsely settled areas at the northern boundary of the state, the Wisconsin flows through rural country, past small towns, hamlets, and small cities, a country that offers, in its harmonious existence, evidence of the successful assimilation of many peoples. Along its shore live Americans who have come in one of the past five generations from Bohemia, England, Norway, France, Sweden, Germany, Austria, Ireland, Poland, Lithuania, Switzerland, and the Atlantic seaboard—the Old Americans, as the sociologists will have it. Throughout the course of my research among them, no one ever spoke to me about the Wisconsin as *our river*, but always *my river*. I offer that as proof of the Wisconsin's intimacy.

Here and there the farmers are united in co-operatives; occasionally the villagers join the organizations, too, and reap the benefits of co-operative living. For the most part, there is a strong communal spirit in the towns along the river, and while there is no formal organization among them, there is always among farmers the fundamental kinship of landsmen. Cows predominate in the Wisconsin River valley, but there are also many pigs and some sheep. Wherever the Wisconsin flows through rural areas—and that is almost everywhere, once the remaining forest areas have been passed —the valley is low, rolling; in upper and central Wisconsin often flat for wide distances, but never beyond sight of hills; along the lower river, the fields patchquilt slopes among woodlots.

Despite the hydroelectric plants, the Wisconsin's aspect is pastoral. Yet there is something of wilderness remaining throughout all its length, from the rapids, where the Wisconsin rushes over hornblende, gneiss, and gneissoid granite rocks, past thickets of birch, alder, cranberry, past elm and pine, fir, spruce and tamarack, through the sandy country of mid-Wisconsin, to where the many-islanded river empties into the Mississippi. On the upper Wisconsin especially, there are many rocks: of sienite and greenstone trap, some of them traversed by veins of feldspar, quartz, granite, and titaniferous iron, the granite veins being sometimes a yard in width, and porphyritic. When the sandy mid-Wisconsin is reached, the rocks end, and the only stone appearing in the river thenceforth consists of droppings from sandstone ledges in the driftless areas, or rounded stones with a few similarly shaped boulders.

The Wisconsin is a pastoral river, a canoeist's stream (above and below the area of the power dams), an angler's river, and, since legislation has begun to eliminate the dumping of sewage and waste products into the river, it is once again becoming a swimmer's paradise. A slow-flowing river in its lower reaches, it bears easily the mark of history. The revenant of the wilderness through which it once flowed lingers along its shores; there are still heavily wooded areas, though most of the forests are gone. The small prairies and the oak openings are host to settlements now, but in many places the oak groves remain, the wild crabapples are pink, aromatic clouds of blossom in May, the poplars and cottonwoods make their windy voices to range the valley.

The river remembers past things, the aspects of life gone by forever—the Indians, the blackrobes, the voyageurs, and the engagés, and traders; the redcoats moving along this wilderness water route to seize the fort at Prairie du Chien; the raftsmen and the lumberjacks, the lead miners, the steamboats and the river pilots who battled ceaselessly against the shifting islands and the sand. The river remembers paroquets, the buffalo, the passenger pigeons—of which John Muir wrote: "The beautiful wanderers flew like the winds in flocks of millions from climate to climate in accord with the weather, finding their food—acorns, beechnuts, pinenuts, cranberries, strawberries, huckleberries, juniper berries, hackberries, buckwheat, rice, wheat, oats, corn— in fields and forests thousands of miles apart. I have seen flocks streaming south in the fall so large that they were flowing over from horizon to horizon in an almost continuous stream all day long, at the rate of forty or fifty miles an hour, like a mighty river in the sky, widening, contracting, descending like falls and cataracts, and rising suddenly here and there in huge ragged masses like high-plashing spray. . . . 'Oh, what bonnie, bonnie birds!' we exclaimed over the first that fell into our hands. 'Oh, what colors! Look at their breasts, bonnie as roses, and at their necks aglow wi' every color juist like the wonderfu' wood ducks. Where did they a' come fra, and where are they a'gan? It's awfu' like a sin to kill them!' " The river remembers the men and women who lived along its shores—Black Hawk and his tragic war, Count Haraszthy and his dream of viticulture, Frederick Lueders standing on his acres watching the heavens night after night, Hercules Dousman and King Joe Rolette and the paradoxical Captain Marsh, John Muir walking its valley, Zona Gale writing in her study overlooking the river where she might see always the broad stream, the islands, the blue Caledonia hills in the distance, Dan Whitney, Amable Grignon and George Stevens, the loggers, lumberjacks, raftsmen and the lumber barons who followed them, Amherst Willoughby Kellogg, with his colleagues, like other contractors, investing his savings to saw lumber on the Wisconsin and take his considerable pay in lumber to be floated down—in the one year of the decade in which there was no rise; the prophet Jenkin with his flowing beard and his eloquent sermons, the five enterprising sons of old August Ringling, the dynamic lion of architecture, Frank Lloyd Wright, old Bob La Follette electioneering along the valley—and all those others who led their quiet or troubled lives along the Wisconsin.

A man who has grown up along the river takes it for granted; it is a part of his daily life though he may never step into it or enter a boat to cross it. Yet he can never be unaware of it, even if his awareness is only such as the experience of this moment, as I write: of having his radio program interrupted by a news bulletin announcing the approach of flood stage in the river for Portage and the lower Wisconsin. But that awareness is evident also in the lives of those who live in the towns of the valley. Not long ago Kate Reely, sitting next to me at a dinner, expressed that cognizance of the Wisconsin when she spoke of her girlhood in Spring Green. "Though we weren't on the river, we were always somehow aware of it—like something just out of sight, something impending." Everything she did not say was implied in what she said. Who could forget the musky miasma rising from exposed stones along the river in low water? Or the wonder of wild grapes and locusts blossoming in late May and early June, the lure of woodruff and the pungence of mints, sending their perfume forth from both shores of the Wisconsin. Or the ominous thunder of the risen river among the piers of bridges, among the boles of trees, for the Wisconsin in flood is formidable, and the surging power of its voice heard in the nights during the spring floods or the June rise is a memorable tribute to its latent potence.

Yes, and there are hundreds of small aspects no one who has ever known the Wisconsin could forget: the sand bars in the early morning sun and the herons fishing there, the catbirds' magic mockery in the willows, the moonlight making new worlds among the islands on a windy night in May, heady with lilac and apple perfume. And the carp fishing—! Once it was catfish, suckers, and sunfish that predominated, and full many a time I took to the Wisconsin or its sloughs for sunfish and bass, alone, or with a friend—though when two of us were out, we lost all sense of time, and were usually fetched home by anxious parents who were fearful and anxious for our safety only until we had been found, and unmistakably irate thereafter. The carp came up along its shores, and wherever the pea canneries used to empty their waste into the Wisconsin, the old gaffers and the small boys fished, and the carp they caught were taken home to be pickled for winter eating. But whether anglers are after sunfish or pike, bass or carp, their habits do not change: out before dawn in the season, and often home after dark, only the creak of oarlocks to betray them in the night folded down over the Wisconsin, a small sound vying with the talk of the water around the piers of the bridges, with the killdeer's nostalgic crying of spring evenings, and the toad's trilling, with the tinkle of cowbells from cattle pastured for the night on the slopes of the moraines. I have come upon lone anglers often on its shores, along its banks, standing in the dusk with cane poles and reel poles, and fly-rods . . .

> Quietly as evening's tree
> the angler gathers dusk
> along the slough's dark shore
> where others of his kind have stood before,
> deep in the fragrant musk
> of prisoned water, stands free
> of time, and with each cast
> brings in a little of the past . . .

From spring to autumn the anglers line the banks, firm in their age-old beliefs—that the fish bite best before rain—during rain—after rain, large numbers of anglers adhering to each theory without regard for the fact that they are contradictory.

And the swimming holes! They are still in use, as they should be. Off Third Island east of Sauk City is Bare-Skin Beach, which is just what its name implies, of course; looking upstream at any time during hot weather from April to October, it is possible to see the lithe bodies of the boys gleaming in the sun, white against the cobalt water and the massed trees behind.

There are others—more, perhaps, on the tributaries. I have no doubt that there will always be old swimming holes. The late comic cartoon artist, Clare Briggs, who made famous *Mr. and Mrs., Skinnay, When a Feller Needs a Friend, Days of Real Sport, et al.,* and who originated the serial comic strip, with *A. Piker Clerk,* in Hearst's Chicago *American* in 1904, was born and spent his childhood in Reedsburg along the Baraboo River, and, returning to his native town in later years, said many times that his *Old Swimming Hole* panels derived from his memories of swimming in the Baraboo. Since his day and since my own, WPA has made it possible for towns along the river to build swimming pools —a project for the authorization of which someone not familiar with the Wisconsin must have been responsible; for no reason exists to justify the expenditure of public money on such projects when supervised swimming in the river for the young could be carried out at considerably less cost and with no more danger to human life and health.

The danger of the Wisconsin's water to life and health was most frequently given as the excuse for the construction of swimming pools. I can remember not so very long ago when tests were made of the Wisconsin's water; this was at a time when a few sewers still emptied into the lower river. It was gravely announced that the river was highly toxic; and, indeed, there were doctors who, when faced with any unusual kind of rash or irritation of the skin, immediately asked the patient whether he swam in the Wisconsin, and, at least by the inference of forbidding him to do so, concluded that the water had poisoned him. As a matter of fact, I know of no case on record, either in local lore or in medical case histories, of disease and contamination caused by the Wisconsin. Secondary infection, perhaps, and even this is dubious. Of course, there is the case of a lad who witlessly went swimming with a bad case of poison ivy, which became worse as a result; but he survived to repeat history.

That the Wisconsin is any more dangerous to human life than any other river is fantastic. In many communities there was held for decades the belief that the river claimed one victim each year for its own—a sort of blood sacrifice, as it were, to propitiate the spirit of the waters. The Wisconsin has taken victims, as have all rivers—but they are not victims of the river, but rather of accident, carelessness, deliberate intent. My grandfather Derleth on one occasion years ago told me that in the early years of Sauk City the suicide rate was as high as one death annually; the river accepted many of these desperately lonely, maladjusted, despairing men and women. Men like the considerate old gentleman who tied one leg to a tree so that people would have no difficulty finding his body. Men and women who walked out into the river from the shore, jumped from the bridges, weary of life, temporarily demented, and from other motives. Who knows? And the early records are full of laconic statements, particularly in regard to the toll of lives taken among the lumbermen. "James Hall drowned while running lumber through the rapids. . . . Three men drowned over Neeves dam near Grand Rapids. . . . Christ Collins drowned while running Little Bull. . . . Charles Schiller got tipped off a raft at Conant's, and drowned there. . . . Port Edwards dam got George Neskin, James Monroe, and Ole Thompson. Six men in one week that time."

Such superstitions in regard to the Wisconsin stem from something that is best described as an instinctive fear of the river; it exists just as commonly as the attraction of running water. There is no reasoning with it, since the victims of superstition find no difficulty in pointing to all drownings as evidence of an incontrovertible malignity that is the river's.

Those who, like myself, represent a fourth generation along the river have in addition to the daily aspects of the Wisconsin itself, the life of the valley. Four generations is not a long time in the stream of history, but it is a tangible time in memory. Here it was, in this valley of the Wisconsin, in the country on the western rim of the Sauk Prairie that my maternal grandfather, Adam Volk, a crack shot, a veteran of the Austro-Prussian War, after the most extreme provocations, killed a man in a formal duel. Unfortunately, he chose the wrong time to do it; Wisconsin had just passed a stringent law forbidding duels, and he was sent to prison, where he died soon after. "I recognize," said the judge in imposing sentence, "that the circumstances which caused you to act were enough to exhaust the greatest human patience, and my only regret is that I cannot follow only my own inclinations; but the law leaves me no alternative, I must impose sentence, I must at least impose the absolute minimum the law allows." Even then a sick man, he was sent to die in prison. I am proud of him, and though he died before I was born, I have never been entirely unconscious of his presence in the valley: the stocky figure with the mass of black, curly hair, the dark, snapping eyes, the saturnine mouth. A Prussian, with the military training and experience, but never an autocrat, rather a German Bauer who became a tavern-keeper, whose blood mingled with that of the square-jawed, pale-eyed, silent locksmith who was my paternal great-grandfather, whose name had become Derleth from d'Erlette, whose family by marriage became as Bavarian as the natives of that land before his impatience and disgust with the oppression of the German rulers spurred his flight to America over a century ago.

The children of these pioneers grew up in the Sauk Prairie country, playing among the Indian mounds, among the cornhills that were left to mark the village Carver had visited in 1766, ("When we were little girls," remembered my grandmother Derleth, "we went out in the evenings—in *die Dämmerung*—and we played a little game there among the corn-hills—that's what they were, those mounds—and we played we were Indians, and jumped from one to the other of them, daring each other, boys and girls together, like children will. Oh, those days! Why, we could still see Indians then, every summer, when they came down from up north . . .") skating on the ice of the river in winter, hunting and fishing in a paradise which, for natural beauty, is exceeded by no other spot save the Dells along the Wisconsin. The lumber rafts took the place of the trains of a later day. "We used to swim out to them," said Billy Ynand, "and sometimes we could get lumber. If we got the men mad enough, they threw pieces at us. Then we took them up to the lumberyards and sold them for a dime or so." Occasionally rafts broke up coming through between what was then Third Island and Second, and then there was a great deal of free lumber to be salvaged. They hunted wolves—even today there are rare times when the howl of a wolf rises among the hills, from the Heights where once Black Hawk stood his ground, from the bluffs to the south of the Sauk Prairie—they hunted deer and bear—as on one occasion, when Judge Irwin was holding court on the Upper Prairie and a neighbor rushed in to announce that a large bear had been seen moving down across the prairie to the river, whereupon the judge immediately recessed court, and he, together with the prosecution, the defense, the defendant, the plaintiff, and all the witnesses took out after the bear, and, after a feast of bear meat, continued the trial. They hunted grouse and prairie chicken, lynx and raccoon.

But they hunted chiefly the passenger pigeons. This was the sport of boys. "Sometimes they would come in late, going south," said my grandfather Derleth. "We boys would go out after a snowfall and there they were in the woods—breaking down the trees, they were so heavy on the limbs. They were snow-blinded. We could just knock them off the branches." All over America this scene was being repeated, though it was not the boys who destroyed the passenger pigeons; it was in large part the greed of men for the little money the birds brought—a small but telling manifestation of that cancerous "merchant philosophy," as Edgar Lee Masters calls it, the philosophy which puts the selfish ownership of dollars above the common good. In 1882, the last flock of passenger pigeons in America was seen at the Dells of the Wisconsin, where they stayed several days and nights, enduring the usual slaughter; and then only scattered birds until 1899, when one pigeon was observed—a last bird. After that no more.

Even then, and long after, they did another kind of hunting—for Indian relics: arrowheads, tomahawks, implements of war and field—for these things abounded on the Sauk Prairie; indeed, almost everywhere along the Wisconsin, excavations in later years turned up everything from flints to skulls, all Indian in origin. These relics were not alone from the early Sauk village and the later Winnebago occupation of the country north of the prairie, but also from the colorful annual summer visits of a small band of Winnebago who, led by their chieftain, spent several months of every year in the lush Honey Creek flats southwest of Sauk

City. Only this year a farmer from that country stopped me on the street to show me a singularly beautiful miniature tomahawk he had found recently in the river bottoms where the Winnebago had summered four decades ago: the plaything of a papoose, beyond question.

The valley drew strange, lonely men. Men who had been young and adventurous enough to fight with Napoleon, who idolized him, who could not bear his defeat and death and became nomadic, taking to the sea in search of new lands. Up and down the Wisconsin, in the south particularly, there are graves of men who fought with Napoleon. Men like old Charlie Schleicher of Sauk City. It was true that people laughed at him, for when he walked down into the commercial part of town, he was followed by dogs, sometimes as many as a score. The only friends he could trust, he used to say unsmilingly. "They ask nothing but my affection, and of that I have plenty going to waste." The village soap-maker, poor as a churchmouse, a little queer in his last years. But he knew several languages, he could recite Homer, Shakespeare, Goethe by the yard in the original, he was not known to lose an argument, and, like most of his fellow soldiers, to the last he revered Napoleon. And old Gasparri, also from Sauk City, a congenial old soul who could on occasion be as sour as a crabapple, who took delight in telling ghost stories with grim realism, who dressed like a tramp six days a week, and on Sunday was elegantly attired in undreamed-of finery, from top hat down, for the sole purpose of attending church services, though he disagreed by nature with virtually everything the harassed pastor undertook to say.

After them, the retired raftsmen. There was Emil Kessler, for instance: a tall, broad-shouldered riverman. He was a legendary figure in my childhood, for he had been struck by lightning and survived; indeed, it was said he had not even been knocked down, but only a little irritated. He haunted the river, understandably; I used to come upon him in the bottom, on the islands, sometimes fishing, sometimes just taking the leisure of his old age. And that descendant who, knowing the river so well that he has an uncanny way of finding the drowned dead, earned for himself the nickname of *Corpse-Finder.*

There are no longer many of them left, though once they were to be found from the Wisconsin's headwaters to its mouth, unwilling or unable to escape those familiar waters so often cursed for willful vagaries in their long journeys to the Mississippi. How gladly they testified before the Federal Power Commission in the case of the Tomahawk Dam! "The river was so winding you might as well call it the duplicate of the intestine of a hog, that was the way it was. We would keep on rolling around below Nekoosa. That is just the first day's work, to get through Grignon Bends. We would buck into it and swing around." ... "A sand bank will shift inside of twenty-four hours, because... the Wisconsin keeps rolling sand, sand, sand. Where we had run one afternoon with a piece of lumber, tomorrow a raft will come through, follow the same track, and get stuck right there because of a new sandbank that has formed right there in the water." ... "Captain Nader told me ... 'Louie, I used to think we could make that stream navigable, but we can't make that stream navigable any more than a dog can use two tails. I will guarantee you that we can't.' ... When he gave it up, Mr. Hinman took over the job, and they thought they were going to make it navigable. ... He didn't do any more than Captain Nader did." Indeed, the Wisconsin was never made navigable for any distance; Major G. K. Warren concluded, after an examination into the navigability of the river in 1875, that there could be no satisfactory improvement by any system of contraction or rectification, and, moreover, that a canal system to improve the lower Wisconsin would cost at least four million dollars!

Nevertheless, despite all the surveys and reports, present-day engineers take time to meddle with the Wisconsin. In May of 1941 I came into Sauk City from the east and saw machines busy hauling sand off the only usable beach near the village, just under the east approach of the bridge. In response to my inquiry, the engineer in charge of the project informed me that the beach was being removed "to make more channel." He explained that the Wisconsin was deeper now, and that there was some menace to the structure of the bridge carrying the heavy traffic of several federal and state highways; so if there were more channel under the bridge, the pools around the piers might be filled with sand. Twenty years ago when the bridge was built, it was scarcely possible to swim across below it; now, save for a very short distance, it is possible to walk across the river below the bridge. Moreover, squarely across the line of the proposed new channel north of the bridge lies Hiddessen's Island; slantwise underwater between the island and the projected channel lie the piers of the old bridge; and directly below lies a high bank. How the engineer hoped to convince the Wisconsin that this section of sandy bottom freed of the bar which was the beach—at the expense of the state's taxpayers, of course —was actual channel, and by what legerdemain he might persuade Hiddessen's Island and the current-directing line of old piers to detour the Wisconsin remains to this day a problem completely beyond my comprehension. I thought at that time that anyone who could have devised such a scheme and put it into practice in such a place to begin with must have recourse to

some further ingenuity sufficient to enable him to con-
jure the Wisconsin to do his will. Quite naturally, as
any amateur could have informed the engineer, by this
time, less then two years later, the Wisconsin has again
begun to roll sand in along the shore to build up a new
beach where his fond hope had been for "more channel."

The Wisconsin's sand has for decades been a bogey
for the boys who haunt the old swimming holes along
the river. I remember in my boyhood being warned not
to dare the river, not to go swimming or even wading
(of course, we did, warnings disregarded), and hearing
the tragic tale of what happened to a young lady of
Sauk City when she bathed two successive days at the
same place—where a sand bar had been on the first day,
and a deep hole to drown her on the second. Quicksand
had drawn her under, said the excitables; but of course,
ultimately it came out that the Wisconsin had rolled
the sand bar away. Overnight. And yet, it would be a
mistake, I think, to assume that this rolling of sand is
the usual thing along the Wisconsin. Possibly because
of all the warnings of my boyhood, I paid some attention to the wanderings of the sand bars, in particular to
the bar behind Karberg's in Sauk City, where we swam
for more than a decade, and to a submerged bar below
Otto Hiddessen's Island—the site of the most attractive
cabin, of logs and stone, built by the hand of its owner,
on all the Wisconsin—where we swam for the following
decade and where we are still swimming despite the
proximity of the public pool at Prairie du Sac. The bar
behind Karberg's underwent only one persistent change
in the last two decades; it grew in size, narrowing the
river across from one of the old wing dams lining its
shores, willows and cottonwoods began to grow, and
finally, in low water, it became part of the shore; the

bar below Hiddessen's Island shifted from one to ten feet from shore, but otherwise changed in no particular.

The wing dams are overgrown with willows and cottonwoods: the haunt of fishermen now; the highways and the railroads carry the commerce that once the Wisconsin bore on its surface; but the essential river has changed perhaps less than many another river of its size on the North American continent.

The river of a thousand isles—sand bars lost in a night, wilderness land overhung with ivy and grapevines, smilax and bittersweet, red in autumn with the wild berries there, willow islands sheltering the herons as the bluffs harbor the bank swallows. All up and down the river the least and solitary sandpipers sing their sweet songs at the bars, along the beautiful, wooded shores where there is no sign of man's passage; cowbells tinkle from the pastures on the slopes; warblers nest in the underbrush on both banks, along the sloughs and backwaters, the secondary streams around the islands. At night barred owls, great horned owls, and whippoorwills haunt the bottoms; by day ospreys, bitterns, herons, killdeers, inhabit the shores; and the surface of the water shelters pied-bill grebes, wood ducks, mallards, mergansers, and coots. Woodcocks, jacksnipes, and nighthawks make their mating flights by dusk and darkness. In the hot days of midsummer the thrushes sing out of the tree-bound shores, the peewees call nostalgically, the catbirds and brown thrashers mock the larks and robins. Secretly among the plants and reeds of the water's edge walk the rails.

Under leaden skies the water's face is leaden, under the clear heaven, cobalt, and the sandbars a dark gold. Among the trees the red barn gables show briefly here and there; sometimes an old cemetery rears itself upon a hillside; in summer the stacked grain is beautiful against earth and sky, and the current swirls and ripples or flows dumbly around trees drawn into the water, dead tree tops projecting sometimes for as much as forty feet from the shore line. Sand bubbles ride the surface of the river, and in early autumn the red lobelias make a bright fire among the green grasses alongshore. Approaching the mouth of the Wisconsin, as many as three channels become evident, some of them flowing deeply, swiftly, narrowly between islands, so that the overhanging trees from opposite shores meet and arbor the way. Cicadas stridulate among motionless trees on windless days, and in the heat of midday, mirages of sand bars lie above the bars and open water where the snakes and turtles are sluggish in the sun.

For over four hundred miles, the Wisconsin, though a river superficially tamed by the dams along its central portion and the reservoirs on its tributaries, is still essentially a wilderness stream, but quiet now, aging, seldom rising to the flood stages of early years, pastoral and beautiful where it flows slowly down between the hills that enclose its valley to give itself through the Mississippi to the sea.

Acknowledgments

I<small>T</small> should be clear readily enough that I have made no attempt to write a comprehensive history of the Wisconsin or its valley, a forbidding task within the self-imposed limitations. I have, however, adhered as closely as possible to history, and to the best of my knowledge there are no historical inaccuracies in this book. Necessarily, I have had the advice and assistance of many people who know their history, and their particular portions of the river's valley, better than I.

I am profoundly grateful to all those who have been so generous with their time and material—to my secretary, Miss Alice Conger, whose research in concise notes came to greater length than the total body of the book itself; to Dr. Louise Phelps Kellogg, Charles E. Brown, and Albert O. Barton, who were kind enough to read the manuscript and make helpful corrections and suggestions; to all those authors and publishers who permitted quotations from their books; to Miriam Bennett for her father's fine *Camera's Story of Raftman's Life on the Wisconsin;* and, for the loan of unpublished manuscripts, privately printed accounts, clippings, and letters, to Dr. P. L. Scanlan, Mrs. Virginia Dousman Bigelow, A. O. Barton, Dorothy Moulding Brown, Steve Fogo, Miss Jean Cunningham, Mrs. Isabel J. Ebert, George P. Steinmetz, Dr. Bertha Reynolds, L. N. Coapman, the Reverend E. C. Dixon, Lyman Howe, George Hagar, Dr. Ruth Marshall, H. S. Tuttle, Fred Heinemann, Herman O. Zander, J. Wesley White, William W. Morris, John Radlund, Miss Grace Munsell, Joe Alexander, W. D. Ryan and others.

Apart from the *Wisconsin Historical Collections* and the *Wisconsin Magazine of History,* I have drawn most heavily upon six books: Dr. Louise Phelps Kellogg's admirable historical studies, *The French Regime in Wisconsin and the Northwest* and *The British*

Regime in Wisconsin and the Northwest; Juliette Kinzie's *Wau-Bun;* the American Guide Series book, *Wisconsin: A Guide to the Badger State;* Frederick Merk's excellent *Economic History of Wisconsin;* and Fred L. Holmes's extremely readable *Badger Saints and Sinners.* Those who might like to know the history of the Wisconsin and its valley in more detail might turn to these books, as those who would wish to know more of the Wisconsin Valley's men should turn to Frank Lloyd Wright's *Autobiography,* the works of Zona Gale, and my biography of her: *Still Small Voice;* Fred L. Holmes's *Alluring Wisconsin,* Dr. P. L. Scanlan's *Prairie du Chien,* and John Muir's *Story of My Boyhood and Youth.*

A special note of gratitude should go to all those who accompanied John Steuart Curry and me down the Wisconsin from the Sauk Prairie to the mouth by canoe and motorboat in the summer of 1941: Miss Conger, Mr. and Mrs. E. A. Ingles, Karl Ganzlin, Jack Stanton, Robert Koenig, Robert Straub, and, for the last lap, Lyman and Bill Howe; and also to all those dwellers along the Wisconsin who were both kind and generous with their time and patience in giving us the information we sought at our various stopping places.

And finally, to John Steuart Curry, my collaborator in this venture, all gratitude for intelligent and unsparing co-operation.

Bibliography

BARTON, ALBERT O., *La Follette's Winning of Wisconsin*. Madison, 1922.

BLACK HAWK, *Autobiography*. Rock Island: American Publishing Company, 1912.

BROGMAR, NEMO N., *Ten Years in North America*. Chicago: Morpheus Publishing Company, 1871.

CANFIELD, WILLIAM H. (ed.), *Outline Sketches of Sauk County; Including Its History, From the First Marks of Man's Hand to 1861, and Its Topography*. Baraboo: A. N. Kellogg, 1861.

CARVER, JONATHAN, *Travels Through the Interior Parts of North America in the Years 1766, 1767 and 1768*. London, 1781.

CRAWFORD, GEORGE and ROBERT M., *Memoirs of Iowa County*, 1913.

DAVIS, SUSAN BURDICK, *Old Forts and Real Folks*. Madison, 1939.

DERLETH, AUGUST, *Wind Over Wisconsin*. New York: Charles Scribner's Sons, 1938.

———— *Restless Is the River*. New York: Charles Scribner's Sons, 1939.

———— *Bright Journey*. New York: Charles Scribner's Sons, 1940.

———— *Still Small Voice, The Biography of Zona Gale*. New York: D. Appleton-Century Company, 1940.

DOS PASSOS, JOHN, *U. S. A.* New York: Harcourt, Brace & Company, 1939.

DRAPER, LYMAN COPELAND (ed.), *Collections of the State Historical Society of Wisconsin*, Vols. I-X. Madison, 1855-1886.

GRENDON, S. G., *Through Wisconsin on a Bicycle*. Sauk City: Arkham House, 1940.

HISTORY OF SAUK COUNTY. Chicago: Western Historical Society, 1880.

HISTORY OF NORTHERN WISCONSIN, 1881.

HISTORY OF CRAWFORD COUNTY.

HITCHCOCK, HENRY-RUSSELL, *In the Nature of Materials—The Buildings of Frank Lloyd Wright 1887–1941*. New York: Duell, Sloan & Pearce, 1942.

HOLBROOK, STEWART H.: *Holy Old Mackinaw*. New York: The Macmillan Company, 1938.

HOLMES, FRED L., *Alluring Wisconsin*. Milwaukee: E. M. Hale & Company, 1937.

—— *Badger Saints and Sinners*. Milwaukee: E. M. Hale & Company, 1939.

ISELY, BLISS, *Blazing the Way West*. New York: Charles Scribner's Sons, 1939.

JOHNSON, REV. PETER LEO, *Stuffed Saddlebags*. Milwaukee: Bruce, 1942.

JONES, JENKIN LLOYD, *An Artilleryman's Diary*. Madison: Wisconsin History Commission, 1914.

JONES, GEORGE O., McVEAN, NORMAN S., & Others (compilers), *History of Wood County*, 1923.

—— *History of Lincoln, Oneida, and Vilas Counties*, 1924.

KEARNEY, L. S. (LAKESHORE), *The Hodag*. Madison: Democrat, 1928.

KELLOGG, LOUISE PHELPS, *The French Regime in Wisconsin and the Northwest*. Madison: State Historical Society of Wisconsin, 1925.

—— *The British Regime in Wisconsin and the Northwest*. Madison: State Historical Society of Wisconsin, 1935.

KINZIE, MRS. JOHN H., *Wau-Bun—The "Early Day" in the North-West*. Chicago: R. R. Donnelly & Sons, 1932.

KOENIGSBERG, M., *King News*. New York: Stokes, 1941.

LA FOLLETTE, ROBERT M., *A Personal Narrative of Political Experiences*. Madison, 1913.

LAUT, AGNES C., *The Fur Trade of America*. New York: The Macmillan Company, 1921.

LYMAN, GEORGE D., *John Marsh, Pioneer*. New York: Charles Scribner's Sons, 1934.

MacDOUGALL, CURTIS D., *Hoaxes*. New York: The Macmillan Company, 1940.

MARCHETTI, LOUIS, *History of Marathon County*, 1913.

MARRYAT, CAPTAIN C. B., *A Diary in America*. Philadelphia: Carey
& Hart, 1839.

MARTIN, DEBORAH B., *History of Brown County*, 1913.

MAZZUCHELLI, SAMUEL, *Memoirs*. Chicago: Hall, 1915.

MERK, FREDERICK, *Economic History of Wisconsin During the
Civil War Decade*. Madison: State Historical Society of Wisconsin, 1916.

MINER, JUDGE JAMES H., *History of Richland County*, 1906.

MUIR, JOHN, *The Story of My Boyhood and Youth*. Boston:
Houghton Mifflin Company, 1913.

MYERS, GUSTAVUS, *History of the Great American Fortunes*. Chicago: C. H. Kerr, 1910.

NUTE, GRACE LEE, *The Voyageur*. New York: D. Appleton-Century Company, 1931.

——— *The Voyageur's Highway*. St. Paul: Minnesota Historical
Society, 1941.

QUAIFE, MILO M. (ed.), Index to Volumes I-XX of the *Wisconsin
Historical Collections*. Madison, 1915.

RANEY, WILLIAM F., *Wisconsin: A Story of Progress*. New York:
Prentice-Hall, 1940.

SCANLAN, PETER LAWRENCE, *Prairie du Chien: French—British—
American*. Menasha, 1937.

SCHAFER, JOSEPH, *A History of Agriculture in Wisconsin*. Madison: State Historical Society of Wisconsin, 1922.

——— *The Wisconsin Lead Region*. Madison: State Historical Society of Wisconsin, 1932.

STEVENS, JAMES, *Paul Bunyan*. New York: Alfred A. Knopf, 1925.

THWAITES, REUBEN GOLD, *Down Historic Waterways*. Chicago:
A. C. McClurg, 1910.

——— (ed.), *Collections of the State Historical Society of Wisconsin*, Vols. XI-XX. Madison, 1888–1911.

TITUS, WILLIAM A., *Wisconsin Writers*. Chicago, 1930.

TORELLE, ELLEN (compiler), assisted by BARTON, ALBERT O. and
HOLMES, FRED L., *The Political Philosophy of Robert M. La
Follette*. Madison, 1920.

TURNER, FREDERICK JACKSON, *The Early Writings*. Madison: University of Wisconsin Press, 1938.

VESTAL, STANLEY, *King of the Fur Traders*. Boston: Houghton Mifflin Company, 1940.

WOODWARD, W. E., *A New American History*. New York: Farrar & Rinehart, 1936.

WORKERS OF THE WRITERS' PROGRAM OF THE WORK PROJECTS ADMINISTRATION, *Wisconsin—A Guide to the Badger State*. New York: Duell, Sloan & Pearce, 1941.

WRIGHT, FRANK LLOYD, *An Autobiography*. New York: Longmans, Green & Company, 1932.

———— *On Architecture*, Selected Writings, 1894–1940, Edited by Frederick Gutheim. New York: Duell, Sloan & Pearce, 1941.

Booklets and Pamphlets

BENNETT, H. H., *The Dells of the Wisconsin River*. Kilbourn, 1927.

BIGELOW, VIRGINIA DOUSMAN, *History of "Villa Louis."* St. Paul, 1936.

BROWN, CHARLES E., *Wisconsin Indian Tribes*. Madison, 1931.

———— *Paul Bunyan: Natural History*. Madison, 1935.

———— *Prairie Stories*. Madison, 1934.

———— *Paul Bunyan: American Hercules*. Madison, 1937.

———— *Moccasin Tales*. Madison, 1935.

———— *Cloud Lore*. Madison, 1935.

———— *Whiskey Jack Yarns*. Madison, 1940.

———— *"Cousin Jack" Stories*. Madison, 1940.

———— *Flapjacks (Paul Bunyan Tales)*. Madison, 1941.

———— *Birchbark Tales*. Madison, 1941.

BROWN, DOROTHY MOULDING, *Wisconsin Circus Lore* (privately printed). Madison, 1937.

———— *Wisconsin Place Name Legends*. Madison, 1936.

CASSIDY, FREDERIC G., *Some New England Words in Wisconsin*. Language, 1941.

COLE, H. E., *Stagecoach and Tavern Days in the Baraboo Region*. Baraboo, 1923.

———— *Baraboo, Dells, and Devil's Lake Region*. Baraboo, 1920.

———— *Baraboo Bear Tales*. Baraboo, 1915.

DAVIDSON, JOHN NELSON, *"Wisconsin"—The Name of a Region, a River and a State*. Madison, n.d.

DERLETH, AUGUST, *The Heritage of Sauk City* (printed anonymously). Sauk City: Pioneer Press, 1931.

EBERT, ISABEL, *The Wanigan Song Book*. Rhinelander, n.d.

EMERSON, CHARLES L., *Wisconsin Scenic and Historic Trails*. Madison, 1933.

FEDERAL WRITERS' PROJECT OF WISCONSIN, *Portage*. Portage, 1938.

GREGORY, JOHN GOADBY, *Jonathan Carver: His Travels in the Northwest in 1766–8*. Milwaukee, 1896.

KEMPTON, WILLETT MAIN, *Before Our Day*. Madison, 1936.

LAPHAM, INCREASE A., *The Antiquities of Wisconsin*. Washington, 1855.

LATHROP, HARRY, *The Yankee Abroad*. Bridgeport, 1927.

—— *Memories of the Wisconsin*. Flint, Mich., 1903.

LEICHT, BRONTE H. (ed.), *Wisconsin*, Bulletin 180, Department of Agriculture and Markets. Madison, 1937.

LUEDERS, F. G. J., *A Memorial to the Representatives of Physical Astronomy*. Madison, 1887.

—— *List of Six Hundred and Eight Auroras*. Madison, 1884.

LUEDERS, HERMAN F., *Floral Structure of Some Gramineae* (n.d.).

—— *Concerning the Structure of Caoutchouc*. New York, 1893.

—— *The Vegetation of the Town Prairie du Sac*. Madison, n.d.

POND, ALONZO W., *Cave of the Mounds*. Milton Junction, 1941.

THWAITES, REUBEN GOLD, *The Story of the Black Hawk War*. Madison: State Historical Society of Wisconsin, 1892.

WAUSAU, WISCONSIN, Illustrated and published by the Art Gravure & Etching Company, 1891.

Periodicals and Newspapers

Architectural Forum, Vol. 68, No. 1, January, 1938.

Baraboo *News*, 1926.

Baraboo *Republic*, 1867–1868.

Capital Times, 1917–1942.

Courier, Prairie du Chien, 1930–1942.

Crawford County Press, 1926.

Fennimore *Times*, 1926.
Green Bay *Press Gazette*, 1927.
Merrill *Herald*, 1920–1928.
Milwaukee *Journal*, 1925–1942.
Milwaukee *Sentinel*, November 13, 1867.
Nation, New York, February 15, 1928.
Pioneer Press, Sauk City, Wis., August 11, 1938.
Republican Observer, Richland Center, Wis., March-April, 1939, July-November, 1941.
Sauk County News, August 11, 1938.
Stevens Point Journal, 1927.
Three Lakes News, Three Lakes, Wis., Vol. 10, Nos. 19–26, 1941.
Time, January 17, 1938; February, 1942.
Wausau *Pilot*, 1920–1927.
Wisconsin Archeologist, Volumes 18, 19: 1937–1939.
Wisconsin Magazine of History, Vols. I-1 through XXV-3, 1917–1942.
Wisconsin Mirror, June 17, 1868.
Wisconsin State Journal, 1880–1942.
Wisconsin State Register, August 29, 1868.

Manuscripts

CHILSEN, W. B., *Log-Driving on the Wisconsin.*
CORS, LYLE and STORY, JOHN ROBERT, *Notes on a Canoe Trip from Portage Down the Wisconsin River.*
CROOKS, RAMSAY, *Letters.*
CUNNINGHAM, JEAN, *The Retreat of the Forest.*
DERLETH, AUGUST, *A Sac Prairie Journal, 1941.*
DIXON, E. C., *Newport: Its Rise and Fall.*
DOUSMAN, HERCULES L., *Letters.*
SCANLAN, PETER LAWRENCE, *Jefferson Davis in Wisconsin.*
―――― *Jean Joseph Rolette.*

Documents

BRIEF ON BEHALF OF THE STATE OF WISCONSIN AND THE PUBLIC SERVICE COMMISSION OF WISCONSIN, INTERVIEWS BEFORE THE

FEDERAL POWER COMMISSION, Docket DI-134 In the Matter of the Tomahawk Dam, Madison, 1939.

BULLETIN OF THE ASSOCIATED STATE ENGINEERING SOCIETIES, Vol. XIV, No. 3, July, 1939.

CRAM, T. J., *Report of Captain T. J. Cram, October, 1840.*

REPORT OF THE RAILROAD COMMISSION OF WISCONSIN TO THE LEGISLATURE ON WATER POWERS. Madison, 1915.

SENATE DOCUMENTS, No. 57, Thirtieth Congress, First Session.

TRANSACTIONS, Wisconsin Agricultural Society. Madison, 1861–1868.

WATER PLAN REPORT FOR THE UPPER WISCONSIN RIVER BASIN IN WISCONSIN. Teper: Horner, Lenz, August 20, 1936.

Index